BALAAM AND HIS INTERPRETERS

Program in Judaic Studies
Brown University
BROWN JUDAIC STUDIES

Edited by
Shaye J. D. Cohen, Wendell S. Dietrich,
Ernest S. Frerichs, Calvin Goldscheider, David Hirsch, Alan Zuckerman

Project Editors (Projects)

Lenn Evan Goodman, University of Hawaii (Studies in Medieval Judaism)
David Hayes, Coe College (Studia Philonica)

Number 244
BALAAM AND HIS INTERPRETERS

by
John T. Greene

BALAAM AND HIS INTERPRETERS
A Hermeneutical History
of the Balaam Traditions

by

John T. Greene

Scholars Press
Atlanta, Georgia

BALAAM AND HIS INTERPRETERS
A Hermeneutical History
of the Balaam Traditions

Copyright © 1992 by Brown University

All rights reserved. No part of this work may be reproduced or transmitted in any form or by any means, electronic or mechanical, including photocopying and recording, or by means of any information storage or retrieval system, except as may be expressly permitted by the 1976 Copyright Act or in writing from Brown Judaic Studies, Brown University, Box 1826, Providence, RI 02912.

Library of Congress Cataloging-in-Publication Data

Greene, John T.
    Balaam and his interpreters : a hermeneutical history of the Balaam traditions / by John T. Greene
    p. cm. — (Brown Judaic studies ; no. 244)
    Includes bibliographical references and indexes.
    ISBN 1-55540-690-4
    1. Balaam (Biblical figure) 2. Bible, O. T. Numbers XXII–XXIV—
Criticism, interpretation, etc. 1. Title. II. Series.
BS580.B3G74   1992
222'.14092—dc20   92-1032
                                              CIP

Paperback edition published 2007 by Brown Judaic Studies.
ISBN 1-930675-41-0 (alk. paper : paperback)

Printed in the United States of America
on acid-free paper

FOR

Martin Dwayne (Bud) Greene

Patrice Lynn (Treesie) Weatherspoon

Erica Yvonne Green

In Memory of

Jamie Julia Johnson Greene

CONTENTS

Abbreviations   iv

Preface   viii

Introduction: A Man, A Monarch, A Marked Paradigm, A Monument: Balaam the Son of Beor   x

PART 1: Background   1

Chapter 1. A Discovery at Tell Deir 'Allā: Its Implications and Significance: The Coming War Between Heaven and Earth   2

Chapter 2. Sacerdotal, Social and Religio–Political Protests in Ancient Israel: Hermeneutical Wars on "Paper"   6

    a. The Friedman Thesis: **Who Wrote the Bible**? Revisited   7

    b. The J Thesis: (A Southern Perspective)

    c. The E Thesis: (A Shiloh Perspective)

    d. The JE Thesis: (A Conciliatory Perspective)

    e. The P Thesis: (A Reactionary Perspective)

    f. The D Thesis: (A Backlash Perspective)

    g. The R Thesis: (A Redactional Perspective)

Chapter 3. The Development of Communication Theories, Praxes and Community Control: Wars for the Fidelity of the People   9

    a. The Priest   9

    b. The Prophet   10

    c. The Diviner   12

    d. Who is the Legitimate Spokesperson for Deity or Deities?   12

PART 2: Prophet, Priest, Diviner: Balaam as Test Case and Paradigm   15

Chapter 4. Philosophies of History and Communication in Ancient Israel: Priestly Wars and Nonaggression Pacts   16

    a.   The Balaam Cycle of Texts (Numbers 22–24): An Exegetical Explication   17

        1) "Balaam" in The Service of J

        2) "Balaam" in The Service of E

        3) "Balaam" in The Service of JE

        4) "Balaam" in The Service of P

        5) "Balaam" in The Service of D

        6) "Balaam" in The Service of R

    b.   Significance and the Connecting Theme of War   65

Chapter 5. Balaam Elsewhere in the Hebrew Scriptures: The War Theme Continues   69

    a.   Numbers 31 and Balaam   69

    b.   Micah 6:5 and Balaam   75

    c.   Deuteronomy 23:4–5 (MT 23:5–6) and Balaam   76

    d.   Nehemiah 13:2 and Balaam   79

PART 3: "Balaam" In Other Semitic Language–Written Materials   82

Chapter 6. Qumran and the Balaam Traditions: The Fantastic War   83

Chapter 7. The Samaritan Literature and Balaam: Warring Priesthoods: The Hermeneutical Debates Continue   101

    a.   The Samaritan Pentateuch   104

b.	The Book of Joshua	123
c.	The Discourse Concerning the Angels	124
d.	The Asatir or Secrets of Moses	124
e.	The Birth Story of Moses and Balaam	125
f.	*Memar* Marqa	133
g.	Summary	134

Chapter 8. The Book of Enoch (I Enoch): The War to Destroy All the Godless   **136**

PART 4: Balaam Hermeneutics for Later Ages   **141**

Chapter 9. "Balaam" During and Beyond the Middle Platonic Period: The Inability to Jettison the Theme of War   **142**

a.	Balaam in The New Testament	142
b.	Josephus' Antiquities and Balaam	144
c.	The North African Platonists and Balaam	145
d.	Rabbinical Literature and Balaam	148
e.	The Medieval Balaam	155
f.	Balaam and Modern Literature	156

Conclusion	162
Notes	170
Bibliography	209
Indices	219

ABBREVIATIONS

ANE	Ancient Near East
BAR	Biblical Archaeologist Reader
BAR	Biblical Archaeology Review
BASOR	Bulletin of the American Schools of Oriental Research
BZAW	*Beihefete zur Zeitschrift für die alttestamentliche Wissenschaft*
D	The Deuteronomistic History or the Deuteronomist
DH	Documentary Hypothesis
E	The Elohistic Source Stratum
HS	Hebrew Scriptures
IDBSV	Interpreter's Dictionary of the Bible Supplementary Volume
IEJ	Israel Exploration Journal
J	The Yahwistic Source Stratum
JA	*Journal d'Archaeologie*
JAOS	Journal of the American Oriental Society
JBL	Journal of Biblical Literature
JE	The Combined J and E Source Strata
JJS	Journal of Jewish Studies
JNES	Journal of Near Eastern Studies
JSOT	Journal for the Study of the Old Testament
JTS	Journal of Theological Studies
MT	Massoretic Text
NT	New Testament
OT	Old Testament
P	The Priestly Source Stratum
Provriediv	Prophet, Priest, Diviner in one
R	The Redactor of the J,E,JE,P, and D Strata
RB	*Revue Biblique*
RQ	*Revue de Qumrân*

RSV	Revised Standard Version
SBL	Society of Biblical Literature Seminar Papers
SP	Samaritan Pentateuch
TaNaK	*Torah, Nevi'im, Kethuvim* (The Hebrew/Jewish Scriptures)
VT	*Vetus Testamentum*
ZAW	*Zeitschrift für die Alttestamentliche Wissenschaft*
ZDPV	*Zeitschrift des Deutsch–Palästina Vereins*
ZThK	*Zeitschrift für Theologie und Kirche*
1Q M	Cave One War Scroll From Qumran
1Q S	Cave One *Serekh* = Community Rule Scroll From Qumran
4Q En.	Cave Four Enoch Scroll From Qumran

PREFACE

One need merely inquire of the existence of sustained scholarly works about Balaam ben Beor to find that there exist one book,[1] and a recently published doctoral dissertation.[2] These two are fairly recent. There exist also several well written, but now dated, articles about Balaam.[3]

Equally dated are most works concerning the relationships between ancient Middle Eastern priesthoods, prophets, diviners, wizards, sorcerers, augerers and other mantic types.[4] An exception to this situation is the anthology which grew out of a conference that took place at Brown University in August of 1987.[5]

Even more recently, interest in Balaam and his relationship to mantological studies has been expressed in three papers growing out of studies executed by members of the Philo Seminar of the Society of Biblical Literature at its 1989 and 1990 annual meetings.[6]

This book grows out of my interest and involvement in the Brown University conference on Magic and Religion, Prophecy and Magic, Science and Magic, my involvement in the Philo of Alexandria Seminar of SBLSP, and my sustained fascination with the subjects of prophecy, divination, thaumaturgy and magic. One of the best figures in ancient (and now modern!) literature around whom to group and study these abiding human concerns is Balaam the son of Beor. But study of literature about him tells the reader much about the social and political climate of a given century or era in the life of ancient Israel also. Moreover, it provides data which addresses the question of why Balaam became fixed as a type to be cast in both a positive and negative light by his interpreters whether ancient, medieval and modern. This modest effort attempts to stimulate a renewed interest in how one faction (i.e., the priestly) of one ancient society (ancient Israel) attempted to solve certain socio-political and religious problems, and how later societies followed in their wake. It also points to ways which modern society, currently grappling with some of the same problems, may acquire problem-solving skills to address contemporary needs.

INTRODUCTION

A Man, A Monarch, A Marked Paradigm, A Monument: Balaam the Son of Beor

The New Testament states concerning Melchizedek, the priest-king of Salem, that he had no beginning and no end.[1] He served as the paradigm for the mysterious, nebulous holy man. Balaam ben Beor of Numbers 22-24 served a similar paradigmatic role. The mysterious, nebulous activities of numerous mantic types were seen to fit his paradigm. In due course, "Balaam" became more than a man, a mantic, a mystery, a master mediator: he became a monument as well. Balaam became many things to many interpreters of many times. Just as each Gospel writer cast "Jesus" in the role of master teacher, master lawgiver, self-confident, pre-existent Christ, and hidden messiah (Luke, Matthew, John, and Mark respectively), a practice carried even further by the author of a given Gospel comprising the Nag Hammadi Library,[2] each "author" of the source strata of the Petatench (i.e., J, E, JE, P, D, and R) utilized "Balaam". He eventually became a marked, paradigmatic mantic for all seasons.

But, like Jesus of Galilee, Balaam was a historical person. He, too, however, became larger than life ordinarily allows one to become, and thereby, has suffered at the hands of many who would chronicle his activities: activities refracted through the prism of a given interpreter's purpose(s). Like historical studies about Jesus, Balaam, too, deserves a new hearing.

A careful reading of the Numbers 22-24 material, as well as the Balaam account from Deir 'Allā,[3] suggests that the historical Balaam was more than a shadowy figure who possessed the ability to effectively curse people until he met Israel. There is the suggestion that Balaam was a monarch! Shedding more light on this issue is a recent work which studied communication techniques in the ancient Near East (hence ANE) for an extended period.[4] It demonstrates that Balak's message to Balaam (Numbers 22:5-7; 15-17) is cast in the form of one equal communicating with another **king**! Allied with this is the possibility that the name, Balaam, might be nothing more than a play on words (or a word). The problem alerts itself in two ways. (1) In Genesis 36:32 one reads about a King Bela, (*bl'*) the son of one Beor who was king of Edom in the 12th or 11th century B.C.E. (2) Balaam (*bl'm*) at Numbers 22:5 is also said to be the son of Beor. The only morphological difference is the final *mem* (i.e., /m/ on *bl'* producing *bl'(m)*.[5] Priest-kings were a common phenomenon in the ANE. (6) Some of them have been extolled for their wisdom (cf. Solomon), their sense of law (cf. Hammurabi, Lipit-Ishtar, Eshnunna, Ur-nammu), their engineering skills (cf. Hiram of Tyre), and their musical abilities (cf. David). It seems likely that underlying the numerous accounts of Balaam was a monarch who was famous for his abilities as a diviner—and who, like the others, became a legend: in his time and, as the following will demonstrate to satisfaction, well beyond.

This study of Balaam will demonstrate that:

(1) Balaam was a famous monarch/seer reputed to have been an effective diviner.

(2) As a result of his divining efficacy, he became a legend among the members, especially the priests, of the petty kingdoms of the eastern Levant between the 10th and 5th centuries B.C.E.

(3) Ancient Israelite priesthoods warred with each other over the issue of sacerdotal hegemony: wars reflected in the source

strata of the Pentateuch and "Balaam's" role within them.

(4) Later priestly trajectories continued to craft insider/outsider arguments around the Balaam figure and type.

(5) In some cases, Balaam's words were severed from his figure and type and were utilized by the Qumranities, the Samaritans, and the writer of 1 Enoch, or

(6) The figure was embellished by later Samaritans (Pilti), Josephus (the Balaam speech), and Al Kisa'i.

(7) Balaam was remotely remembered by certain writers of works contained in the New Testament, the Babylonian Talmud, and medieval Samaritan works.

(8) Modern short story and political-scientific writers found Balaam the figure, or words attributed to him, helpful in articulating social and political concerns.

The ancient Middle Easterners were interested in world-building and world-maintaining systems (i.e., **religions**). Their ancient kings' preoccupation with law-giving, gardening (maintenance of the **Sacred Tree**), fertility, shepherding, and war testify to these overarching concerns. Their priests, working within the framework of these concerns, focused on the issue of maintenance of secure and effective lines of communication between the otherworld and the world-builders/maintainers. For many of them, as we shall observe time and time again below, Balaam the figure and Balaam the type served as an excellent paradigm around which to group their explanations of how their world was or was not to have been maintained.

PART 1 : BACKGROUND

Chapter 1. A Discovery at Tell Deir 'Allā: Its Implications and Significance: The Coming War Between Heaven and Earth

> This inscription, as we have reconstructed it, provides us with what is probably the best example we have of the appearance of an eighth–century B.C.E. northwest Semitic manuscript in Aramaic, Phoenician, or Hebrew. At that time, the differences among these three scripts were minimal...[1]

Thus described André Lemaire an extra–Israelite text concerning Balaam ben Beor produced by archaeological research in present–day Jordan. The text was written on a plastered wall in bicolor: black and red. Black was used for writing the majority of the text, while red served for writing titles and key words intended by the scribe(s) to stand in relief. The Balaam text occupied one of four columns. The remaining three columns need not detain the reader, for Balaam was not their subject.

The Balaam text, the latest ancient Middle Eastern text concerning him to be found (March 1967), describes the activities of a *hzh*, a seer/prophet. He is specifically termed *'š hzh 'lhn*, the man who was a seer of the gods. It is generally agreed that the text of Deir 'Allā is a copy of a much older text.[2] A reconstructed text follows.

> The account of [Balaam, son of Beor], who was a seer of the gods. The gods came to him in the night, and he saw a vision (2) like an oracle of El. Then they said to [Balaa]m, son of Beor: "Thus he will do/make [   ] hereafter (?), which [ ]."
> (3) And Balaam arose the next day [   ] from [   ] but he was not ab[le to   ] and he wept (4) grievously. And his people

> came up to him [and said to him, "Balaam, son of Beor why are you fasting and crying?" And he sa(5)id to them: "Sit down! I will tell you what the Šadda[yyin] have done.] Now, come, see the works of the gods! The g[o]ds gathered together; (6) the Šaddayyin took their places in the assembly.[3]

This account depicts Balaam having much in common with several ninth-century to sixth-century prophets mentioned in the Hebrew Scriptures. 1) He sees visions which are like oracles. 2) He responds to bad tidings by not eating, and by weeping, because he must retail these tidings to his people, and he, too, is subject to any coming calamity he must proclaim. 3) He (through his vision) gained entry into the assembly of the gods.

The superscriptions of the prophetic books of the Hebrew Scriptures (hence HS) may be likened to the first characteristic. Jeremiah 36:24; Isaiah 20:2-4; and Isaiah 37:1-2 show similar responses to the second commonality. The third places Balaam in a class with Michaiah the son of Imlah of 1 Kings 22:19-22; Isaiah 6:1-4; Jeremiah 23:18, 23:22; Psalm 82:1, 89:7; Job 15:8 and the picture painted by Job 1:6-12.[4]

The last observation may be expanded. Following the final sentence of the above-quoted Balaam text, the account continues: "And they said to Š[ ]: "Sew up, bolt up the heavens in your cloud, ordaining darkness instead of (7) eternal light!"[5] Apparently, the council of gods gave a directive to one of its members to cause the calamity which was designed to punish Balaam's people. This recalls a similar scene in Job 1:6-12. Through a series of such images as "the deaf hear from afar" and "a fool sees visions" (lines 13 and 14 of the reconstructed text), existence is depicted as topsy-turvy.[6] That this sole deity's name commences with the letter Š, and that deity is depicted as playing a "spoiler's role" opposite humankind, it is very tempting to see a connection with another figure in a similar role in the Prologue of the Book of Job: the **satan** (=adversary). We need not yield to this temptation, however.

The Balaam of the Deir 'Allā text is depicted as a seer who has a dream vision at night. He is frightened by its contents, for his people are to be chastised by fire as punishment for somehow having rebelled against their gods. This so unnerves the seer that on the day he arose from his sleep he was unable to eat and drink, but spent much time weeping in sorrow. After describing (the reconstruction contains numerous *lacunae*) the nature of the punishment which is to befall his people, he states also that it will be meted out on a specific date. Regarding what will happen specifically, the sun god, Shamash, will shut the skies with a cloud. This will bring on utter darkness. Mindless terror will result, his people will be thrown into derision, and a plethora of winged saurians will fill the skies. It is at this juncture, unfortunately, that the badly damaged text breaks off and becomes unreadable. Speculating about what possibly followed, one scholar wrote: "Perhaps by execrations or other forms of magic, Balaam attempted to avert the disaster."[7] Thus, one view of Balaam as magician.

The Balaam text from Deir 'Allā, though new and recent, is rooted in images which have long been familiar to the reader from the prophetic and wisdom literature of the HS. Rebellion against the gods by humans, and the gods' reply by cosmic conflagration allow one to see that the themes of covenant and war are combined in the text. The ancient Israelites and Judaites would not have found its contents foreign. Although the Deir 'Allā text of Balaam dates to the eighth century probably, it is argued that this is merely a copy of a text which was considerably older.[8]

BACKGROUND

The Deir 'Allā text suggests strongly that this figure was important and relevant during the eight century B.C.E. Moreover, its existence at Deir 'Allā suggests that its writer(s) had inherited an even older text and tradition about a famous prophet, priest, diviner (i.e., *propriediv*!)[9] who must have been considered quite a phenomenon to his contemporaries and beyond.

Deir 'Allā presents the interested reader with the latest discovered installment of an interpretation of Balaam's position and role. It takes its place among many, many others already extant which one reads throughout the literature of ancient Israel (employed here in its broadest sense). It can also be demonstrated that interest in the Balaam type **and** character continued to titillate the imagination of various post–Israelite writers and thinkers, even to modern, present times. Yet, this account is *sui generis*.

The account of a Balaam ben Beor found recently in the present Hashemite Kingdom of King Hussein–ruled Jordan, then, will serve as an excellent *Eintritt* into the fascinating and labyrinthine subject of prophecy, divination and magic. The figure **and** type, **Balaam**, will be shown to have lent themselves well to the analytical and hermeneutical needs of several generations of ancient Israelite thinkers who found it both necessary **and** convenient to group certain problem–solutions around him.

Chapter 2. The Sacerdotal Class: Social and Religio-Political Protests in Ancient Israel: Hermeneutical Wars on "Paper"

Jeremiah 18:18 mentions three of the social estates in ancient Israel: the priest, the prophet, the wise one. And the tripartite division of the HS is said to have derived from these three worldviews. Although there is merit in making such a connection, it distracts attention from a more important observation: almost all of the thirty nine works which comprise the *TaNaK* anthology were written by priests, either practicing or non-practicing. Most, then, of the HS/Old Testament reflects a priestly *Weltanschauung*. What has perhaps been most misleading is the use of the word **prophet.** Amos, Micah, Isaiah of Jerusalem, and Jeremiah are known to have been prophets: oracles and prophetic discourse ascribed to them comprising portions of the Prophets section of the *TaNaK*. But, there is evidence to support a claim that Amos, Micah, and most certainly Isaiah of Jerusalem were priests. [10] Jeremiah's family is counted among the priests of Anathoth in the superscription to the book of Jeremiah. **Priest** points therefore to a social class within ancient Israel, while **prophet** points more toward a more specialized **activity** engaged in by a person who may or may not have been a priest also. Since members of this class would have been the best educated also, one should not be surprised that the wise ones would have also been members of this class. Who were they? One obvious reply would be those (sons) who had physical deformities, great or small, which prevented them, had they so desired, from serving at the altars of religious sites of the sacrificial cult. Though perhaps physically scarred, their minds remained unblemished.

Thus, the picture becomes somewhat clearer why we state with some degree of confidence that the *TaNaK*, for the most part, is a priestly-written—and, for that matter, priestly-edited—anthology. Failure in the past to appreciate fully this fact has led many who would plumb the depths of meaning of any given page of the *TaNaK* into serious error.

a. When one considers the HS in light of this argument, it is nowhere more clearly and entertainingly argued than in Richard Elliott Friedman's book **Who Wrote The Bible?** [11] how much a priestly product is the *TaNaK*. This book revisits the Documentary Hypotheses, and makes to stand in clearer relief some of the problems glossed over by earlier schools of researchers into the identities of authors of various *corpora*. The earlier progression from J to E to JE to D to P received some updating which resulted in the Friedman schema as

b. J (A Jerusalem-based work reflecting a southern perspective.)

c. E (A work reflecting the critical perspective of the Shiloh-based priesthood.)

d. JE (A work reflecting the interfacing of the J and E source *strata*.)

e. P (A negative reaction by Jerusalem-based, Aaronid priests to the conciliatory perspective of JE.)

f. D (A Shiloh priestly backlash reaction to P.)

g. R (A redactional attempt, accredited to the priest-Scribe Ezra, to bring the preceding hypothesized strata into harmony.)

For Friedman, each *stratum* was the result and product of priestly concerns for the present and future well being of Israel. Simultaneously, however, each *stratum* was crafted as an argument, a full statement designed to articulate a particular program and position in the world opposite opposing programs, and to expose the opposing programs' flaw(s). Friedman's work shows that the *TaNaK* contains, unfortunately, a priest's-eye view of the world of ancient Israel. It tells the reader little, if anything, about the *Weltanschauung* of the poor, the villager, the business person, the soldier, the woman, the teacher, the shepherd, the foreigner in their midst, the **King as King even**! A clearer picture emerges, then, that what most readers of biblical literature thought was before them is in essence a series of priestly, polemical works which cast aspersions on the articulated worldviews of other priests. It is not argued by J that s/he fabricated a worldview out of wholecloth and wrote the view of every person. And in no wise does R pretend to provide **his** readership with a view of the political-religious life of Persia-ruled Israel which was democratic and all-inclusive. Each, however, like poets of a given society, does serve as the literary and cognizant point of confluence of ancient Israelite society. Like Wagner after hearing one of his works performed, the writers of J, E, JE, P, D, and R could likewise exclaim, as the former did for Germany, "Israel," *daB hast du gedichtet* !" Israel you wrote these pieces! These priestly writers will all opine concerning Balaam ben Beor. Below I will present a thesis which argues how each of these priestly writers opined concerning Balaam.

Chapter 3.   The Development of Communication Theories and Praxes: Community Control: Wars for the Fidelity of the People

a. The Priest

It is a *pondus* upon one's shoulders and one's soul to have the awesome responsibility of maintaining constantly a ritually–pure individual status before a given deity. How much more weighty the *pondus* when one is responsible for maintaining the ritual purity of an entire people! Such was the position and purpose of practicing priesthoods about which we shall learn more below.

The pursuit of the maintenance of ritual purity was such an important one that various priesthoods serving the same deity disagreed, sometimes violently, as to just what constituted --as well as guaranteed-- ritual purity. In time, in ancient Israel, this concern reached the fever pitch of interpretive battle. As alluded to above, the hypothesized J through R documents are in essence literary weapons in the service of various priestly groups: groups at war with each other for community control. "Balaam", for each group, will serve various purposes at various times within a period of priestly, polemical activity in ancient Israel ranging from the tenth to the fourth centuries B.C.E. The time or "season" determined how Balaam was viewed and utilized. For many of the priesthoods of ancient Israel, the Sinai–Horeb covenant was a one–time affair which bound two parties inextricably forever. The god of Israel would be their god, they would be his people: exclusively. As long as the proper ritual relationship existed between the two parties, Israel would prosper and the universe would be in perfect balance. Evidently there arose within the ranks of the priests those who took issue with their fellow priests over the veracity of their arguments concerning the "one–timeness" of the affair. They observed the activities of their fellows and those of the highest and lowest **strata** of their society, then proclaimed in the midst of the market place of Israel's existence, "It ain't necessarily, like you tell it, so!" A serious bifurcation occurred within the priestly ranks over a period of time, resulting in specialization of activities. One such specialized group came to be known as prophets. All prophets in ancient Israel were not priests, but priests were those most inclined to become prophets.

b. The Prophet(ess)

Seers, gazers, dreamers, augurers, interpreters of dreams, and "those who enter heaven" often are assigned the title **prophet** in English. Likewise, those who advised monarchs, such as Nathan, Isaiah of Jerusalem and the 400 counselors to King Ahab are called **prophets** also. Hulda's counsel was sought in a similar manner.

The terms *ro'eh*, *hozeh*, *yo'etz*, *hartum* and *nabi'*, are familiar to the student of prophecy in ancient Israel. Although they are generally rendered prophet or counselor -- a prophetic function -- a more specialized function was implied in their use in ancient Israel. Thus, the writer of 1 Samuel 9:9 must inform his readers that he who was formerly known as *ro'eh* is now a *nabi'!* A change in function occurred. For analytical convenience, the epoch of major prophetic activity in ancient Israel is divided into three periods: preexilic, exilic, and postexilic.

The preexilic literature depicts many people engaged in prophetic activity. Moses, known for his lawgiving and covenant making, was also said to have been a prophet. Moreover, his prophetic spirit was poured out onto the heads of some seventy elders of Israel at the Tent of Meeting. Nowhere is it argued that elders would not have been suitable candidates for prophethood. But, then enter Eldad and Medad, two unlikely candidates. Engaged in other activities near the tent, some of the poured out prophetic spirit "splashed" onto them as well. And, like the seventy, they, too, began to prophesy. The story demonstrates the author's view that not every prophet had to have an official position. Non officials, even regular citizens, or rascals!, could prophesy. One onto whom the deity had poured out the prophetic spirit could but prophesy. The reader is not told, however, just what this prophesying consisted of. Yet, an important socio-political statement had been made.

The story involving the anointing of the first **permanent** leader of Israel, Saul, continues the understanding that he whom the deity chooses as a prophet, even for a short time, becomes in fact a prophet. In addition, the story tells us something of the beginning of a "wedding" of two endeavors, the kingly and the prophetic, a wedding which lasts until the death of kingship in ancient Israel in the sixth century B.C.E. Opposite each subsequent king was a prophet. Thus, famous pairs came to exist: David and Nathan, Solomon and Ahijah, Ahab and Michaiah, Ahaz and Isaiah of Jerusalem. The final Judean monarch, Zedekiah (Mattaniah), was opposed by the prophet Jeremiah. And Saul, anointed by the prophet Samuel, eventually came to be opposed and denounced by him.

During this period, prophets are depicted as having been organized into either bands operating at various rural sites of religious importance; bands or guilds located at various royal courts; or as individuals who acted independently.

Prophets continue to be active long after the prophet/king forced "divorce". During the exilic period, ca. 597-539 B.C.E., two prophets, one the priest Ezekiel, the other termed Deutero-Isaiah, were among those active in Babylonia. Both longed for Jerusalem and its temple. One warned that Jerusalem and its inhabitants could be swept away; the other provided a blueprint for Jerusalem's restoration.

Following Deutero-Isaiah's pronouncements of restoration, the new Jerusalem temple was rebuilt between ca. 520 and 515/14 B.C.E. Again, the names of two prophets loom large in post exilic times: Haggai and Zechariah. They appear to have been prime movers in maintaining high morale during this period of restoration.

From these glimpses, one intuits that much prophetic activity took place in ancient Israel. Moreover, one gathers that "prophecy" meant engaging in different activities at different times between the 11th and 5th centuries B.C.E. And we stated earlier that many of these prophets were priests.

c. The Diviner

If **priest** and **prophet** presented Janus faces of the same phenomenon, **diviner** became a third face grafted thereon. The meaning of the Hebrew word, *qsm*, appears to be one who divines by the use of a rod, one who reveals, one who cuts wood into pieces for the purpose of making lots (i.e., lot cutter), and one who conjures by magic. Depending on the time and place, these characteristics are equally applicable to priests and prophets also. A picture will slowly emerge which demonstrates that one person's priest or prophet is merely another's diviner, and vice-versa.

With diviner, as with prophet, one notices another fine-turning of priestly activity. This activity is brought on by the exigencies of the times and situations faced by various groups or individuals. Instead of viewing prophet, priest, diviner, and so on as different, as pursuing different, separate trajectories through the life of ancient Israel, one has greater success viewing each as various points on the same circle: a circle on which every point was in constant flux.

d. Who Is the Legitimate Spokesperson for Deity or Deities?

Let us place our study of the background to the hermeneutical history of Balaam in proper perspective. Prophets, priests, and diviners must be understood as part of a greater concern for ancient Israel: the question of how the deity communicates with the created order. For Israel, this was apparently an important and serious question.

Beginning with the stories of Genesis and ending with the exclamation of Deutero-Zechariah 13:2ff., the reader is able to see just how many answers to the question of communication the *TaNaK* anthology provides. In the "garden" story, the deity walks the earth, speaks with the man and woman directly, and is informed by the "blood from the ground" that Abel has been heinously murdered. Showing a move toward transcendence on the part of deity is the story of Noah, for it is the deity who closes the door of the ark. A different picture of semitranscendence emerges when one considers the story of Abraham and the three "angels". Each angel (=messenger) speaks for the deity, but no **one** provides the reader (or Abraham!) with a full account of what is planned for Sodom and Gomorrah. All three together allow Abraham to speak with his god.

Heaven and earth are connected by a ladder upon which messengers move busily up(ward) and down(ward) in the dream of the patriarch Jacob. The deity is nowhere to be found, but the reader is led to think that somewhere beyond the uppermost portion of the ladder was the abode of Jacob's god. The ladder answers the question of **how** heaven and earth were connected.

Following the dreamer is the interpreter of dreams, Joseph. "Are not dreams the property of (the) god? Tell me your dream." (Genesis 41:16). With this story one encounters the **human** mediator of a deity's communiqués at Deir' Allā. It sets into motion a movement whereby many specializations within the mediator frame of reference are noticeable. Enter the mantic personality; the animist, the augurer, the wizard, the sorcerer, the reader of the signs of heaven, the shaman, the priest and priestess, the prophet, the diviner, the one who "inquires of the Lord". Standing somewhere just off center stage is the "detached voice" of the "burning bush".

In all this, two overarching concerns were repeatedly addressed: whether the deity had distanced himself from the earth, and if not, who was (were) his legitimate, earthly spokesperson(s). We stress here **spokesperson(s)** because the ultimate debate between priesthoods will be centered on the *dbr yhwh*, the **word** of Yahweh, and not on ritual. Various priesthoods, it will be demonstrated below, took each other to task both inside and outside Israel as they wrestled with this, for them, life and death issue. The fascinating role played by "Balaam" in all this will be unpacked systematically in what follows. It should be noted, however, that the debate continued in ancient Israel long after the office of **prophet** ceased to exist. The debate between priests, prophets and diviners, therefore, had a limited historical life during the period in which ancient Israel attempted to communicate effectively with its god.

PART 2: PROPHET, PRIEST, DIVINER: BALAAM AS TEST CASE AND PARADIGM

Chapter 4. Philosophies of History and Communication in Ancient Israel: Priestly Wars and Nonaggression Pacts

Henri Frankfort and others have long since demonstrated that discursive thought was evident in the ANE long before the classical Greek philosophical tradition got under way.[1] If "What is truth?" seemed to have been the most overarching question raised by the ANE intelligentsia, "How can one know that truth when one hears it?" occupies a close second-place position of importance. In either case the questions were posed in all sincerity and in earnest by the sacerdotal classes. They stood in constant danger of being denounced by colleagues within their ranks, as well as by detractors from without for not being able to provide an acceptable answer. Oftentimes, the outside detractors were priests belonging to competing priesthoods within the kingdom, or to conquering kingdoms, countries, or empires.[2] Priesthoods which appeared unable to answer both questions to the satisfaction of all concerned were constantly in danger of being replaced.[3]

But there was a second danger, intimately bound up with the first, but providing a separate danger or threat all its own: internal politics. Priesthoods and their efficacies were therefore threatened when Saul, David, Solomon, Jerboam I, Ahab and Jezebel, Manasseh, Hezehiah, and Josiah all ascended thrones. These were crucial times for the sacerdotal classes: some were empowered, others passed by the way side. During these tenures operated the Shiloh priesthood with its Mushite orientation and the Hebron-based Aaronid priesthood: major priesthoods serving the Israelite and Judahite tribal confederations respectively. There were others as well. After the monarchy was established and a state priesthood was established with David as king **and** highest priest, the fortunes of these two major priestly groups changed for the better and for the worst, with the Shiloh group receiving the worst. From the tenth through the fourth centuries B.C.E., these two major priesthoods waged sacerdotal warfare against each other. All types of aspersions were cast, and the seemingly clear terms **prophet, priest,** and **diviner** took on new meanings as weapons in the mouth and hand of those who would dispute their meaning and legitimacy with opposing groups. Present, and at center stage of these debates was the figure Balaam as the ubiquitous test case and convenient (though necessarily nebulous) paradigm.

a. **The Balaam Cycle of Texts (Numbers 22-24):**
    An Exegetical Explication

> ".... it is not necessary for the written work into which living tradition is translated to become a dead letter. This written word carries within it a germ of spiritual energy capable of generating a new living tradition, which in turn should breathe new life into the word."
>
> Geza Vermes [4]

In deuteronomistic circles, all known or acknowledged oracles were reassessed in light of concerns about legitimate communication and communicator(s).[5] Deuteronomy 18:21ff. holds "How may we know the word which the Lord has not spoken?" – When a **prophet** speaks in the name of the Lord, if the word does not come to pass or come true, that is a word which the Lord has not spoken; the **prophet** has spoken it presumptuously, you need not be afraid of him." As to the nature of a *bona fide* oracle spoken by Yahweh, the Deuteronomist identifies certain terminology which had to be present when one spoke of or retailed an oracular experience. The *shoresh* or "root" for these technical terms follows. The *dbr* or "word" "comes" (*bw'*, cf. 1 Sam. 9:6; Jer. 15:15); "comes to pass" (*hyh*, cf. Deut. 18:22a); is "done" (*'sh*, cf. Num. 23:19); is "fulfilled" (*ml'*, *nfl*, cf. 1 Kgs. 8:56; 2 Kgs 10:10), but is, rather, "established", "brought to fruition" (*qwm*, cf. Isa. 44:26; 2 Sam 7:25), does not suffer the fate of returning to Yahweh "unrealized" and "unfulfilled" (*l' yshwv*, cf. Isa. 45:23; 55:11). These characteristics are enshrined in the words placed in the mouth of the nebulous figure Balaam ben Boer. Addressing Balak, his employer, the King of Moab, in Num. 23:19-20, he asks of Yahweh: "Would he speak and not act (*y'sh*), promise and not fulfill (*dbr wl' yqymynh*)? Truly, my message was to bless: and when he blesses, I cannot reverse it (*wl' 'sybynh*).[6]

Immediately, then, one notices that a deuteronomistic programmatic appears to exist here. The Balaam cycle of oracles at Numbers 22-24 appears to be a part of that programmatic. Further, Balaam- at least here- is touting the party line. A mantic personality, and an outsider to boot!, is depicted as uttering oracles in the name of the insider deity, Yahweh. Adjusting our focus to pan the producer of this Balaam cycle of texts, one sees that the programmatic is framed by the activity of those engaged in mantological exegesis (or perhaps eisegesis). Mantology and its concerns at a specific time in the life of ancient Judah is reflected in the cycle of texts.

This section has the limited purpose of being an exegetical essay in its own right on the meaning of the Balaam cycle for the circle(s) which produced it, to describe and analyze that database, and to state what happened to it as it survived later mantic traditions and interpretations of them in ancient Israel. It has the further purpose of introducing a new series of data which provide meanings and uses for the Balaam cycle by certain priestly groups (especially) in Judah, and there, primarily in Jerusalem. To my knowledge, meanings have not been proposed or presented which state how the Balaam cycle functioned within the inter-and intra-priestly circles' polemical debates. The present work makes that contribution as well.

This section lays the groundwork for all other arguments this work will contain. It is an exegetical essay on the meaning(s) of this the most sustained biblical text concerning Balaam for the circle(s) which produced it. Moreover, I will describe and analyze this database and explain what happened to it as it survived numerous mantic traditions and interpretations of it in ancient Israel. This section has the further purpose of introducing a new series of data which provide meanings and uses for the Balaam cycle by certain priestly groups in Israel, but primarily those in Jerusalem. My conclusions state how the Balaam cycle functioned within the inter-and intrapriestly circles' polemical debates.

The Text

The Massoretic Text (hence MT) of the Balaam cycle presents a nightmare to those who would analyze it critically. Of the many pitfalls, words make no sense (*bny 'mw*, i.e., sons of his people) at 22:5; phrases appear gratuitously ("And Moab said to the elders of Midian," at 22:4) which appears to be a unexplainable intrusion; elders from Moab and Midian depart to visit a diviner with divinations in their hands! (22:7-14); these elders do not appear to be quite certain of their destination (i.e., whether it is in Ammon or in Aram); Yahweh allows Balaam to accompany the messengers of Balak (elders once [2:7-14] and princes another time [22:15-21], and then is angry (22:20) because he goes (22:22)). But it takes a *mal'ach*, a "messenger" of Yahweh, to finally let him go (22:35). That is, he is given permission to go twice! Balaam speaks of himself in the third person (24:3;15); and oracles dangle like marionettes at the end of this cycle as it presently exists. And then the prophet, priest, sorcerer, diviner, seer, gazer just leaves; he goes home and leaves Balak's life in a shambles! Seen this way, the MT paints two portraits of Balaam: (1) He is a known territory-wide mercenary, diviner/sorcerer, mantic hit man, or (2) he is a prophet plus who, though an outsider, exhibits the traits of one on whose head the ominous hand of Yahweh rests. The reason for this quandary is the nature of the text before the reader. One critical reading suggests the existence of a text mosaic: a text mosaic which must be unravelled.

Debates about, and learned opinions concerning, the state of the text are legion. Sandwiched between the 1773 study by Verschuir, *Dissertatio de oraculis Bileami*, and von Gall's *Zusammensetzung und Herkunft der Bileam-Perikope* of 1900 are a number of studies which have grappled with the text.[7] Since 1900 numerous studies have also appeared. Among the most stimulating and probing are found the works of McNeile (1932);[8] Cazelles (1958);[9] Vermes (1961);[10] Sturdy (1976);[11] Leibowitz (1980);[12] and Fishbane (1985).[13] It is therefore somewhat surprising that Von Rad in **The Problem of the Hexatateuch and Other Essays**[14] devotes space to the text on only two pages. Of the first (p.7) he writes: "Here ....we have.... the major features of the story of redemption, from the patriarchs to the entry into the promised land. The minor accretions–details concerning...the meeting with Balaam and so on...." shows this cycle to be a minor issue for him. Of the second he writes:" A second major complex of tradition which the Yahwist found more or less readymade is to be seen in the Balaam story,..." and then sees the writer/editor's problem as being merely one of fitting it into a certain scheme (p.52).

The most common learned opinions as to why the text exhibits its particular characteristic find it having been compiled from two hypothesized documents, J (Yahwist) and E (Elohist.)[15] According to one scholar,[16] the J document may be traced to the courtly circle of the Judean Kingdom, while the E document's origin is said to be the circle of Mushite priests at the cultic center Shiloh in the Kingdom of Israel. Various times are offered for the appearance of both hypothesized documents and again, it is evident that interpretive battle rages on.[17] Thus, R.F. Johnson writes: "The two poems in Numbers 23, usually attributed to E, are obviously acquainted with the story of Balaam in the employ of the King of Moab, while the J poems in Ch.24 could have originated apart from this particular tradition about Balaam."[18] Likewise, Gray [19] maintains that "It is true, however, that the characteristics of E are more apparent than those of J." Without providing a rationale for why one passage or another is either a part of the J or E strand, McNeile [20] merely labels each verse as belonging to one or the other throughout his entire commentary.

Backing away from the importance of assigning the J or E designation to the text of Numbers as a whole, Sturdy [21] states: ". . . material has traditionally been divided between two early sources, which have been called J and E. It is not, however, necessary to assign passages between J and E in this commentary." Friedman [22] assigns the entire periscope to E. And neither Vermes [23] nor Leibowitz [24] considers the Documentary Hypothesis at all.

In all, one may state with some certainty that the text is readable. It exhibits clear signs of being a literary mosaic. Whether pieces making up the text come from a P (priestly) source [25], a J source or an E source learned opinions differ widely. There appears to be no unanimity of opinion looming on the near horizon either. Source conflation is obvious, but whether that conflation is to be sought in various hypothesized P, J, and E documents or source strata remains to be cogently argued. It is perhaps an exhibition of wisdom which heretofore has been given little credit when we repeat the words of Von Rad quoted earlier "A second major complex of tradition which the Yahwist (i.e., J) found more or less ready-made is to be seen in the Balaam story." [26] The story seems to appear in material characteristic of J, but J is depicted as merely carrying a story forward which was already the result of a conflation of earlier separate stories.

Linguistic Analysis

For the Balaam text to be intelligible, analysis of the key terms is necessary. When this is performed, several layers of the text are exposed. This once again points to the text's mosaic character, and puts us in a better position to understand the text and its purpose in the hands of those who produced it in the present form. Although a more through discussion will follow in the section devoted to the literary form(s) of this cycle below, linguistic analysis will be approached by dividing the cycle into (1) narrative framework, (2) fable, and (3) poems.

(1) Narrative Framework

One raised on the Documentary Hypotheses will naturally attempt to unravel a text such as the Balaam cycle by recourse to searching for the presence of divine appellations, in the text and then grouping certain literary characteristics around them. [27] Doing so, one finds that *yhwh* (Yahweh) occurs 29 times; [b] *'elohim* ([the] deity) 9 times (and twice with a suffix); 'l (El, i.e., deity) 8 times; *shdy* (Shaddai, i.e., mighty one) twice; and appearing only once is the term *'lywn* (Elyon, i.e., the eternal one). One bears in mind, however, that the MT is a 7th to 9th century of this era product: it is a very late text.[28] Comparing the divine name occurrences of the MT with their counterparts in the other major codices, i.e., the Septuagint(s); the Samaritan recension of a Hebrew text; the standard Jewish recension of a Hebrew text (unvocalized); the Syriac (Peshitto) Version; the early Aramaic Versions or Targums; and the Vulgate, one notices numerous variant readings, and thereby occurrences, of the divine names. The history of why this is so need not detain us here. [29] The Qumran, the Peshitto and Septuagint codices preserve a text earlier than that in hand (i.e., the consonantal text) underlying the MT.[30] All of this suggests strongly that conventional methods of approaching this text will not suffice here. All of these texts and versions do not read the same.

Most instructive is the presence of the term *mshl (mashal)* at Numbers 23:6 (here *meshalo*, i.e., his *mashal*). Proverbs, the biblical anthology, is called *mishle shlomo* or the *mashal* of Solomon (plural *smihut* of *mashal*). As one reads them in Hebrew, it becomes clear that they were composed using *parallelismus membrorum*, i.e., synonymous parallelism and that one is working with a literary type which implies more than its surface or "obvious" meaning. One is in the presence of a wisdom saying, a gnome, an aphorism.[31] *Mashal*, therefore, may be rendered as discourse," "parable," or "proverb". *Caveat emptor!*

The translator of this cycle is also confronted with the possibility that the name of the main character might be nothing more than a play on words (or a word). The problem alerts itself in two ways. (1) In Genesis 36:32 one reads about a King Bela, *(bl')* the son of one Beor who was king of Edom in the 12th or 11th century B.C.E. (2) Balaam *(bl'm)* at Numbers 22:5 is also said to be the son of Beor. The only morphological difference is the final *mem* (i.e., /m/) on *bl'* producing *bl'(m)*.[32]

Here one also becomes aware of a problem similar to the one encountered in Deuteronomy 26:5–10. There the MT states: "An Aramean about to **perish**, or a **perishing** Aramean...." Many English interpretations/translations render this: "A **wandering** Aramean....", since it is reasoned that this cultic recitation refers to Jacob, and Jacob is depicted in biblical literature as a seminomadic sojourner. The challenge presented by the MT is the word *'bd* (perish). Most translators/interpreters intuit a scribal error and read *'br* (cross over, wander [with a purpose]). The printed Hebrew letters for /d/ and /r/ are very similar and may be easily misread by a scribe working in haste. The same is true for the old Hebrew alphabet where /d/ is rendered by ∆ and /r/ is rendered by ∆. It is an easy error to make. It remains to be demonstrated by cogent argument, however, that a mistake **was** made in the text.

This same possibility of error exists in relationship to the name of the supposed homeland of Balaam. It centers on the names Edom and Aram. Balak, in which ever version (both having been combined in the Numbers account), sends embassies to Balaam to request his divining services. Words such as "Pethor," "the River", and "Amaw" in the present version have led many to suppose that Balaam's homeland was somewhere in present-day Syria near the western bank of the Euphrates.^{33} We are presented with a case similar to the crossing/wandering/perishing, for *'dm* and *'rm* demonstrate once again just how much difficulty some ancient scribe might have had with ∆ and ∆$_t$. The orthographic difference between "Aram" and "Edom" in either old or Massoretic Hebrew is ∆ and ∆! But elaborate explanations have been offered by numerous scholars to demonstrate that Balaam's home was in Syria (Aram) somewhere near the Euphrates; all on the assumption that the MT is flawless.^{34} The area of the would-be confrontation between "Israel" and the Balak coalition is depicted as being south (Edom), southeast (Moab), and possibly southwest (Amalek) of Judah. A donkey ride by an embassy to Syria would be ridiculous, especially in light of the simple morphological clarification and its attending concluding possibilities. Whether it was a donkey ride by elders or by princes really doesn't matter. Edom, not some territory near the Euphrates, appears to be a more sensible location for the geographical setting for this cycle. (Deir 'Allā text.)

Shedding more light on this problem is a recent work which studies communication techniques in the ancient Near East.^{35} It demonstrates that Balak's message to Balaam is cast in the form of one equal communicating with another: that is with another king! This supports the earlier discussion concerning the *bl'* –*bl'm* identification. At Genesis 36:32 Bela or Bala (*bl'*) is named as one of the kings (i.e., equals! to Balak) of Edom, a near neighbor of Moab and Amalek. Priest/kings are nothing new to the ancient Near East.[36] Some of them have been extolled for their wisdom (cf. Solomon), their sense of law (cf. Hammurabi), their manual skills (cf. Hiram of Tyre), and their musical abilities (cf. David). It seems likely that underlying this cycle before us was a monarch who was famous for his abilities as a diviner–who, like the others, became a legend.

The narrative section frames the *meshalim* by providing a geographical backdrop. From (as I argue above) Edom, Balaam makes a journey to "the (nebulous) city of Moab (*'ir moab* [= the capital city), then on to a cultic site, *Kiriath–husot*, where what appears to be a state banquet was held (22:40). The next day the scene unfolds at *Bamot–ba'al*. After the *mashal* delivered there, the group moves to the field of *Zophim*, to the top of *Pisgah* (23:14a). *Peor* which overlooks the desert (or Jeshimon)[37] at 23:28 is the next locus. It is the scene of several, among which is the final, *meshalim*. Then, according to this narrative framework, Balaam, having accomplished Yahweh's, not Balak's work, departs for home.

Kiriath–husot means City of Streets. It appears only in this cycle, and the site is unknown.[38] *Bamoth–ba'al*, the raised mounds or altars (dedicated to) Ba'al (of the region) designates a well–known shrine. It lay near Dibon (present–day Diban in Jordan) where the Deir 'Allā texts concerning Balaam were discovered.[39] The field of *Zophim*, that is the field of gazers (*zophim* [and even *hozim*])[40] adds to the significance of what Balaam was understood to be and to do. *Pisgah*, which means peak, summit or branch, is the height from which gazers delivered their utterances. It was located north of the Arnon River. *Peor*, like *Ba'al, Nebo*, and *Pisgah*, is also the name of a deity of the region,[41] and identified as well another "summit" in the region. The writer of this cycle has provided the careful reader with at least one part of the overall thesis of the work; Yahweh is able to enable Israel even at sites known or reputed to be the haunts of other deities, generally of the agricultural, fertility cult variety. It depicts a higher purpose on Yahweh's part: the casting down of high places.

(2) Fable

Numbers 22:21 is the end of a section which tells of Balaam agreeing to accompany Balak's embassy. The preceding verse 20 has explained why he is undertaking the journey. Thus, the first part of verse 22's contents are quite the *non sequitur*, especially if one were to argue that this work is seamless wholecloth.[42] It does provide a literary bridge across which one may travel into pious Fableland. Numbers 22:22b through 35 contains the fable which has been augmented by more narrative material.

The important terms here are *stn* (22:22 & 22:32b), *pth* (22:31), *yrt* (22:32b), and *bt'* (22:34) and *glh* (22:31). *stn* is translated "adversary" and not the personalized Satan.[43] This term appears elsewhere in biblical literature [44] with the same meaning as that in the book of Job (1:6).

pth is here employed in a standard phrase used to show that a person (usually a prophet) is speaking a *dbr-yhwh*, that is, Yahweh-word. [45] It is translated "open" with Yahweh doing the opening.

The *hapax legomenon*, *yrt*, presents a problem. Much ink has been employed in attempts to explain it. Arabic *wrt*, "to throw, cast headlong" is generally preferred as a possible cognate, suggesting a translation such as "to rush headlong (into something)." More research is needed before the meaning of this term becomes clear.

"To rebel" is probably the best way to render *ht'*. It is a common term used in language relating to a convenantal understanding, or a world view at the center of which is understood to be a covenant. *ht'* is an acknowledgement by one covenant member to another that that member has abrogated covenant responsibilities agreed to at the making of that covenant. It is therefore a legal term, and it is so used here. The only reason, however, that Balaam has come to understand what is going on is because his eyes have been opened. The Hebrew expression is *glh 'ynym*, "to uncover the eyes." Only then does the person who is paid to gaze see, with an inner eye as it were. Balaam is repeatedly cast as the bungler whose long-standing reputation is repeatedly castigated until he is humbled into the dust of derision. A reputation as diviner, mantic, gazer, magician, and seer has not impressed the compiler and editor of this narrative material. These, like sending one on a trek through (let us utilize the standard term) the "wilderness" and leaving such a one to his/her own devices, are only sufficiently pliable, nay, malleable to serve as instruments/partners (by way of covenant [always lurking in the background in this material]) for Yahweh's expressed *telos*. This fable casts Yahweh as the master teleologist.

Those five terms summarize the fable. An **adversary** opposes Balaam; **opens** the mouth of an (empowered to be wise) ass to impart otherworldly wisdom to a reputedly wise man who is; rushing headlong foolishly against the superior adversary; only to force the reputedly wise man to admit that he has rebelled. that is, abrogated his part of a sworn to agreement. We as readers have not been given text which depicts the making of the covenant between Balaam and Yahweh, but *ht'* certainly implies such an understanding on the part of the writer who crafted this cycle. The only way that the reputation of Balaam can be salvaged is through the medium of divine intervention. The reputed wise one is enabled to be wise by the omniscient Yahweh, and then become an instrument/channel for that greater wisdom.

(3) Poems

Two *mashal* poems appear in Chapter 23, with the remaining five being embedded in Chapter 24. In the first, Balaam is certainly cast as a gazer, a hozeh, for from the tops of the mountains, from the hills (in *parallelismus membrorum*) he observes "Israel". The presence of Jacob and Israel suggests that this poem has a northern provenance. Verse 10's "Let me die the death of the righteous (*yshr*) puts one again in the midst of covenant language. "Upright" means having the ability to hold one's head up before the law to which one has adhered unswervingly. The poem opens with the statement that the speaker is from Aram. It is well to keep in mind that Balak in the first colon is in synonymous parallelism with the "king of Moab" in the second colon. There is no emphasis on Aram. Thus, our earlier arguments concerning Balak's homeland in the narrative discussions still hold.

The second *mashal* of Chapter 23 presents no linguistic problems. There is in the doublet at verse 23 and the appearance of *nhsh* in the first colon which is balanced by *qsm* in the second. They are terms which refer to the practice of magic and divination. *nhsh* is translated elsewhere (cf. Genesis 3:1 and Numbers 21:6) as serpent. Then in Numbers 21:19 and following one reads that Moses must fashion a bronze serpent to eradicate the menace of the serpents which are plaguing Israelites. The term, a play on words, is *nhsh nhshym*. Both serpents and bronze have the same root. This bronze serpent was used for cures and was reputed long after the time of Moses to have had curative powers. It was destroyed during the reign and reformation of King Josiah ca. 639–609 B.C.E.

qsm may be rendered as (1) one who divines by the use of a rod (noun), (2) cut (i.e., cut wood into pieces for the purpose of making lots), and (3) magical conjuration. Much of this is based on the Syriac *qsm* which means to exorcise or to swear, or Arabic *qsm* in its second and fourth forms meaning an oath.[46]

shtm, 24:3's "man of opened eyes(s)," presents the reader with another term of nebulous meaning in Hebrew. It may also be rendered "closed" or even "perfect". Its sense is wholeness, completeness with reference to understanding the workings of deity. Once this man has been enabled by Yahweh to see, it denotes a person whose eyes therefore have been *glh*, "uncovered", or "revealed" (to). In addition, this person has *shm'*, "heard" with an inner ear as it were. These terms denote prophetic activity of the type and caliber in which an Isaiah, a Jeremiah, and a Micah, to name just three, would have been engaged. Here Balaam is so cast.

The fourth *mashal* essentially introduces Balaam in the same way. There is an extended version of the lead in which adds the expression *d't 'lywn*, "knowledge of the eternal one." Once again, it denotes covenant language (cf. Hosea 4:1b), and implies that the speaker is a party to a covenant which is still in force. This *mashal* ends at 24:19.

The remaining three *meshalim* occupy 24:20–25. Only the final one contains an expression worthy of some discussion. The first portion of verse 24 contains the word *Kittim*. Oftentimes it is written *ktyym*, and is derived from *kty* (in Greek, *Kition*), a town on Cyprus. At least this is the apparent sense of Isaiah 23:1; 12. But *Kittim* is a pregnant concept in the Hebrew mind, and the term takes on a number of nuances as the history of Israel develops. Progressively in the literature, *ktym* will come to mean the Western seagoing peoples (Jer. 2:10; Ezek. 27:6), the Romans (Dan. 11:30), and the Greeks (1 Mac. 1:1;8:5). *Kittim*, then, in biblical literature, depending on which historical period, essentially means (seagoing [but not exclusively]) Westerners.

The preceding approximately thirty five terms were isolated because it is impossible to understand the cycle as it has been preserved in the MT without some discussion of them. Some researchers might have chosen more, some less, and their works would have reflected the fruit of that choice. We have elaborated the essential terms necessary to continue a serious discussion of the Balaam cycle, and we may now proceed.

The Literary Form(s)

Above, we alluded to enough information about literary form to enable us to engage in analysis of the important linguistic phenomena. Normally the present concern could be cast in the form of a simple question, Is the text prose or poetry? Again, through linguistic analysis it is clear that the question is far more complicated. How many literary forms are evident to the text? appears to be a more precise question in light of that analysis. A reading with an eye for terminology has revealed three major literary forms comprising the text. These forms have helped delineate the text as well. The forms are narrative fable (which depicts an ass imparting other-worldly wisdom to one who is reputed to be this-worldly wise using human speech), and a series of poetic *meshalim* of varying lengths and contents.

(1) The Narrative Framework

The narrative framework directs both the fable and the poetic *meshalim* in a specific direction. Otherwise, one would have nothing more than a fable and a series of individual *meshalim* with no apparent connection between them. It is in the framework, therefore, that one finds whatever purpose the compiler/ author/editor of this cycle had in engaging in this enterprise.

The cycle is part of a much larger story. This larger story wants to tell how Israel under the leadership of first Moses, then Joshua, succeeds in moving ultimately from Egypt to the land of the Canaanites. It wants to explain, however, a number of vicissitudes, institutions, challenges to both Moses as a leader, and to Israel as a people, engagements with peoples who occupied territories along the route from the mountain of Yahweh to their final destination, the land promised to Abraham and his progeny, and their success both enroute and in that land which had been promised.

Following a route itinerary which would make sense to only a priest, Israel is depicted as moving from locale to specific locale. Shortly before the text of Numbers arrives at our cycle, locales such as Kadesh(-barnea) (Num. 20:1); Edom (20:14); Mount Hor on the border of Edom (20:22); (by way of the Red Sea to) Oboth; Lyeabarim east of Moab; valley of Zered; and then settled for a time north of the Arnon River which, according to 21:13b, "is the boundary between Moab and the Amorites." Curiously, at this point, if the object of all this movement had been to occupy the land of the Canaanites, all Israel would have had to have done was move due westward! Instead, 21:20 names two places where Israel dwells for some time; Bamoth and the top of Pisgah which looks down upon the desert. In the narrative as it continues, these are two places from which Balaam will deliver *meshalim* (22:41 and 23:14). Here, the Moses host desires to travel northward through the land of the Amorites, is denied access, fights against them and defeats them, occupying the land between the Arnon in the south and the Jabbok in the north. The story does have a point to which it is rapidly moving: the land bounded on the north by the Arnon and how the Arnon came to be the northern boundary of that land: Moab, over which Balak now rules. That sets the stage for the present cycle of texts. A clue as to the device utilized by the narrative writer is found in 21:14a. It would appear that at the heart of his narrative framework is the Book of the Wars of Yahweh. The itinerary which one has been following was probably provided by sites named in an extended poem (or series of poems) with this title.[47]

(2) The Fable

Aesop readily leaps to the Western mind when one begins to speak of fables, and this is understandable. But students of the MT and its variants think first of the *nahash* (serpent) in the second creation story (Gen. 3:1 ff.), and the ass in the cycle under discussion. The presence of the fable *(mashal* also) is not by accident; it belongs with the other *meshalim* which are in poetic form, for all have the same purpose of teaching an important point in the crafting scheme of the editor/writer. The fable/*mashal* sets the tone, then, for the following *meshalim* and anticipates them. The difference between the ass fable and the serpent fable is also instructive. The serpent speaks of his own accord and is characterized in the material as the most shrewd (*'rwm*) of all the animals made by Yahweh. The ass must have her mouth opened by Yahweh. It is therefore a *mshl–yhwh*, a Yahweh discourse, with the ass being merely the medium for non–human thought and instruction. This is an important difference, and once again gives evidence why it was appropriated by the editor/writer for his/her purposes.

(3) The Poems (in the form of *meshalim*)

The *meshalim* form a major part of the cycle. Their purpose here is to drive home (almost rub ones's nose in the dust!) the point that Yahweh (as invincible divine warrior [following the earlier clue from the Book of the Wars of Yahweh]) [48] accomplishes complete victory and hegemony over his adversaries by not only warfare, but also by wisdom. Yahweh is both physically and intellectually superior to all who would oppose his divine purposes; especially where Israel fits into those plans. Let us approach each *mashal* individually and observe its particular characteristics.

(a) mashal 1

mashal 1 is contained between 23:7a–10. It is written in poetry in the first person. The *locus* is a "bare height" which is known as Bamot Ba'al, that is, a cultic center dedicated to the local manifestation of the agricultural/fertility deity of the Canaanites, Ba'al. According to this *mshl*, Balaam has been recruited from the district of Aram. Although one would like to make more of this than can be demonstrated, all boundaries of political entities of the ancient Near East were always fluid. Today their boundaries could be measured this. Tomorrow, in light of a new political development, the boundary could be measured that. Such was the nature of political influence tied to the dependence on happenstance in the ancient Near East (henceforth ANE). The exact boundaries of Aram are therefore undeterminable regardless of time period.

At a Ba'al cultic center, a foreigner acknowledges that the "righteous" experience the most rewarding end existence. Since there is no Ba'al activity depicted in the *mshl*, the site has been transformed (for the editor/author's purposes) into a site for Yahweh's use. A "decontamination" of the site appears to be the purpose of this discourse.

All of "Israel" was supposed to have been at this locale.

(b) mshl 2

Numbers 23:18b–24 is also a *mshl* cast in the first person. Here the *locus* is the "Field of Zophim", atop Mt. Pisgah. The major theme is antidivination, representing a time when the author/editor is an exponent of a radically different view of the expected efficacy of spells and curses. The *mshl* praises the existence of "Israel" and argues for its inviolability. References to the "lioness" and to the "Lion" may be a plug for Judah (and its totem), and may signal one of the contributing parties to the JE material. Cursing the small didn't work any better than cursing the large.

(c) mshl 3

24:3b–9 contains *mshl 3*. It refers to Balaam in the third person. Its *locus* is the top of Peor. It would appear that two separate poems have been brought together, one which aggrandizes Jacob/Israel, reflecting a northern concern, and one which expresses the southern importance, since the lion and lioness are placed in prominent position in the second half of the poem(s). This would appear to signal Judah's importance (through its totem). In essence, the form betrays a poem/*mshl* about, not by, a Balaam.

(d) mshl 4

Another third person–cast *mshl* whose *locus* is at the top of Peor is located at 25:15b–19. An (from the literary frame) unsolicited (=freebie) oracle (damnation type) projected to be fulfilled, i.e., the latter days (= those of the apocalyptic writer interpreting his own times) appears here. The beginning of the oracle is the same as that of the previous, solicited oracle. Added to the introductory of the oracle is the idea that now Balaam reflects *d't yhwh*.[49] Covenant terminology is again evident here.

(e) mshl 5

According to the narrative framework, the *locus* of the *mshl* located at 24:20b is also Peor. This *mshl* departs from the preceding poetically–written ones in that it exhibits the characteristics of lyrical prose.[50] It is cast as a separate pronouncement against Amalek. According to Exodus 17:8–16, "The Lord will have war with Amalek from generation to generation." The *mshl* appears to have had a separate existence as perhaps an oracle fragment.

(f) mshl 6

The contents of 24:21b–22 are also cast as having been delivered at Peor. This *mshl*, also written in lyrical prose, is a separate pronouncement against the Kenites. There is reference to them as a mountain/hill–dwelling people.[51] Assyria, which flexes its muscles ca. 850–600 B.C.E., is to be their undoing.

(g) mshl 7

The final *mashal* is located at 24:23b-24. The *locus*, according to the narrative framework, is the same. The lyrical prose-written piece is a pronouncement against Asshur and Eber who will meet destruction at the hands of the ship traveling *Kittim*. Thus, the agent of Yahweh's punishment (Asshur) in the previous *mshl* becomes in turn punished by another of Yahweh's later agents, the Kittim.[52]

The seven *meshalim*, the fable, and the narrative framework, which shapes and provides direction for the wise sayings occupying Chapters 22-24 of Numbers, offer a variety of literary forms in so short a space. The reader notices a masterful blending and choreographing of separate wisdom pieces (the fable is also an example of the *mshl*) all of which point beyond themselves to a member of the *literati* in ancient Israel (here employed in the broadest sense of that term) who knows how to do theology, battle, and polemics through storytelling.

The Setting

Ascertaining the setting of the author/editor of this cycle is necessarily and understandably an involved exercise. As to the date and culture context of the completed cycle, both narrative framework and the *meshalim* provide clues. Clues may be read in numerous ways, however, so differences in informed opinion abound in such an exercise as well.

(A) J, E, JE, and *Balaam*

(1) Narrative

Since there are arguments for J and E strands,[53] and even arguments for P being present as well in this cycle,[54] one would begin to search for the probable setting in Judah, and then, some time after 722 B.C.E. Strong arguments suggest that the narrative exhibits the traits of JE.[55] The major characteristics of this combined North/South document is its conciliatory tone and tenor. The Shiloh (Mushite) priests of the North and the Judaean (Aaronid) priests of the South, former adversaries, ceased their mutual antagonisms, and joined forces to heal the politico-religious rift between themselves.[56] JE is thought to have mirrored just that. In this case, then, it would seem that the setting for the writer/editor of the present Balaam cycle would be the Judaean priestly circle dominated by the conciliatory Aaronid/Mushite faction, and is part of the post- 722 B.C.E. presentation of the traditions of surviving religious "Israel".

Since the reader is aware that at least two separate stories about Balaam have been woven together, it is reasonable to state that traditional material about a Balaam lies at base of both the separate J and E accounts. This material, because of the *locus* of its concerns, appears to have as its traditional homeland the region northeast of the Jordan, and east and southeast of the Dead Sea.[57] That is, influences on the author/editor's work are from non-Israelite as well as Israelite sources. It is quite possible that the (not available to us) complete northern (E) version would have had a northern homeland for Balaam. A pastoral scene near "the River," as it were, is in keeping with the northern Israelite writer's (geographical) setting.[58] In keeping with the southern version (J), the context clues of *bene 'ammo(n)*, i.e., the inhabitants of Ammon, and "Edom" (which for northern use could have very easily been altered to "Aram" [as shown in the linguistic analysis above]) keep the *locus* in the South. Portions of J and E, then, reflect some altering of non-Israelite traditional material which has been (pre-722 B.C.E.) recast for use by northern and southern writers.

The J document contained a story about a Balaam ben Beor who was reputed to have been an effective prophet, priest, and diviner. (Let us combine portions of each title and produce [in good Jewish fashion] the word *"propriediv"* to refer to all three functions simultaneously).[59] But J has recast the eastern, traditional, non-Israelite material to tell a different story for his/her[60] purposes. The J version made use of the Balaam figure some time after 843 B.C.E. [61]

Likewise, the E writer made use of some existing tradition about a Balaam also. His[62] Balaam appears also to have been a *"propriediv"*. This Balaam figure served the needs of a Shiloh priestly group to 722 B.C.E. As to assigning a more precise date, more recent scholarship is less adventurous than earlier students of the Documentary Hypotheses. [63]

In essence, readers of the MT have before them at least two recastings of an older, non-Israelite tradition about a Balaam (ben Beor). Like an old wine skin, the Balaam figure—and the tradition about him—has been refilled with two different vintages of new wine, one from northern (literary) vineyards and one from corresponding southern vineyards, first as separate vintages, then blended after 722 B.C.E. by cooperating vintners in the South to produce a new vintage which (following this analogy) we call *"Propriediv Nouveau!"*

J and E, as well as JE, reflect three phases of mantological exegesis at three different times, but in only two locations. A *propriediv* subject would certainly have been of interest to the Aaronid and Mushite priestly/prophetic groups performing exegeses of outside traditions. This issue of when all three phases could have taken place, and a plausible rationale for each will be taken up and offered below.

(2) meshalim

Before discussing the setting for each phase and providing the rationale for it, some attention must be paid (here in a general way) to possible context clues to the various writers' settings which may be provided by the poetic and lyrical prose sections of the present MT cycle.

MT poetic texts—and the Psalms are the best examples of this—are the most unreliable texts out of which to tease a plausible date.[64] Yet, one cannot just cease to probe, give up, pack up, and go home.

(a) There are no reliable clues provided by the first *mshl* as to the time it was produced in this form.[65]

(b) What is present in the second *mshl*, that is, "Jacob," "Israel," and "king.....among them," suggests strongly the existence of the kingdom of Israel. So long a period of possible setting (922–722 B.C.E.) also provides too wide a historical window through which to allow the viewer to see anything safe to use.[66]

(c) *mshl* number three mentions Israel's tents/tabernacles, seeming to point to Confederated, Tribal Israel (ca. 1250–1050 B.C.E.).[67] Also mentioned is a king who shall be higher than Agag, which seems, once again, to presuppose a monarchy. Since no specific monarch is named, however, this *mshl*, too, allows one to make no defensible statements about its usefulness in ascertaining the historical setting of its author.

(d) The contents of the fourth *mshl* also appear to assume a northern monarchy. It goes even further and assumes that Moab has been defeated by a northern monarch who would also have subdued the children of Sheth, Edom (which clashes greatly with studies concerning Balaam's homeland and position in it), [68] and Seir.[69]

(e) If one can verify a total defeat of the Amalekites, *mshl* number five will have been the most helpful thus far in providing the date(s) for the setting of the writer of this piece.[70]

(f) Likewise, if one can document a time when Assyria vanquished the height–dwelling Kenites, a reliable *datum* would be provided the researcher in the case of this *mshl* as well.[71]

(g) The final *mshl*, which refers to Asshur, Eber and the *Kittim*, provides the same possibilities and challenges as the preceding two *meshalim*.[72]

Of the *meshalim*, terms such as "Israel's tents," a king Agag, (3); king, Moab, Sheth, Edom (4); defeat of the Amalekites (5); Assyria–vanquished Kenites (6); and *Kittim*–vanquished *Asshur* and *Eber* (7) are all that provide any material which alludes (regardless of how nebulously) to possible historical occurrences, thus suggesting a possible setting for the writer of each.

When the context clues provided by the narrative (including that which cements the fable to the overall cycle) and the sum of that provided by the *meshalim* are viewed as a completed mosaic, the following picture of a time slowly begins to develop clearer outlines.

From historical sources [73] which focus on the region of Syria–Palestine, one learns that most of this region, by 966 B.C.E., was under the control of Emperor David, and from 960 to 922 B.C.E. would also be under the control of Emperor Solomon. The region from the Euphrates in the North (i.e., Syria) to the River of Egypt in the South (i.e., the *Wadi Maghara*) was under the control of these two rulers. That included the region which provided the geographical setting for the MT Balaam cycle. The recently new priesthood of the United Monarchy (ca. 1000–922 B.C.E.) would have taken an ardent interest in existing traditions about other and, especially legendary *homines religiosi*, such as the *propriediv* Balaam of Transjordania.[74] The very fact that traditions about this outsider were first preserved by priestly circles within "Israel," then transformed by these circles to depict him as performing the duties of an exponent of the now national deity, Yahweh, signals a formidable threat by this mantic personality, and official attempts to bring his legendary character and reputed efficacious skill "to heel." Phase one, then, the J phase,[75] has an understandable politico-religious urgency about it, and existed to defang a powerful legendary figure, then depict him as a faithful convert to state Yahwism.[76] Like the law during this period, the Balaam legend might have served the official purpose of being a propaganda piece for converting regional priests to the priesthood of state Yahwism. This is an issue which has received little attention.[77]

Israel the kingdom also dominated portions of the Transjordan between 922 and 722 B.C.E.[78] Since it has been shown that E was opposed to, and criticized both the producers of J and the official priesthood of Israel, it is difficult to determine whether E's source(s) about the legendary Balaam was/were borrowed from the southerners who produced J, or came from the same source(s) as that/those tapped earlier by the J circle.[79] Since JE depicts the two strands as having been woven together and brought into harmony, it is very difficult to determine from the existing MT form just what use an independent Shiloh-oriented E document would have made of the non-Israelite Balaam tradition(s), for E was an independent tradition, not a state-controlled, state-oriented apology.[80]

JE, like J, has a southern provenance,[81] and what one argued is E material about Balaam is only encountered in the anthology, the tone of which, we repeat, is conciliatory. It has been suggested above that one possible use of the Balaam tradition and its reshaping by the J circle was in the service of the state, specifically in retooling state priests of conquered (now), vassal states for service as priests of the imperial Yahwistic state religion, and that prior to the beginning of the Divided Monarchy.

The post 722 B.C.E. situation for priests in the territory of the former kingdom of Israel, whether the Shiloh-oriented Mushites or the remainder of the former Israelite state priests (now unemployed) would, if my suggestion is correct, have provided a second use of the Balaam tradition as reworked by J.

It would now serve as a device for "repatriating" such priests and reabsorbing them into the surviving Judaite state priesthood's service.[82] The lyrical prose *meshalim* (6 & 7) which mention Assyria (*Asshur*) would certainly point to such a time as the possible setting for their having been written.[83]

The second and third *meshalim*, at least in part, glorify Israel and her king. Since the Shiloh priesthood was anti king of Israel[84] and anti Israelite state priesthood, these two may be traced to either (1) Israel during the United Monarchy (especially since Judah seems to be given equal though second serial status), or (2) from Israel state religion traditions preserved by the Israel state priests who had also come to the South.

Although Moab, Sheth, and Edom lie east and southeast of Judah, *mshl* 4 depicts a northern monarch as having conquered them. This, too, would be the contribution of Israelite traditions.[85]

In all, then, three of the seven *meshalim* come plausibly from the North. Their probable historical settings range over a period which covers the United and Divided Monarchies up to the destruction of Israel of the North. Another two of the *meshalim* (6 & 7) have a post–722 B.C.E. setting and appear to reflect southern concerns. Finally, *mshl* 5 reflects a southern setting, a southern concern with a traditionally southern antagonist. When is impossible to say.

Having examined the possible settings for the individual *meshalim* and possible purposes for each source stratum's existence, all that may be safely said is that the author/editor's historical setting is post 722–B.C.E. Judah at a time when the Assyrians rule the majority of the Levant. In addition, and to consolidate our gains, the conflated JE anthology places the setting of the writer at a post–722 B.C.E. date. Again, recent research has dictated that an attempt at providing a more precise (and unnecessarily forced) date is imprudent.[86]

The argument that Balaam appears to have been (1) a king of legendary mantic fame,[87] (thus providing a possible clarification of the seeming problem of identifying Bela, king of Edom and Balaam [both named "the son of Beor."], (2) the connecting of the deuteronomic circle's programmatic to an intensified interest in directing the course of official priesthood and prophecy (and why such a programmatic would have focused on a Balaam–type character),[88] and (3) the suggested uses for the J and JE Balaam tradition(s) in the hands of the Jerusalem based, Aaronid priesthood during the United Monarchy and post–destruction of Israel (the kingdom) periods all[89] deviate from usual treatments of the Balaam cycle. They are the results of the cycle being critically revisited. They augment previous research and clarify various internal problems occurring in individual *meshalim* or the narrative framework, but all this is understood to fine tune an essentially JE cycle. From the beginning of this essay to the present line, however, only the "first shoe" has been allowed to drop.

(B) P and Balaam

The "second shoe" begins to drop when one reconsiders the Documentary Hypothesis. Richard Friedman [90] has stated that Eduard Reuss's insistence that the Prophets section of the *TaNaK* was not quoted in the Law section was a mistake which precipitated misunderstandings about the theses and time of writing of the document called P or the Priestly Document. Even today, the preponderance of the OT/HS scholars hold that the four "documents" which comprise the first five biblical books were produced in the order J,E,D, and P. Most would further assign the dates ca. 950, 850, 650, and 550, B.C.E. respectively to them. [91] These dates suggest strongly that P is a post–exilic document, and that it contains a literary constellation of concerns and issues designed to buttress Zadokite priestly claims to head the theocratic government in Jerusalem.[92] This has been the prevailing picture for some time. Friedman's study takes this picture and the scholarship which produced it to task. In

Chapter 11 of his work he writes, under the heading An Alterative Version,: "P was written as an alternative to JE.[93] In Chapter 12 Friedman argues convincingly that this alternative to and polemical work against JE was produced during the reign, and at the court of King Hezekiah (ca. 715–687).[94]

It is known and acknowledged that ultimately P incorporated much of the J,E and JE material into his "document,"[95] and that P is the largest of the four documents. It was assumed, however, that this incorporation took place after 550 B.C.E. Friedman argues that "P was produced after 722 and before 609 B.C.[96] The upshot of all this is that J,E,JE,P, and, as he argues in Chapters 5 and 6, D1[97] were all produced prior to 609 B.C.E. They are all pre–exilic. Exit an old theory that had been around in one form since Reuss, Graf, Wellhausen and their *epigoni*, and enter the new, more plausible theory of **Who Wrote the Bible?**[98] The "second shoe" has finally dropped.

This "second shoe" situation calls for a corresponding rethinking of the setting of the writer of the Balaam cycle, and the purposes for including it into his cycle. It is to P one must turn to ascertain toward what uses the Balaam strands woven together into JE were directed in the author/editor's programmatic prior to 609 B.C.E.

E had challenged J on the issue of legitimate priesthood (especially, but not exclusively in the South). The legitimacy issue was actually a canopy under which were sheltered a *plethora* of subissues in a priestly polemical duel. E had cast serious aspersions on the ancestor (Aaron) of the ruling Jerusalem priesthood;[99] had elevated the figure of Moses (to whom he traced his ancestry) to a position of priestly preeminence; and had given priests other than those from Shiloh and it associates [100] a bad name and reputation by questioning the pedigree of the Aaronid priesthood.

And then, the J circle after 722 B.C.E. had collaborated with the E circle (its former detractor!), and by producing the JE anthology, had given the appearance that at least some of what the E circle had maintained was still correct.

In either case, J or JE, the Balaam tradition was an important segment of either document's mantology, but that mantology was used to convert foreigners to the state priesthood controlled from Jerusalem. In either case, aspersions cast on the figure of Aaron had not been retracted by the time of the writing of P prior to 609 B.C.E. An Aaronid long-standing grievance still needed to be addressed, if not adjudicated.

P, chaffing from all this, took JE to task. P also took thereby JE's Balaam cycle to task. By scholars having focused on a JE Balaam cycle as the finished product, P's influence on and use of this cycle has either been overlooked, ruled nonexistent or ignored. This has been due to the heretofore held J,E,D,P chronology, and the history of Israel reconstructed from these documents.[101]

It becomes clear that one of the reasons scholars have had so much difficulty separating E from J material in the Balaam cycle, and assigning only snippets such as Numbers 22:1 [102] to P in this three chapter work, or not knowing what to do when suspected "J material" appeared in the middle of suspected "E material" (for all the categories and context clues appeared to have been scrambled), is because solid P material mirroring a pre 608 B.C.E. situation and polemic was also present but undetected.[103]

As an Aaronid priest during the reign of Hezekiah, P would have had motives and opportunities to engage in mantological exegesis, and to use the Balaam material(s) in that exercise. Centralization, in a word, characterized the rule of Hezekiah. Centralization of the state cultus was the concern of P.[104] If the Balaam traditions transformed and preserved by J and JE had functioned to integrate non state priests into the official state priesthood centered on Jerusalem, making all priests legal, equal, and able to offer sacrifices on behalf of the state at all official cultic centers, then P was committed to bringing about the antithesis of that situation.[105]

(C) P in the Balaam Cycle

Any clue(s) to identifying P's "thumb print" in the Balaam cycle must be sought carefully in material of a polemical nature, a nature which supports centralization of priestly control, especially sacrifices, and which makes the opposition look ridiculous. If J and JE had an official purpose regarding priests, it had been to legitimize them where they functioned within or without Jerusalem. The specific mentioning of specific religious centers dedicated to specific deities was intended to neutralize them. It was a form of exorcising a site of any former religious significance, and then rendering any further activity there an ignorant, empty act.[106] This was a form of site exorcism and deity assassination.

Indissolubly linked to these sites was the practice of offering sacrifices. Major sacrificial animals such as oxen and sheep (22:40); bullocks and rams (23:4; 14; 29; 30); high places of Ba'al (22:41); (7)altars (23:1; 4; 14; 29); catchwords such as every altar (23:2; 4; 14; 30); burnt sacrifice (23:6); and burnt offering (23:15) mirror priestly concerns used (contextually) polemically. In addition, anti purity laws are expressed in 23:14. All this was designed to belittle sacrifice offered anywhere except Jerusalem.

There appear to be no context clues to priestly concerns in the fable material **at first reading**. No sacrifices or sacrificial animals are mentioned. Nothing is said about centralizing anything. But a P "thumb print" is detectable nonetheless. To "lift it", attention must be directed to what Friedman has convincingly shown are additions to the story of the rebellion against Moses in Numbers 16.[107] P augments what is essentially a J text. Studding the P literary style in the reworking of the J text are the expressions:[108]

a. "princes of the congregation..."(16:2)
b. "And he fell on his face..." (16:4)
c. "And they fell on their faces..." (16:22)
d. "In the morning Yahweh will make known who is his..."(16:5)
e. (Gives orders) "Do this: Take incense burners..."(16:6)

Of the above expressions, Numbers 22:8b's "and the priests of Moab abode with Balaam"; inclusions of princes at 22:13; 14; 15; 21; 35b; 40b; 23:6; and 17 combine with (a) above to show P's preoccupation with princes.[109] Expressions (b) and (c) above surface also at Numbers 22:8 (first part) and 13 (conclusion); 19 (first part) and 21 (conclusion); and 41. Finally, like (e) above, orders (i.e., directions in the imperative) are given by Balaam at Numbers 23:1;3; 15 and 29. Of these "thumb prints" characteristic of P, b) also appears in the narrative material which is associated with the fable. Plausible evidence has been presented, then, to argue forcefully for the presence of P in the Balaam cycle as well as JE material.[110]

To summarize the evidence from the setting analysis, it may be stated with some confidence that the date of the Balaam cycle in its present form is between 715 and 687 B.C.E. during the reign of Hezekiah, king of Judah. Looming large in the background, and insinuating itself into the politico-religious affairs of the smaller, formerly independent states of the Levant was neo-Assyria, bent on empire building. During this period, major cities of Judah had been subjugated to Assyrian military supremacy, and Jerusalem herself, to which siege had been laid in 701 B.C.E. under Sennacherib, had experienced Assyria's pulse-quickening presence firsthand.[111] Internal disruptions within a neo–Assyria experiencing the alternating contractions and periods of calm associated with giving birth to a new empire, had periodically given a false sense of hope of continued autonomy to the small kingdoms of the ANE which thought that an abortion would result instead. During one such period of Assyrian withdrawal, Hezekiah had sued for independence, and had launched his reform. P had launched a corresponding one, and the Balaam cycle played a part in that reform. Complementing Hezekiah's political/religious efforts [112] were the priestly/polemical efforts of P. If the JE material of the Balaam tradition had reflected a liberality toward the priestly office in former times, in the hands of P it championed conservatism, exclusivity of Aaronid priestly prerogatives, and the reforming efforts of the "second Solomon." [113] The outsider, Balaam, who had been made to deport himself like an (earlier) insider, now looked like a dupe. All priestly functions performed by Balaam (and Balak, for that matter), and *sacerdotal* machinations engaged in by him were shown to be impotent.

P, and the Balaam figure within it, has an urgency about it. Not all of this can be explained between 715 and 687 as a serious reaction to JE or JE's paradigmatic figure. Balaam the foreign *propriediv* now represented the foreign Assyrian *propriedivs!* And they were the greatest threat to an Aaronid priesthood if Assyria's might asserted itself in Jerusalem. The reign of Hezekiah's successor, Manasseh, demonstrates that P had not been paranoidal or over–reactionary. He deserves more credit than he has heretofore been given. This, then, was the general setting of the more recent writer/editor of the Balaam cycle. Below, a more detailed recapitulation of immediate events surrounding P's times will be provided for the reader.

Meaning(s)

A

The Balaam cycle contained in Numbers 22–24 of the HS/MT was used several times by several circles. It is a patchwork of fable, *meshalim* (written at various times, and in various regions), and narrative (which serves to cement all three constituent parts together). The narrative shows signs of having been reworked by JE and P more recently, although J and E had produced traditions about Balaam some time earlier. In its present form, the Balaam cycle is an overworked (i.e., *überarbeitete*) tradition stemming, **it would appear**, from P.

Approaching the Balaam cycle within the framework of recent studies on the Documentary Hypothesis, it became apparent that the language of the cycle accommodated already known characteristics of J, E, and therefore, JE "thumb prints." Studies from Astruc (1753)[114] to present had added more language clues to help identify J or E more readily. *yhwh* and *'elohim* were viewed as reliable indicators, when present in the Pentateuchal text of J and E material respectively, or so it was thought with reference to the Balaam text. This can no longer be thought the case, especially where *'elohim* occurs, for instance.

The linguistic analysis of the present cycle yielded a sufficient amount of material to help clarify certain problem-causing peculiarities. Among these were Balaam's homeland, his social position, his probable identity, the location of various locales in Transjordan which are prominent in the cycle: all in the narrative material.

In the fable, a number of terms reflected convenantal concerns, a *hapax legomenon, yrt* (=rushing headlong into something?), provided as much a stumbling block to linguistic analysis as the *ml'k yhwh* who impeded Balaam's advance in this fable. Unlike Balaam's ass, however, the researcher had no clarifying data which "spoke" so clearly as to bring enlightenment concerning the meaning of this term.

In the various *meshalim* contained in Chapters 23 and 24, the language analysis produced nothing solid in each *mashal* as it appeared which provided a clear route toward ascertaining meaning of the cycle. When combined, however, *yshr* (upright), *nhsh nhshym* (bronze serpent) and *qsm* (divining by rod or staff; and one who reveals), *shtm* (one of opened eyes) and *glh* (uncovered, revealed), *d't 'lywn* (knowledge of the eternal one), and finally *ktyym* (Westerners [i.e., west of Syria–Palestine]) reveal the concerns of some whose thoughts were always framed within a convenantal *Weltanschauung*. The combined *meshalim* could be crafted to state the following. When one is a covenant member, one has been exposed to *d't 'lywn*, which requires one to live the life of the *yshr*. *nhshym* wielded by a *qsm*, while at one time characterizing Moses, are no longer necessary, for the *yshr* has the status of *glh* and *shtm* and will therefore live and die the death of the righteous. For all who break Yahweh's covenant, there is the rod of his wrath, the agent whereby Yahweh redresses his grievances as injured second party in the covenant. Here the *Kittim* represent this (in the history of Israel) changeable agent.[115] It is the whole covenant (as presented in the literary anthology known as the *TaNaK*) story in miniature.[116]

The exegetical method holds that the goal of the four previous analyses (i.e., text, linguistic, literary form(s), and setting(s) of the writer(s)/editor) is to enable one to state the meaning(s) of the text. One necessary step in arriving at that "meaning" is (1) asking what the work(s) meant, and (2) asking what the text as a whole meant to the author and/or reactor who put it into its final form. By bringing the key terms of the narrative together, we actually get three different programs.

1) Narrative   A famous monarch is invited to participate in a special

coalition with other monarchs from Moab and Midian to halt the advance of a potentially (and demonstrably) dangerous, and bellicose foe. By the means of prophecy, priestly cultic activity, and divination skills, all combined in *propriediv* fashion at specific and holy spots of demonstrated/designated efficacy, Yahweh, through Yahweh/Holy War, [117] and through this mantic medium as human instrument, realized his desired ends.

2) Fable

A famous mantic personality (here cast as a member of a covenant community, and held responsible for that membership) is shown "rebelling" (misunderstood to be sinning!) against the one who empowers him. Moreover, this mantic personality, on his way to serve as facilitator between Yahweh and his (i.e., the *propriediv's*) client, is unable to perceive Yahweh! Serious aspersions are therefore cast on this seer's ability to see.

meshalim

shtm and *glh* are the outstanding terms which sustain the theme carried through in all the *meshalim*. The "open eyed one" to whom wisdom, or better *d't 'lywn* has been revealed, is the antithesis of the closed eyed "bungler" of the fable. In fact, the fable may now be understood to precurse the contents of the following *meshalim* (individually and/or collectively). The invisible watchman behind all this is the covenant understanding, determined to maintain itself against all who would storm its citadel.

Seen in this light, asking what the (important) words meant still leaves us with a tripartite division which comprises this cycle. We are somewhat enlightened about perhaps heretofore nebulous characteristics of each section, but the fact that each of the three sections has existed has not escaped any critical reader. What that text (cycle) as a whole meant to the author/editor who put it into its final form (as we have it in the MT) should indubitably bear more fruit.

B

The cycle of texts has dictated just how it must be approached if anything useful is going to come out of it. Narrative, or fable, or *mashal* alone would present any researcher with enough of a challenge to plumbing the depths of its literary form and teasing out a plausible meaning. We have observed with this cycle that three major *strata* constitute it, and that each had a separate life. Because of this, we resorted to the archaeological method, superimposed it upon this cycle, and set about a stratum by stratum investigation, seeing each literary *locus in situ*, as it were, against the backdrop of its time and probable use.

The linguistic analysis and analysis of the literary form notwithstanding, it is the setting of the writer/editor of the Balaam cycle which provides the most reliable data as to one possible meaning of this cycle. The reign of King Hezekiah of Judah is the kernel around which everything else grows. A brief summary of the events leading up to Hezekiah's bold actions during the period from the death of Ahaz (715 B.C.E.) to the death of Hezekiah (686 B.C.E.) will be helpful.

The prophet Isaiah (of Jerusalem) shows marvelous understanding of the political machinations of Hamath (north of Israel) and Egypt (southwest of Judah) as they engaged in the political science of the day. Both fomented insurrections among the smaller states of the region. Egypt was particularly eager to establish the smaller states which made up Syria–Palestine as a buffer between itself and the Assyrians. To this end, a deputation from Egypt arrived at the court of Ahaz (Isa. 18:1-2) armed with convincing arguments why Ahaz should throw his lot in with that of Egypt. The prophet diplomatically rebuffed this overture, then stated that Egypt herself would meet defeat (18:3-7). Ahaz eventually rejected the Egyptian offer. But that was only one possible crisis averted.

Around 722 B.C.E. Shalmaneser V (727-722 B.C.E.) of Assyria died while Assyria's western armies were besieging Samaria, the capital of Israel. His successor, who would eventually assume the throne name Sargon II, defeated Israel, but then returned to Assyria in order to consolidate his empire. That was to take some time. While this process of consolidation was taking place in the East, small states in the West looked upon the lack of a menacing Assyrian military presence there to foment rebellion against Assyria. One of the first was Philistia which, by 714 B.C.E., withheld its tribute money. Both Isaiah of Jerusalem and Sargon II mark this withholding. In Isaiah 14:28-32, the oracle against Philistia, he states:..."and the first born of the poor will feed, and the needy lie down in safety (showing that Assyria will not redress this breach of covenant immediately, and thus give Philistia a false sense of success, but that once consolidation was complete) "For smoke comes out of the North, and there is no straggler in his ranks." One of Sargon's annals states that: "Azuri, king of Ashdod, had schemes not to deliver tribute [any more] and sent messengers [full] of hostilities against Assyria to the king [living] in his neighborhood."[118] This king was deposed, another placed in his stead, who was also deposed by the Philistines, who elevated a pretender to the throne named Iamani, who ruled for about three years.

Hezekiah was a nationalist and a Yahwist. Ahaz, his father, had scouted Isaiah's advice, and had voluntarily become the vassal of the king of Assyria (then Tiglathpileser III). Hezekiah, viewing the machinations of

Ashdod, also examined possible ways of divesting himself of his inherited vassalhood. A Philistine embassy sent from Iamani, the anti-Assyrian party in Jerusalem, and the revolt by Moab and Philistia against Assyria, combined to bring severe pressure to bear on Hezekiah and his own personal ambitions. The period 713-711 B.C.E. therefore had been crucial years in the early reign of Hezekiah. He had seen what could befall one (and one's country) who tried the might of Assyria. Whatever the reason (maybe the constant tauntings of the prophet Isaiah of Jerusalem counseling him not to do anything rash), Hezekiah watched the developments of the time, and refrained from committing himself or his resources to either the Moabite or Philistine rebellions. About ten years of peace for Judah was the result.

But to lead directly to the issue at hand now that some recapitulation of major events leading up to the setting has been provided, the words of one writer admirably sum up the immediate background to the meaning of the Balaam cycle for P.

> Isaiah unquestionably approved of Hezekiah's reforms which consisted of regulating religious practices in the villages and in the Temple itself. He destroyed cult centers where Yahwism and fertility goddesses were worshipped side by side. He stripped the sacred serpent, reputedly made by Moses himself, from the Temple (2 Kings 18:1-8; cf. Num. 21:5-9). These reforms were undertaken guardedly at first in order to see what reaction Assyrian political agents in Jerusalem might have. Since no reaction set in, Hezekiah continually pushed the nationalization of religion and politics until at the death of Sargon II in 705 B.C., he was ready to announce his independence.

He refused tribute money to Assyria and simultaneously attacked her Philistine provinces in a bid to expand his territory and to collect revenue from the rich harvests in the Shephelah.[119]

Sargon was killed on a campaign to Elam. He was succeeded by Sennacherib (705-681 B.C.E.), an equally aggressive ruler. During this time many former vassals of Assyria revolted. Among them was Marduk-ipal-iddina (the biblical Merodachbaladan), king of Babylon, who sent an embassy to Hezekiah, entreating him to join a coalition against the new Assyrian ruler. Where Ashdod and Hamath, as well as Moab, had been unsuccessful some decade earlier, the Babylonian ruler triumphed. Egypt, too, (Isaiah 30: 1-7; 31: 1-3) participated in the machinations, and promised a military contingent. Isaiah the prophet of Jerusalem, our main literary source here, was not impressed with these maneuvers. (31:3).

Sennacherib defeated in rapid succession, and to the surprise of especially the Babylonian who thought that he would first campaign in the West against the smaller states and exhaust himself and his forces, Babylon, then all of the states in the West. He did not have to effect a military defeat everywhere, however, for many merely offered tribute and capitulated out of their own instinct for survival. Assyrian political agents in Jerusalem, however, had apprised Sennacherib of Judah's and Hezekiah's involvement. In 701 B.C.E., therefore, Sennacherib and his forces were wreaking havoc all over the countryside of Judah. In the same year his chief military officer, the Rabshakeh with a large Assyrian force, was standing before the walls of Hezekiah's Jerusalem. After listening to Hezekiah's officers who made counter proposals as to why they should not capitulate, the Rabshakeh was prepared to accept nothing short of total surrender. Yet at the very moment when Jerusalem seemed to be facing utter defeat, the Assyrians retreated, they left off what was to have been the certain and successful siege of Jerusalem. Whatever the reason, the Jerusalemites interpreted it by refracting current events though the prism of their own hermeneutic of the time. Jerusalem was saved miraculously, and obviously Yahweh was directing events. This encouraged many observers of the times, and is probably responsible for creating the idea of the inviolability of Zion.

Against this backdrop, then, an Aaronid priest apparently started his own minor reformation, which corresponded to, and probably was an integral part of the national reformation. The religious side of that reformation saw priests who officiated at cultic centers outside of Jerusalem disenfranchised. At most of these centers, a sort of syncretistic religion was practiced which included elements from national Yahwism, fertility religions of various varieties, and traditional religious practices associated with individual sites. Officiating at many of these centers were the descendants of priests from Israelite national religion, as well as contingents of Shiloh priests. Many of these centers were simply destroyed. The aftermath of 722 B.C.E. had witnessed scores of priest/refugees from the north arriving at Jerusalem and other religious centers in the South. Where else could they have gone? The document JE was the eventual literary outgrowth of this post-722 crossfertilization of J and E. Reading it, one sees that "Zadok" and "Abiathar" had been reunited.[120] In the opinion of P, "Abiathar" had, since 722, not only been returned to a position of favor at court, he had also garnered a considerable amount of sacerdotal power in the meantime as well. Recent events, however, which had been brought about by the spirit of nationalism, religious and political, had produced a King Hezekiah who would set things right. Centralization, the keystone of the king's plan, also meant centralization of the priesthood at Jerusalem. That office, since the year 966, had been firmly in the hands of the Aaronid, Zadokite priesthood until its dilution by refugee priests from the North. E elevated the Shiloh priesthood over both the Jerusalem and Samaria/Bethel/Dan priesthoods, and tauted the Mushite party line. JE did not back away from this line either. Now events made it possible for an Aaronid priest to "set the record straight".

Friedman has demonstrated that the JE document was overworked by P.[121] In this overworking, Aaron, not Moses, is cast as the central figure. All E "insults" to Aaron have been overturned. P refers to non Aaronids throughout his overworking as **Levites**, and to the Aaronids as **priests**. This literature reflects a corresponding politico-religious situation at the court of Hezekiah. It had been Solomon in his role as regent who had banished the co-High Priest, Abiathar, to Anathoth, to remain under the watchful eyes of the Aaronid priests there. That action had elevated Zadok, the remaining (and loyal) co-High Priest, to the position of undisputed High Priest. This Aaronid, Zadokite priesthood became the national, hereditary priesthood, and Solomon was remembered by subsequent generations of Zadokites who continued to enjoy this sacerdotal hegemony for several centuries, as their enfranchising patron. The conditions of the setting, and the contents of P suggest strongly that Hezekiah, through his policy of centralization, had reinfranchised the Aaronids. P's denigration of Moses (as, among other things, a "bungler",[122] and elevation of Aaron makes it clear who is his champion. P reflects, thereby, the setting wherein the Aaronids are again what their first royal patron, Solomon, had made of them over two centuries earlier.

Having identified P's setting, a more specific sacerdotal program within that setting, and within Hezekiah's reforming program, one would search the literature for signs of priestly concerns. This would isolate much literature which comprises the Pentateuch as well as other documents of the *TaNaK*. But narrative literature responds to given times, and the times generally dictate specific responses, even when a piece of literary tradition is reworked or overworked several times.

The important question is what did the Balaam cycle mean to P who shows signs of having overworked it during the backdrop of Assyrian expansion? Continental reformers like Luther, Calvin, and Zwingli had been bothered by much contained in the Old Testament, and had chafed under the rules of conduct traced to the laws therein. As reform leaders on the european continent, they had had the power to abolish the Old Testament in order to present no opposing or competing anthology of scripture to that of the New Testament.[123] They could have, but they didn't. Their rationales for not doing so would fill numerous tomes. What is important is that they included what at first was understood to be competitive material from another scriptural anthology in **their** anthology within which was granted honored place to the New Testament. P likewise, included rival traditions in his document as well. He, too, had the option of jettisoning material such as JE, but, like the sixteenth-century reformers, he chose to keep it and overwork it. The result is the Balaam cycle of P.

Realizing that P was an important contributor to the already-existing Balaam written traditions, it is tempting to attempt a total reconstruction of the cycle, and to raise in bold relief the P traditions thereto. Here, we need not yield to this temptation. Above we have provided enough of P's "thumb print" to convince the reader that P's program is also present in the Balaam cycle. Since the Balaam material was kept, we must merely look for the meaning of Balaam for P the priesthood reformer.

P's overworking of the Balaam cycle employs the figure of Balaam, the *propriediv*, as the archetypical adversary to his priestly reformation. Prophets had attacked the Aaronid, Zadokite priesthood to which he belonged on several occasions. One need only recall the words of a Micah of Moresheth, an Amos (in his oracles against the nations), or, in P's own time, his fellow priest/prophet, Isaiah of Jerusalem. There were no doubt others who spoke out against the

Jerusalem priesthood. We are bereft of their recorded words, however. Prophets, some of whom came from priestly ranks, presented a formidable challenge to the programs of the state priesthood. There is nothing worse, some say, than to be criticized by one who was formerly a colleague, and who now has become a public advocate. There is evidence to support a claim that Amos, Micah, and most certainly Isaiah of Jerusalem were priests.[124] Other priests, who did not display the tendency toward prophethood, also threatened to dilute the ranks of the priestly courses in Jerusalem. These were the priests who had come from the north on the one hand, (both from Shiloh and from the state priesthood[s]), and others who had been long before legitimized when J was first employed in the service of incorporating other, former foreign priests into the service of the empire, then later in service to the Kingdom of Judah after the death of Solomon. Since P worked and reformed within the reform of Hezekiah, it is quite possible that on many issues raised by the social activist prophets he was in agreement. But these prophets delivered oracles with such sweep and broad stroke that it was impossible for the conscientious state priest in Jerusalem of the eighth century B.C.E. not to feel having been indicted along with those who were demonstrably corrupt. Once, the legitimate state priesthood had to accept other priests into its ranks. Under Hezekiah's reform, there would hardly be a need for most non–Aaronids; they had become supernumeraries. Levites were an exception.

The Balaam cycle does not pullulate with the word *qsm (qesem)*, or diviner. Nor are the terms *me'onen* and *mekashef* (found especially at Deut. 18:10 before which *qsm* stands) which also are translated **diviner** to be found there. When *qsm* is found in the Balaam cycle (cf. Num. 22:7 and 23:23) the first occurrence is in what might be seen as a corrupt text, the result of trying to weave J and E together.[125] The other occurs within one of the *meshalim* where the writer of the *mshl* holds that there will be "no divination against

Israel". If we look further afield literature wise, but remain within the historical setting, one finds other eighth century writers concerned with *qsm* as well. Isaiah of Jerusalem talks about a diviner (3:2) and diviners (2:6). Micah mentions divination at 3:6; to divine at 3:11; and diviners at 3:7.[126] It is the isaianic passage (2:6) which may contain, the clue[127] to why diviners were a topic of concern in the eighth century, and therefore in the P Balaam cycle. The passage refers to diviners from the East, most probably from Assyria.[128] P would have had every reason to be concerned with such people, given the spirit of the times, for it was known that if Judah became a vassal of the Assyrians (as she had already been under Ahaz, and would be again under Manasseh), Assyrian overlordship included religious overlordship to varying extents. In fact, some of these Assyrian diviners and possible enthusiastic Judaean disciples would have also been present in P's Jerusalem certainly before Hezekiah's reformation, but during as well.[129]

The already legendary figure of the *propriediv*, Balaam, suited P's needs perfectly. He attacked all those who did not conform to his view of legitimate mantis with this figure. That included Isralelite prophets, priests and foreign priests, especially from Assyria. For P Balaam was his foil. He was cast as a foreigner. P made him appear as a **foreigner** from the region near Assyria ("at Pethor, which is near the River, in the land of Amaw..."(22:5) He was cast as a **priest** ("and Balak and Balaam offered on each altar a bull and a ram"(23:2). He was cast as a **prophet** (all seven *meshalim)* "and I will bring back word to you, as to Lord speaks to me," "The word that God puts in my mouth" (23:5); "must I not take heed to speak what the Lord puts in my mouth?" (23:12); "and the Lord...put a word in his mouth," (23:16). He was cast as a **diviner** "prepared the seven altars, and I have offered upon each altar a bull and a ram." (23:4)) The sacrifices serve a different function in the mind of P than they serve in this cycle. He casts Balaam performing sacrifices or directing the sacrifices of Balak in order to open some mysterious portal through which Yahweh communicates directly with him at some specific spot some distance away from the spot of sacrifice. For P, however, there can be no legitimate place for sacrifice other than on the altar before the Tabernacle.[130] Moreover, only an Aaronid priest can perform a sacrifice.[131] P therefore renders the sacrifices unnecessary which are performed by Balak or Balaam, for there is no necessary connection between the sacrificial act and the "word" of Yahweh in the cycle. Prophet, priest, (local Israelite variety and Assyrian) and diviner—a term used here in a derogatory sense to serve as a boundary marker between insider priest and outsider priest, although there is no such inherent difference deriving from the use of the word *qsm* in biblical literature—are all attacked in the P overworking of this text.

There is more in the cycle which appears to serve P's purposes, and as far as I know, no one has made the connection. Above (C. P in the Balaam Cycle), I made reference to five characteristic concerns and/or expressions which characterize P's writing style, the so-called "thumb prints". The first (a) was the expression "princes of the congregation..." In noted P material[132] such as Numbers 20:2-13 (compare with Exodus 17:2-7 which is written by E, but also covers the same topic, Water from the Rock), the words congregation and community occur eight times in thirteen verses. Likewise, in the Heresy at Peor story (Num. 25), verses 6-16 belong to P.[133] Therein "congregation" occurs twice. The Rebellion of Numbers 16:1-35 also contains P material.[134] Congregation occurs in verses 2 (also assembly); 3; 5; 6; 9; 11; 16; 19 (twice); 21; 22; 24; and 26. "Princes of the congregation" also occurs specifically in this passage at verse 2. Congregation, for P, refers to the entire citizenry of "Israel". It means nothing less than the sum of the subjects of the ruler of Jerusalem. Kings ruled with the assistance of princes (those exalted in the community, as well as the sons of a given king), and counselors.[135] A careful reading of the

MT, where the word princes occurs eight times throughout the Balaam cycle, reveals that the word always appears to have been brought in gratuitously. The implication is that certain "princes" did not enjoy the favor of P, and that during P's lifetime. These princes were culpable along with Balaam and Balak for attempting to manipulate Yahweh through divination. But then Balaam is depicted as having gained enlightenment (=d't 'lywn or d't yhwh). Once this occurred, "he did not go, as at other times, to meet [Yahweh] with omens, but set his face toward the wilderness." (Num. 24:1) This verse serves as a value judgment of the sum of Balaam's mantic activities, then delivers the death knell to them. They are overturned. After depicting this, P employed another one of his characteristic "thumb prints," the Spirit of God (i.e., *ruah 'lhym* [cf. Gen. 1:2 *et passim* in P] to show how one must qualify to be in proper communion with Elohim; one must be chosen by deity or by deity's authorized representative. The Aaronid priesthood in Jerusalem had been so chosen by deity's representative (and son by adoption!), Hezekiah, King of Judah, as far as P was concerned.

One last expression then I'll drop my "third shoe" to demonstrate what I think is the full meaning of the Balaam cycle for P. The expression is "If Balak should give me his house full of silver and gold,". It occurs at Num. 22:18; and 24:13. The expression recalls the most valuable objects in a typical temple in the ancient Middle East[136] which one sent to another asking for services. These two occurrences of this expression, coupled with the evidence presented in the foregoing analysis, supply the reader with the meaning of the Balaam cycle for P.

P was an Aaronid priest who was active during the administration of Hezekiah. We need not assume that he began his priestly activities at the same time that Hezekiah assumed his kingly (i.e., messianic) activities as Ahaz's successor. In fact, P shows signs of having served as a priest long before

Hezekiah assumed office. The P overlays alluded to throughout this analysis of the P material, reveal a man concerned with the full reestablishment or restoration of the Aaronid/Zadokite priesthood to the enjoyment of its full sacerdotal status. That status had been endangered each time Judah had been conquered. Each time that had occurred, sacerdotal elements from he suzerain appeared at Jerusalem to oversee certain priestly functions, the major public exercise of which were the daily sacrifices. Whatever the number of such sacrifices in a given ancient Middle Eastern country, several more were added when that country became the vassal country of a more powerful ruler. Daily (or at least specified periodic) sacrifices were offered by the vassal king (or his representative) on behalf of the suzerain. Certain representatives of the suzerain were on hand to make certain that the vassal's sacrifice was offered in the prescribed manner to make it efficacious.[137] Isaiah 7:1–9 tells of a time when Israel, Syria and Edom formed a coalition against Assyria as well as against Judah, ruled at that time by Ahaz. Ahaz, against the advice of Isaiah, voluntarily became the vassal of the king of Assyria. By so doing, Assyrian priests, among other representatives from Assyria, would have appeared presently in Jerusalem. Their assignments would have been to assist the new vassal to adjust to the new order of "business" as a vassal. P contains, as we have demonstrated, material which is concerned with Assyria as the place (or at least direction, if we understand the presence of "Aram" in the first *mshl* at Num. 23:7) from whence "Balaam" had come. But when would the sensibilities of an Aaronid have been so taxed? Anytime during the immediate period before Hezekiah succeeded Ahaz. P was reacting to actual Assyrian agents headquartered in Jerusalem. He was not reacting to a phantom.

It is difficult, therefore, not to look for correspondence between figures in the Balaam cycle and figures during the time of P. Here is my reconstruction. For P, Balak recalled Ahaz. Balaam recalled all the mantics whom P saw threatening the Aaronids. Sacrifices of rams and bulls by Balak, and by Balak and Balaam on another occasion, recalled the sacrifices that Ahaz would have offered on behalf of the Assyrian monarch on the one hand, and perhaps some joint sacrifice by Ahaz and an Assyrian agent respectively. Since the princes of Moab labor under P's indictment also, these recall the political support Ahaz would have had to have in order to "send all the gold and silver" to Assyria. 2 Chronicles 28:16–27 sums up the events which brought Assyria to Judah, as well as Hezekiah's inherited duties as a result thereof. Chronicles is also a work written by a priest.[138]

Under the patronage of the antithesis of Ahaz, Hezekiah, P told a story which held that "Israel," (the cryptic threat) here meaning (the Kingdoms of) Israel, Syria, and Edom, had encamped (i.e., laid siege during the Syro-Ephriamitic War) before "Moab" (for P, Jerusalem). The king of "Moab" (i.e., Ahaz) had sent for the mantic "hit man" from "Pethor–in–the–land–of–Amaw–which–is–near–the–River." (i.e., Assyria) to come and "curse" (i.e., defeat) these people for him, for he knew that whomever he (i.e., the king of Assyria) "blessed (i.e., favored by his protection) was "blessed", and whomever he cursed was "cursed". This desire to have "Israel" cursed had to be paid for by all the gold and silver in the king of "Moab"'s house. The king of "Moab", having done all this, still had no guarantee that services paid for would, or could be rendered by "Balaam." Why? Because "Balaam" was an outsider/instrument of Yahweh's will, and plans for "Israel" (i.e., Judah), and as such could do only what Yahweh allowed his instrument to do. "Balaam" had indeed responded to "Balak"'s call, yet "Israel" had not been "cursed" but "blessed". Hezekiah and his reformation were proof of that for P. P alludes to this king at 23:21, 24:7b, and 24:17. All the gold and silver that Ahaz had sent to the king of Assyria was to no avail, for Hezekiah wrenched freedom from vassalhood from that suzerain. It is as if the money had not been paid. On this point P made an interesting, and in light of these developments, important emendation in the existing text tradition before him (i.e., JE). To show his great disdain for Ahaz's move toward vassalhood, P has the king of "Moab"'s messengers depart for "Balaam's" homeland, not with, as one would expect, the fees for "Balaam's" divination (i.e., the temple treasures) services in their hand(s), but makes it obvious that they already have been bribed into having earned a part of this money for their own services![139]

P writes of the futility of Israel, Aram, Edom, and Assyria in their attempts to control Judah. Although scattered throughout the Balaam cycle, he alludes to all of them. *mshl* 1 identifies "Balaam" as coming from Aram. Numbers 24:18 holds that "Edom shall be dispossessed." And although Asshur (i.e., Assyria) oppressed "Kenites," in the end, the *Kittim* would be Yahweh's instrument of justice for Judah. It is far more difficult to tease out of this material just when Israel the kingdom is alluded to. There might have been less urgency concerning this Israel, because since P challenges the contents of JE, a post-722 B.C.E. document, Israel, would not have existed any longer. It is significant, therefore, that P's overworking of the Balaam cycle ends on a high note. "Balaam" returns to his home (which is located in the East), but will suffer distress in the future at the hands of the *Kittim*. At the time of P's writing, Assyria was indeed involved in internal affairs, and had ceased to actively direct the course of affairs in the West. It reflects P's optimism during the Hezekian administration. This is understandable. What had happened to Philistia and Moab had happened because they were not under the protection of his Yahweh. Let us hope that P, after exercising himself so brilliantly in his overworking of the Balaam cycle, was "sleeping with his fathers" when Hezekiah was succeeded by Manasseh, for he would more than likely have never gotten over the shock to his system.

b.   **Significance and the Connecting Theme of War**

The Balaam of Numbers 22-24 was a figure utilized by various **warring** groups of priests/prophets against each other's ideal self-concept and type-concept. One group saw in him an archetypical priest, prophet, diviner, magician to be emulated. Another perceived in him the archetypical outsider and mantic type to be vigorously spurned. Thus, the word and concept of **war** link all of the material we have just considered. Let us consider how they assist us in providing a significant summary of the foregoing.

The war theme was already there demonstrably in one of the source strata underlying the Numbers 22-24 Balaam text used by either faction: specifically the **Book of the Wars of Yahweh.** And recent evidence concerning the fine-tuning of the Documentary Hypothesis (DH) assisted immensely in unraveling the meaning and uses of the Balaam cycle of Numbers 22-24. Thus Numbers 22-24 remains the pivotal yardstick whereby all other uses of the Balaam figure and type may, and indeed must, be measured until earlier versions of the Balaam story are unearthed and brought to light.

Balaam is located within a long list of encounters with the enemies of Yahweh, the entire list of which constitutes that which makes up the **Book of the Wars of Yahweh.** The most sustained piece concerning Balaam casts the encounter between the Moses host and Balaam near the end of that host's sojourn in Transjordan. Thus, the Balaam cycle relates an episode shortly before the host (later under the leadership of Joshua) crosses the Jordan river to begin its most significant Yahweh war phase: The exegetical essay produced the following scheme and use(s).

a.   The Numbers 22-24 cycle was a literary mosaic.
b.   That mosaic could be subdivided into three distinct parts: a narrative

framework, a fable, and a collection of *logia* or *meshalim*.

c. The "glue" which held these three components together was the wars of Yahweh itinerary.

d. Balaam was probably a famous priest–king who also demonstrated mantic traits of the "seer," the "gazer", the "*nabi*'", and the "wizard".

e. Balaam was probably king of Ammon in Transjordan at one time.

f. Numbers 22–24 shows signs of having undergone four major recensions:

1) a tenth century version wherein the Balaam figure was presented as a type of acceptable, formerly non–Israelite priest who was now accepted as a legitimate priestly colleague by the official national priesthood under either David or Solomon. He might well have been typed as the local Yahweh–loyal prophet/priest/diviner (propriediv) in the territories conquered or controlled by David. Thus, a Judean version, a J source *stratum* was proposed.[140]

2) a later than 922 B.C.E., but earlier than 722 B.C.E. version which concentrates on a northern homeland for Balaam. This northern work is the most nebulous of the discernible recensions. This recension was probably produced by the Shiloh priests. Had we more information, the Balaam type would most certainly have been cast in a negative light. These priests were known to have been rigid in their fierce zealousness and jealousness for Yahweh. Outsider mantics would not have been welcomed by these insiders. An E source stratum was proposed.[141]

3) a post-722 B.C.E. recension which was conciliatory in intent. Therein, Balaam once again served as the type *par excellence* of the priesthood member in Judah after the destruction of Israel the northern kingdom. It was a time when refugee priests appeared in large numbers in Jerusalem. Once again outsiders were absorbed into the body of the Judean state priesthood and given legitimacy. A combination of the above two *strata* was proposed which resulted in a JE proposition.[142]

4) a post JE response to JE identified as the P source *stratum*. This recension is characterized by its anti outsider priest stand, as well as its preoccupation with inefficacious sacrifices offered by other than *bona fide* priests of Yahweh. Its concerns with Assyria as an agent of Yahweh war, on the one hand, while stating confidently that Assyria shall be trodden down by the Kittim, betrays its production during the period of King Hezekiah of Judah.[143]

5) a very subtle response to the P recension. Linguistic analysis provided the program of this last recension writer. Balaam of his product is made to ask questions which marked the major thrust of the deuteronomistic reform movement. Thus, Balaam is made to ask Balak in Numbers 23:19-20 about Yahweh's actions in the following way: "Would he speak and not act (*y'sh*) promise and not fulfill (*dbr wl' yqymynh*)? Truly, my message was to bless: and when he blesses, I cannot reverse it (*wl' 'sybynh*)." This recension bore all of the characteristics

of the D source stratum.[144]

In neither case did those who produced the recensions I have proposed see any need to change the war setting of the story about Balaam. In fact, it appears that Balaam apart from a war setting was quite unknown to those who employed the story.[145] These recensions were produced over a period ranging from the tenth century (the first recension) to the sixth century (the fifth recension) B.C.E. Other than the nebulous E recension (2), three of the others correspond to periods of war in which the southern kingdom of Judah was embroiled (1, 4, and 5).

Only one of these war periods was offensive: the tenth century (holy/Yahweh) wars of conquest under David (1). Recension 3 was produced during the aftermath of a war which resulted in the total destruction of the kingdom of Israel in 722/1 B.C.E.

The present form of the Balaam cycle (the product of R=Ezra) is the result of several overlays or recensions of a basic story about a Balaam ben Beor (i.e., results of hermeneutical arguments and applications of hermeneutical arguments and applications of hermeneutical conclusions) produced between the tenth and eighth–centuries B.C.E. Several hermeneutical recensions existed which demonstrably corresponded to (and were the fruit of deliberations which produced the hypothesized J, E, P, D, and R documents of Pentateuchal criticism studies.

Chapter 5. Balaam Elsewhere in the Hebrew Scriptures:
The War Theme Continues

Other material contained within the HS acknowledges the specific itinerary for "Israel" enroute to the land of the Canaanites, and each writer takes for granted the targeted reader's knowledge of the general tradition about Balaam. Yet, the tradition is focused in such a way that one of two different Balaam trajectories is followed. The following analysis examines their trajectories closely.

a. Numbers 31 and Balaam

Numbers 31 opens on the theme of war. In fact, the word war assaults the reader's senses numerous times. Thus, one reads, "Arm men from among you for the war..."(31:2), " You shall send a thousand from each of the tribes of Israel to the war" (31:4), "...twelve thousand armed for war" (31:5), "And Moses sent them to the war,...." (31:6a), "They warred against Midian,..." (31:7a). All of this positioning for war resulted in the account contained in verse eight: "They slew the kings of Midian with the rest of their slain, Evi, Rekem, Zur, Hur, and Reba, the five kings of Midian;..." And, as if in an afterthought, the account continues: "and they also slew Balaam the son of Beor with the sword." This is also the sentiment found in the book of Joshua 13:22 where one reads ". . . and all the kingdom of Sihon king of the Amorites, who reigned in Hesbon, whom Moses defeated with the leaders of Midian, Evi and Rekem and Zur and Hur and Reba, the princes of Sihon, who dwelt in the land. Balaam also, the son of Be'or, the soothsayer, the people of Israel killed with the sword among the rest of their slain." Joshua 24:9 and 10 reflect the usual view of Balaam expressed in the cycle. Two observations are necessary. Balaam appears to have been brought in gratuitously; there is nothing in the text to prepare the reader for his being present in Midian, especially since he has been depicted as having departed for his "homeland" in the earlier Numbers 24:25 account.

Moreover, this Balaam is accused of a different "crime". More will be stated concerning this problem below.

In an earlier work, I argued that Balaam was treated and addressed as an equal by Balak in the early verses of the Balaam cycle of Numbers 22–24.[146] I based that argument on an analysis of the language employed by King Balak, which I compared with the message to one of equal status or standing studied within the framework of communication practices in the ancient Near East (ANE).[147] I stated further that evidence pointed, then, to Balaam having been a monarch to be compared with Solomon, David, Hammurabi and Hiram, other great kings, yet kings famous for seemingly unkingly or atypical activity for kings.[148] In the case of the above-named that was an intellectual and proverb writer, a musician and song writer, a great lawgiver, and an architectural engineer respectively. King Balaam, I argued, left an impression as a priest/prophet/diviner. The apparent afterthought, "and they also slew Balaam the son of Beor with he sword," [149] appears to betray this same knowledge, i.e., that Balaam was known to have been a monarch, for here he is, albeit gratuitously, depicted as having met the same (deserved) end as other Midianite! monarchs. As for Balaam being depicted as a traveling monarch, found first in Moab (Num. 22:36), then in Midian (Num. 31:8), it should be remembered that Hiram was depicted as being physically present in Solomon's Jerusalem actively engaged in the building projects being carried out by Tyrian artisans and craftsmen (1Kgs. 7:13–14).

At verse sixteen of Numbers 31 Balaam is mentioned again. This time he has been assigned equal guilt by Moses with the Midianite women. The specific charge is: "...these (women) caused the people of Israel, by the counsel of Balaam, to act treacherously against the Lord in the matter of Peor, and so the plague came among the congregation of the Lord." In order to unravel this problem one must first return to Numbers 23:28 where Peor is mentioned for the first time in relation to Balaam. There one reads that Balak takes Balaam to the summit of this mountain named after a deity. According to this account, Balaam has an overpowering experience which has been prompted by Yahweh's Spirit. The following *mashal* depicts Balaam as blessing and not cursing. Thus, in the Balaam cycle, the Peor incident did not result in any harmful side effects for Israel. Whatever the counsel of the Balaam of 31:16, his counsel resulted in what was perceived to be the necessity to kill young male offspring of the Midianite women, as well as sexually experienced Midianite women to reverse its harmful effects. Only women with no sexual experience were allowed to live, but then as booty of war! [150]

But why does this Balaam differ from the one(s) of the cycle? Only the names Balaam and Peor are common to the two versions. A closer view of the Numbers 31 account within context shows that its setting is one of the numerous battles contained in the **Book of the Wars of Yahweh**.[151] That work was produced by priests, and most certainly those priests who were in charge of the ark and related visible symbols of war associated with the divine warrior, Yahweh. [152] These are mentioned as Phineas the son of Eleazar the priest (31:6), the Levites who have charge of the tabernacle of the Lord (31:30), the (relevant) vessels of the sanctuary (31:6), and the trumpets to summon the tribal levies to war (31:6). A rereading of the story betrays the stereotypical language of the priest/scribe: the need to spell everything out as if the unity of the universe was riding on each detail of the narrative presentation (because for priests this **was** the way to maintain the unity of the universe). This whole episode is crafted around certain laws of purity which are at the heart of Yahweh War, such as sexual abstinence on the part of each warrior during Yahweh War, the disposition of women as spoils of war, period of time to pass before warriors and spoils may be allowed to come within the central area of the camp without contaminating (ritually) the ritually-pure maintained center and sanctuary, as well as how the spoils are to be divided. All of these ingredients are present in this story. One also notices that Moses (as priest) and Eleazar the priest legislate everything which is to be accomplished. [153]

The careful reader will continue to note, however, that something is still missing from all this analysis. Granted, priests are responsible for this story having been written. But why does the story not tally with the Numbers 22-24 story at the point of Peor? That question must still be answered. The key to the purpose and meaning of this story lies in the presence of the expressions Eleazar the priest (31:6; 13; 21; 26; 29; 31; 41; 51; 54) and the Levites who have charge of the tabernacle of the Lord (31:30; 47). A fine distinction, therefore, is being maintained here by the writer(s) between priests on the one hand and Levites on the other. The average reader knows what a priest is. Moreover, such a reader knows what the function of a priest was in ancient Israel. But what, then, is a Levite? The most direct answer is that a Levite is also a priest. What, then, is the difference between a priest and a Levite? Functionally, none! But the reader is unknowingly being drawn into making value judgments dear to the heart of the writer, is being manipulated ever so subtly to appreciate priests as a sacerdotal class more highly than Levites (the subtle suggestion is that they are an underclass of priest assistants or something). Looking for information concerning Balaam, one has stumbled upon literature crafted by one group of priests to discredit or belittle another group of priests. It has been demonstrated conclusively during much of the United Monarchy, as well as during a large portion of the Divided Monarchy period, that the Zadokite/Aarnoid, Judah-based priesthood, and the Shiloh-based; Mushite priesthood in the territory of Israel (both tribal and monarchical) exchanged barbs and darts. [154] Raising the question about authorship of the Hebrew Scriptures ultimately revealed serious priestly wars of a polemical/mantological nature. The crystallization of the verbal barbs and darts took the form of what students of the DH would recognize as the J, E, P, and D source *strata* of the Pentateuch. Fine-tuning his thesis, Friedman argued that one of the polemical devices of the author of the P source *stratum* was to refer to his Aaronid colleagues (past and present) as priests, and to refer to his Mushite antagonists as Levites. [155] The Balaam of Numbers 31 is being presented to the reader by the author known as P. What would move P to create a new version of Peor?

Peor occurs only once in the Balaam cycle of Numbers. I have discussed Balaam's relation to it above. Peor occurs outside of the cycle in the chapter of Numbers presently under discussion, in Numbers 25:3; 5; 18 (twice), in Deuteronomy 4:2, in Joshua 22:17, and in Psalm 106:28. Let us study the relevant Numbers material.

Leaving the Balaam cycle, a new P story begins at Numbers 25 wherein the "daughters of Moab" (v.1) invited members of Israel "to the sacrifices of their gods, and the people ate (contaminated food [i.e., which had been sacrificed or offered ritually to Ba'al of Peor]) and bowed down to their gods". (v.2). The expression "So Israel yoked himself to Baal of Beor" (v.3a) suggests that some members of the Moses host accepted formally and publicly this specific form of the Ba'alist worldview. Moses' reaction to this rebellion (against the covenant with Yahweh) was to: "Take all the chiefs of the people, and hang them in the sun..." (v.4), as well as to demand that each of the judges of the host "slay his men" (v.5) who participated in the Ba'al Peor ritual. This series of executions at first glance would appear to have been the sole and "appropriate" response to the rebellion. Apparently it was not.

Numbers 25:18 states why (holy/Yahweh) war was declared on Midian. They (i.e., the Midianite women) have "harassed you with their wiles, with which they beguiled you in the matter of Peor." (v.18) This whole episode is exemplified by the relationship between Cozbi, the daughter of a prince of Midian and Zimri, a man of Israel (vv. 14–15). No Balaam was implicated in the Numbers 25:18 account. Numbers 31 purports to be the culmination of the Ba'al Peor incident. Why, then, is Balaam implicated? The reply lies in an understanding of how Balaam was employed as a *typos* by each of the authors/producers of the four source *strata* of the Pentateuch. Of these, P, the priestly writer as he is known, has been identified more specifically as a(n) Aaronid/Zadokite priest.[156] An analysis of P's program reveals that he guarded jealously/zealously the purity of the Jerusalem-based, national priesthood. P represented a group of priests and supporters who were opposed to any other type of priesthood within or without "Israel". In fact, it has been argued the P's *stratum* and concomitant program of reformation paralleled the contemporaneous political reformation of King Hezekiah, during whose time he wrote.[157] Foreign priestly influence (especially from neo-Assyria), as well as intra-Israelite priestly competing influence, was vigorously lambasted and lampooned in P's literature, but ever so subtly and skillfully. I argue, on the basis of P having been identified as an Aaronid, that "Balaam" served as a code for outside sacerdotal types which combined the characteristics of priest, prophets (here understood in the broadest possible types understood by the ancient Israelite priesthoods), wizards, magicians, and diviners which P and his associates opposed.[158] When this is grasped, and the question of why "Balaam" was seemingly brought into the Numbers 31 text gratuitously is raised, all pieces fall into place. When all of the Midianite monarchs have been put to death, according to P, all of the Ba'al priests and their professional associates should suffer the same fate. P's simple, yet far-reaching and strongly-implying literary device for indicating the Ba'al Peor priestly culpability in leading many of "Israel" astray is "...and they also slew Balaam the son of Boer (i.e., the five dispatched Midianite kings' priesthoods [or, conservatively, their chief priests]) with the sword". (v.8). P is concerned that "Balaam", his competitor, be brought to justice under the rules and demands of Yahweh/holy war, just as the victorious Judaite or Israelite king must slay his vanquished and defeated counterpart. [159]

b. Micah 6:5 and Balaam

The Balaam of Micah 6:5 is mentioned within the framework of a *rîb* or covenant lawsuit. [160] This is stated in verse 2c and d wherein one reads the bicolon cast in *parallelismus membrorum*: "for the Lord has a controversy with his people, and he will contend with Israel." It is probably the least problematical of the biblical texts concerning Balaam. He is mentioned in the section of Chapter 6 which recapitulates in capsule form the major mighty acts of Yahweh upon having brought "Israel" out of Egypt. Moreover, Balaam is here cast in a good light if one reads the text carefully, for Balaam not assisting Balak in carrying out his "devised scheme(s)" must be counted among Yahweh's "savings acts" of verse 5b. It should not escape the reader's attention that these "savings acts" belong to the activity of Yahweh/holy war, the specific itinerary being the war against Midian and Moab. Thus, although the writer of Micah 6:5 is not concerned with forwarding a *typos* argument here, he does reveal that he has invested in the view of "Balaam" contained in Numbers 22-24, and has accepted it as historical fact within the activities of the mighty acts of Yahweh on behalf of the Moses host. [161]

What is different about this account has more to do with where it was produced. Research can place each of the Balaam recensions in either Jerusalem at specific times, or in (most probably) Shiloh at a specific time. [162] Thus, at first sight one might get the impression that the literary Balaam type is passed back and forth between only two camps: "Balaam" concerns were centered on two *loci*. The *locus* of Micah's activity and writing is the rural city of Moresheth, located at some distance southwest of Jerusalem. A critical reading of the Mican material shows that he is at odds with the priesthoods (who support the monarchs) of both Israel and Judah. [163] Whether his views represent the Shiloh worldview, or whether he includes that priesthood in his condemnations also, is difficult to argue If the former, we have an extra–Samarian, antagonistic–to–state–priesthood and extra–Jerusalem, antagonistic–to–state–priesthood, priestly/prophetic viewpoint expressed in Micah. [164] That would mean the two state priesthoods' activities had been monitored by two outside priesthoods which considered themselves having remained loyal to Yahweh and his covenant: one centered on Shiloh and one centered on Moresheth. If the latter, the Mican tradition would be understood to have been hostile to three priesthoods; the Shilonite, Samarian (including Danite and Bethelite), and Jerusalemite priesthoods.

What either possibility does for the *typos* issue is to cast "Balaam" in the role of being any and all of these outside–of–Moresheth priesthoods. Since Micah's activity is located in the eighth century B.C.E., the circle of priesthoods included in this condemnation and represented by "Balaam" would also have to include the Assyrian priesthood which was accompanying the Assyrians as they conquered all in their path. [165]

c. Deuteronomy 23:4–5 (MT 23:5–6) and Balaam

Within the deuteronomic program Balaam was also important. Therein, one reads of a charge to Israel to engage in a holy war without end against the age–old enemies Ammon and Moab. Deuteronomy 23:2–4 reads:

> No Ammonite or Moabite shall enter the assembly of the Lord; even to the tenth generation none belonging to them shall enter the assembly of the Lord forever; because they did not meet you with bread and with water on the way, when you came forth out of Egypt,

and because they hired against you Balaam the son of
Boer from Pethor of Mesopotamia, to curse you.

Verse five of this account holds that Balaam's intentions came to naught: intended curse became transformed into definite blessing due primarily to the love of Yahweh. The statement of verse six: "You shall not seek their peace or their prosperity all your days for ever" declares war on these two groups, and locks them and Israel in mortal combat.

The statement in verse 4b, "...Balaam the son of Boer from Pethor of Mesopotamia,..." is noteworthy. This writer appears to be unaware of another tradition about Balaam's homeland being "near the River in the land of Amaw..." at Numbers 22:5. Although his Balaam also comes from Pethor, that Pethor is located, for him, in Mesopotamia. What is obvious once again is that a number of Balaam traditions existed. In Numbers 22-24, several were woven together, and then these were expanded on by at least five recensions noticeable in my critical reading of that text mosaic. [166] More precise identification of the writers program concerning Balaam comes from two observations.

First, scholars of Deuteronomy the book, and the deuteronomistic history have long been aware that Deuteronomy 1-11 is written as a sort of preamble to a core of earlier-written material comprising Chapters 12-26, the literary home of 23:3-6. [167] This core comprises what are held to be the contents of the scroll discovered in the Jerusalem Temple during the early years of the reign of the young Judean monarch, Josiah. Josiah brought about a long range reformation, using this core as the hub around which his reforming efforts revolved. Text historians argue for a northern provenance for this core sometime prior to 722 B.C.E. The most likely candidate for having produced this core was the Mushite priesthood located at Shiloh. This Shiloh priesthood criticized both the contemporaneous Jerusalem-centered priesthood and the

Samaria/Dan/Bethel priesthoods of chapters following Chapter 26 were also added later. The author/collector/editor of Deuteronomy has been identified as Jeremiah the priest/prophet of the sixth century B.C.E.[168] The author of Deuteronomy is also identified as the collector/writer/shaper of a body of materials now comprising Joshua, Judges, the Samuel books, the Kings books and more. This is what is known as the Deuteronomistic History. Still other literature, such as the Book of Jeremiah, and the Book of Lamentations, continued to make up altogether the literature reflecting the concerns of the "deuteronomistic school". This school was highly influenced by what is known to have been the worldview of the Shilonite priests.[169]

Second, one of the recensions of Numbers 22–24 also reflects the deuteronomistic outlook and program, especially in its use of language conventions. That overlay would have to be a sixth century B.C.E. product. Here I don't argue that Jeremiah is the author of this recension, but I do elsewhere.[170] My focus here is merely on time.

The deuteronomistic material was produced at a time when one Mesopotamian power, neo–Assyria, was ruling much of the A.N.E. and when another, neo–Babylonia, was awaiting its turn on the conquering stage. Balaam material concerning Assyria, and the Kittim was more than likely produced at this time. Thus, in the Balaam cycle, the question of Numbers 24–22: "How long shall Asshur take you away captive?" asked of the Kenites, and verse 24's: "But ships shall come from Kittim and shall afflict Asshur and Eber; and he also shall come to destruction" are arguably seventh to sixth century concerns. A Balaam of Mesopotamia, as the Deuteronomy 23 passages present, would reflect the outlook of the same period as the Numbers material. In other words, both bodies of Mesopotamia–oriented Balaam material smack seriously of the Shilonite stamp.

Concerning typology, if the above time line is correct, Balaam of

Mesopotamia, *170* a construction we read nowhere else in biblical literature, may represent the Assyrian mantic in general, or the chief Assyrian priest in particular. Since all of the biblical Balaam material betrays its having been written by priests, if the pronouncements of Balaam of Mesopotamia (i.e., the priests who most certainly accompanied the Assyrian conquering armies) against "Israel" had been allowed to stand, it would have meant the obliteration of that "Israel". Since Israel the kingdom was destroyed by Assyria in 722/1 B.C.E., the "Israel" which received Yahweh's blessing would have been Judah the kingdom. This provides another reason why I argue for a post 722 B.C.E. period for the Balaam accounts involving a Mesopotamian power, and then, specifically Assyria.

d. **Nehemiah 13:2 and Balaam**

Nehemiah 13:2 reads:"...for they (i.e., the Ammonites and Moabites) did not meet the children of Israel with bread and water, but hired Balaam against them to curse them–yet our God turned the curse into a blessing." Immediately one may state that this writer, too, has accepted the contents of Numbers 22–24 to be true. He reveals his knowledge of another tradition concerning Balaam, the Ammonites and the Moabites, for he quotes from a specific part of that tradition embedded in the book of Deuteronomy. Nehemiah 13:2 parallels Deuteronomy 23:3–4 which reads: "No Ammonite or Moabite shall enter the assembly of the Lord:...because they did not meet you with bread and water on the way..." In addition, the work unwittingly helps correct the text of Numbers 22:5 which relates that Balak "sent messengers to Balaam the son of Boer at Pethor, which is near the River, in the land of Amaw..." We stated elsewhere that Amaw, translated as "of his people" in the expression land of his people was unsatisfactory. *171* A better rendition, taking possible text flaws as well as geographical considerations into account, was proposed which resulted in the suggested revised translation to read simply "...which is near the River (now meaning the Jabbok in Transjordan and not the Euphrates [Which produced more geographical problems than solutions]), in the land of Ammon." Ammon and Ammonites are not mentioned at all in the Numbers 22–24 cycle. However, Balaam arrives at the city of Moab by traveling southward from his homeland. Ammon was located immediately north of Moab.

One other observation is in order here. This text's writer does not betray an awareness of a Ba'al Peor incident for which "Balaam" is to be held culpable as we observed above in the Numbers 31 account. Like the Micah 6:5 account, the account contained in the verse currently under discussion appears to reflect a Peor incident which simply surprised both Balak and Balaam by having Balaam's *brk*, i.e., (intended) curse became transformed into a *brk*, i.e., blessing (seen in Numbers 24:3b–10). Nothing more than this is certainly intimated by the present text. The Balaam of Micah 6:5 and the Balaam of Nehemiah 13:2 are the Balaam figure of Numbers 22–24 and grow out of that tradition. The "Balaam" of Numbers 31 appears to be solely a P *typos* useful to the P and Hezekian mutual reform efforts.[172]

The Numbers 22–24 Balaam cycle became a core text tradition which apparently gave rise to what I have demonstrated were probably two different tradition trajectories through later Israelite and early Jewish history of mantological exegesis of the Balaam text(s) prior to P's editorial overlay. It would be an oversimplification to argue, however, that these two trajectories could be designated priestly and prophetic. The Numbers 31 trajectory is hostile toward Balaam (as were E's and P's) and is not based on anything discernible in the material of Numbers 22–24. It might have grown out of an oral tradition given rise by the P material. The Mican and Nehemian materials do not reflect this hostility, but see Balaam (regardless of what might have been a touted reputation *au contraire)* as a helpless figure made pliable and malleable by the power of Yahweh, to accomplish that deity's bidding and to communicate that deity's will of mighty acts on behalf of his people.

Concerning the theme of war, Nehemiah 13:2b's: "– yet our God turned the curse into a blessing" appropriately falls within the purview of the mighty acts of Yahweh, and as such belongs to the activities of Yahweh/holy war.

Before departing the Nehemiah text, we address the issue of its meaning and use. The portion of text in which it is located was read on a specific day (Nehemiah 13:1) before a gathering among which were the responsible heads of households. Apparently, what was not known to theses responsible heads of households was that contact with the contemporaneous Ammonites and Moabites (with whom they had engaged in at least social and business [if not other] intercourse) was henceforth no longer to be a common practice. Moreover, instead of a decision reached by Balak and his counselors to summon the notorious services of Balaam, this text lays blame at the feet of any and all Ammonites (not implicated in the main document concerning Balaam) and all Moabites (a term here which might also include Midianites). Thus, Ammonities and Moabites are held culpable for (1) joining in a (made useless!) conspiracy to *brk* "Israel", and (2) lacking in civility (offering "Israel" no bread and water)! *173*

PART 3: "BALAAM" IN OTHER SEMITIC LANGUAGE – WRITTEN MATERIALS

Chapter 6.   Qumran and the Balaam Traditions:
               The Fantastic War

All of the literature which contains an account or mention of Balaam ben Boer thus far has had one characteristic in common: these accounts are all located within literature which is not intended to be understood as historical. Most of the literature of the TaNaK may be separated into two main groups: 1) historical (into which would fit 2 Samuel 9–20; 1 [Kings 1–2 the first real attempt at historiographical writing in the Hebrew Scriptures], Ezra, Nehemiah, and the Chronicles books), and 2) non–historical. The non–historical books have essentially theological agenda. Although the Balaam material examined to this point is purported to have taken place within a specific time in ancient Israelite history, one fact does not escape us: the literature which enshrines it is essentially nonhistorical in character, and therefore may not be trusted to present historical fact and sequence.[1] The *agenda* it does present have been discussed already. The historical worth of the already studied material has come through analysis of the contents of each given piece and that content's program and intended use. We were also able to identify tentatively author/editor/concerned group on this basis. Turning to extra–HS materials concerning or mentioning Balaam, we must subject them to a rigid scrutiny also to determine why and how he––as either figure or type––continued to be useful to those who employed traditions concerning him.

The Balaam Materials From Qumran

In taking up the issue of the Qumran Balaam here, I depart from what has been a chronological approach to this point. The Numbers 22–24 cycle with its overlaid recensions ranged from the tenth to sixth centuries B.C.E. With this body as a core, I took up the issues of the Balaam of Numbers 31:8 and 31:16. This material was most certainly later than the Balaam cycle material, and also differed radically from it with reference to the Peor issue. The Mican material came from the eighth century B.C.E., which was followed by (and maybe produced during the same century as) Deuteronomy 23:4-5. The core material of the present Book of Deuteronomy was probably produced long before the Deuteronomist pre and affixed *addenda* to it and made it part of the Deuteronomistic History during the sixth century.[2] The Nehemiah material comes from the post exilic period somewhere between 444 and 398 B.C.E. or even later.[3] If the chronological treatment were to continue, we should take up next the material from Deir 'Allā, which is generally believed to be eighth century B.C.E. material.[4] I employed the Deir 'Allā material as the *Eintritt* to the present book. My rationale for departing from my chronology is based in part on the similarity of language and contents between the materials studied up to this point and the corpus of writings from the Wadi Qumran. The rationale is also based partially on the fact that the language of the War Scroll from Qumran[5] reflects the language characteristics of a particular earlier priesthood which contributed a Balaam recension overlay available in the Numbers 22-24 account: the P overlay.[6]

The most famous body of extra-HS materials is the corpus of writings produced by the Qumran community located near the Dead Sea. This community existed between 150-140 B.C.E. to the middle of the first war against Roman domination, C.E. 68. With the Nehemiah Balaam recension the reader is still presented with ancient Near Eastern influenced portraiture of this *propriediv*. The Balaam of Qumran appears in material which has been influenced by Hellenistic culture. The War Scroll which mentions Balaam comes under the category of nonhistorical literature, also.[7] Thus, the type of literature in which Balaam appears continued to be useful for those writers not concerned with historiography. Below, however, I shall fine tune the nonhistorical types of literature, and demonstrate major differences.

The Qumran community was the product of war, and it was destroyed by war. Between these wars the community became so influenced by the actuality of war that it on one great literary occasion, produced a work employing the genre of the futuristic, cataclysmic war to end all wars. That is, the Qumranites created their own fantastic war between actual wars!

a. The Actual Wars

The ideational war created in the minds of the Qumran writers was preceded in actual historical times by Jewish wars of either independence, conquest, or collusion, on the one hand, and was followed by the first war between the Jews and the Romans on the other. The Qumran community came into being during the reigns of Jonathan Maccabaeus and his brother/successor Simon Maccabaeus, that is, between 153–52 B.C.E.[8] Jonathan, a non–Zadokite priest, was elevated to the High Priesthood in Jerusalem by Alexander Balas. Balas had usurped the Syrian Greek Seleucid throne, and Jonathan had supported his bid with Jewish troops which had fought formerly against Balas' predecessor. When Jonathan was assassinated by a Syrian Greek general named Tryphon in 143–2 B.C.E., Simon was elevated to the position of High Priest and leader of the people by the Jewish government itself. So strong and confident had the tiny nation of the Jews become since the outbreak of the Maccabean wars against (originally) religious oppression under Anthiochus IV Epiphanes (ca. 167 B.C.E.). The successors to Simon the High Priest recouped much territory around Jerusalem and Judah. Under first John Hyrcanus I (134–104 B.C.E.) and then Alexander Jannaeus (103–76 B.C.E.) territory which included Samaria, Galilee, and Edom, to mention just three areas, came under Jewish domination and control. Between the reigns of these two occurred the short reign of Aristobulus I (104–103 B.C.E.). Aristobulus has the distinction, according to many historians of this period, of being the first ruler of Jerusalem since

Zedekiah/Mattaniah of Jerusalem before the main Babylonian deportation, to wear the title *priest–king*. War, then, was the order of the day: wars of religious freedom under Judas and Jonathan Maccabaeus; wars of collaboration under Jonathan Maccabaeus; and wars of conquest under Simon Maccabaeus, John Hyrcanus I, Aristobulus I, and Alexander Jannaeus.

Upon the death of Alexander Jannaeus, his able and capable widow, Queen Alexandria Salome, mounted the throne in Jerusalem.[9] This move led in a direct way to another series of wars. These wars pitted Jews in a bloody civil war. At the center of the conflict was a war between two brothers, John Hyrcanus II and Aristobulus II, sons of Alexandria Salome. In short, Alexandria could be king without being contested. However, no woman could attain the title of any kind of priest. Since that was impossible, and the High Priesthood was such an important and powerful position, unlike her predecessors, Salome had to appoint a male to this position. She appointed the weaker of her two sons in order to maintain a firm grip on the position, and it angered the stronger son, Aristobulus. Factionalism resulted, political lines were drawn, Aristobulus attempted to usurp the High Priesthood, and formed an army willing to help him do so. This filial and familial conflict unleashed hatreds and greed which resulted in an adjudication by the Roman general strongman, Pompey.[10] Although, the High Priesthood office would continue for another three decades, Pompey's actions in 63 B.C.E. of turning the heretofore independent Jewish state into a Roman province effectively ended the battle for the High Priesthood. Rome now controlled the office and appointed the High Priest at its pleasure.

It is not difficult to understand how preoccupation with war for so long a period of time (ca. 167–63 B.C.E.) would move even the intelligentsia to also incorporate it into their writings. The difference between seasoned military men and scholars viewing war is that the scholar attempts to manipulate war safely in the library through writing about it, and to ultimately find some positive use for it. Within all these historical local wars, the Qumran producers of the **War Rule** conceived a war of cosmic proportions. Employing a genre of literature borrowed from Persia [11] on the one hand, and from the Hellenists [12] on the other, they crafted a war scenario in which they, as one of the most injured parties as a result of all these wars, would direct the ultimate war: a war which would result in their being restored to what they understood as their rightful place at the head of the Jerusalem priesthood. Thus, on numerous battlefields, both actual and conceptual, Jews were engaged in combat.

b. The Imagined War(s)

The war(s) imagined by the writers of Qumran is/are contained in what is known as the War Scroll. The fullest study of this scroll was produced by Y. Yadin in a Hebrew-written work published in 1955.[13] The scroll itself is identified in literature by the *siglum* 1QM,[14] and is preserved incompletely in nineteen columns. Rarely has a war been so well described, down to the vivid descriptions of vestments of the combatants and horses. Yet, 1QM is not a military manual. It belongs to the genre of literature known as apocalyptic: a genre which requires some comment.[15]

The "Balaams" of the Hebrew Scriptures, as I shall refer to the types of the various recensions and allied literature discussed under A, above, appear in all three divisions of the TaNaK. The chief work, the Balaam cycle, is imbedded in Numbers, as a part of the *Torah*. The Deuteronomy 23:5 passage belongs both to the *Torah* as its last book, and to the *Nevi'im*,, as the first book of that section. Moreover, the D recension of the Balaam cycle belongs to the deuteronomic outlook. Thus, the *Nevi'im* perspective is also contained in *Torah* material. Micah, as a scroll contained within the Twelve Prophet Scroll, most certainly takes its place within the *Neiv'im* worldview. These *Torah*,

Torah/Nevi'im, or *Nevi'im* works represent outlooks that are unhistorical. Nehemiah 13:2 is located within the *Kethuvim* section, and is one of the few works purporting to "do" history.

The material of the *Nevi'im* section revolves around the view that at the Mountain of Yahweh two parties, Israel and Yahweh, entered into a covenant.[16] No specific date is provided the reader in relation to some known occurrence, and two names have been assigned to the name of the mountain: Sinai in one tradition, and Horeb in another.[17] Without sacrificing the importance of the priestly office and its duties of maintaining a ritual relationship between the two covenanted parties, the prophetic stamp of this sacerdotal responsibility focused more on "grass roots" issues equally important to maintaining the covenant relationship. Thus was born a movement of specialization within the priestly ranks.[18] The "prophetic" priests focused on ethics, i.e. oughtness, as needing serious and omnipresent cultivation. This stance and decision was especially true when wealthy middle classes emerged during periods of prosperity in Israel and Judah which gave rise to new moralities and concomitant conduct. The "prophetic" gauged all actions of members of the covenant by the laws of the covenant, and made no exceptions in terms laying blame, i.e. rebellion, against the covenant demands, at the feet of the proper offender whether that offender were a priest–king or a simple farmer. The most obvious body of literature to view this "prophetic" concern about flagrant violation of covenant rules and requirements is the corpus of writings known as *melachim*, (I and II) Kings. Therein, each of the kings of Israel and Judah is subjected to criticism of rebellions characterizing their period of tenure, and are assigned a "report card" grade. Few of these monarchs received a good report. Among those who do are David, Hezekiah, and above all, Josiah. Thus, this "prophetic" view was written during the age of Josiah (ca. 639–609 B.C.E.).[19] although the subject of each critique is a king, it is not the kingly of their office which interests the writer of these critiques. Rather, it is the priestly side of their office which receives stinging rebuke. These kings did not live up to their priestly responsibilities *vis-à-vis* the covenant they had sworn publicly to uphold. A further litany of rebellions is available in the writings of such "prophetic" literature as Amos, Hosea, Micah, Isaiah 123; 28-39, and Jeremiah. What the reader must not lose sight of is the fact that the "prophetic" critiques the "unpriestly," i.e., the irresponsible acts of priest-kings. The reason lies in the fact that most (if not all) of the prophets, after whom biblical books have been named, were themselves priests! The term "prophetic," unless strictly understood and adhered to, can be most misleading to the uncritical reader. The author/collector of the Kings books referred his readers to the archives (both the Chronicles of the Kings of Israel and Judah were located in Jerusalem in the days of this author/collector) if they wanted to pursue the issue of how these kings functioned as kings. He did not clutter up his critique of them as highest priests with their kingly accomplishments, which for some of them were considerable. [20]

The "prophetic" kept company with the "kingly" and "priest-kingly". As soon as the first king of Israel, Saul (ca. 1020 B.C.E.), had been anointed, he combined with a band of prophets.[21] He thereby effected a "wedding" between the two functions and worldviews which was to last until the last king of Judah, Mattaniah, was taken in chains in an ignominious fashion to Babylonia in ca. 587/6 B.C.E.

Although the office of "prophet", and the "prophetic view" resurfaced during the exilic and post-exilic periods in the writings of Ezekiel and Deutero-Isaiah on the one hand, and Haggai and Zechariah (including Deutero-Zechariah) on the other, the "prophetic" characteristics of the participants remained the same. They were all still priests, however. What had changed was the focus of their writings and their critiques. For one thing, there were no more priest-kings to critique. Their role as "consumer advocates" of Israel was over. A late glimpse into the "prophetic" worldview is contained in the Book of Deutero-Zechariah 13:2ff. There one reads of the death knell which was delivered to that worldview and activity. Most literature on the subject intimates that the prophets should be pitied as having outlived their usefulness, as having fallen prey to their own devices, as being an example of being on top in May, and having been shot down in June.[22] Nothing could be farther from the facts. What probably occurred is that the former, pre-exilic preoccupation of priest and (priest)-prophet under the monarchy responded to the post-exilic preoccupation first of priests at the center of a theocratic government,[23] then[24] sacrificial priests, then scribal priests. "Prophets," then, did not disappear in ignominy, they merely joined the scribal side of the priestly equation.

This scribal side of post-exilic priestly activity appears to have developed along two trajectories. Following one trajectory, one entered the *arcana mundi* of the Torah of the God of Heaven, a *torah* which under Ezra the Scribe had become nothing less than a written constitution of the small Jewish government of Jerusalem sometime between 444-398 B.C.E. This *torah* gave rise to attorneys-at-*torah* whose job it was to constantly update it and make it useful as a constitution in the face of numerous political and social changes.[25] These attorneys-at-*torah* were priests who specialized in scribal functions. Of course, the ruler of Jerusalem, the center of this constitutional government, was the High Priest. The other trajectory of the post-exilic priestly concern crystallized into what one may term the apocalyptic worldview. It focused on a specific time in a relatively-understood future. They counted themselves among this elect group which had been selected, and which had been vouchsafed certain key, and heretofore unknown-to-the-public-at-large information about coming events of a cosmic nature. It was their unquestioned piety, faithfulness to the (still in force) covenant, and personal deportment which had caused them to be selected by the deity. Their knowledge guaranteed that they would be at the cutting edge of any new theocratic government established in Jerusalem after the pivotal godly intervention established on earth a Jerusalem after his heart and desires. After this, nothing would ever be as it had been before. Literature expressing such a worldview is legion.[26]

The 1QM scroll belongs to this apocalyptic genre. It tells of events which will occur, not of events which have already occurred. That is the first and major characteristic of this apocalyptic material. Specifically, it describes in futuristic terms, a spiritual battle between two ongoing adversarial forces: The Sons of Light and the Sons of Darkness.[27] At a time only known to those who have advanced knowledge of the *apo kalyptein*,[28] the God of Heaven will intervene in what will surely appear to those on the earthly plane as more of the ongoing struggle between the two equally-matched camps (i.e., life as it has been known until the time of the apocalypse), and turn the tide of the battle in favor of his Sons of Light bringing an end to the conflict.[29]

1QM quotes three passages from the Balaam cycle: Numbers 24:8 at 1QM 12:11; Numbers 24:17 at 1QM 7:19-20; and Numbers 24:18 at 1QM 11:6-7. This is typical of the whole Qumran literature which employs numerous glosses, expands parallel passages, and excels in editorial-type activity.[30] The Balaam we study here must be understood within the framework of apocalypticism: herein we encounter the apocalyptic-relevant Balaam.

Red flags should go up immediately when one begins to read the War Scroll after having read to his point in my work. The first engagement of the Sons of Light in the futuristic war is against the troops of Edom, Moab, and the Ammonites, the Philistines and the **Kittim of Assyria**.[31] All have a connection with my study of Balaam interpretations and uses so far. Edom and Moab (and sometimes thrown in for good measure, Amalek) have been the "scenes" of the desired cursing by Balaam, and Balaam arrives in the city of Moab from

Ammon (cf. the Balaam cycle material). The Philistines were one of the first groups—along with the Moabites—to rebel against the Assyrians under whom they labored as vassals during the days of Hezekiah, king of Judah. In fact, both the Philistines and the Moabites sent envoys to Hezekiah attempting to lure him into their political intrigue.[32] Hezekiah merely studied the situation from a safe distance (cf. Numbers 24:22–24 and the analysis of the P recension of the Balaam cycle). The Kittim (cf. Numbers 24:22 and the P recension of the Balaam cycle) underwent development in the minds and interpretation schemes of Israelite priestly groups as well. Essentially, the Kittim went from meaning a group of Mediterranean, Cyprus–dwelling warriors who reached the shores of the eastern Levant in the seventh–sixth centuries, to any invader of the eastern Levant from lands located to its west (which later even included the Romans), to **foreigners in general** with hostile intentions toward the Israelites.[33]

The various interpreters of the Balaam material and the Qumran writers who "penned" the War Scroll had much in common, and their concerns about the (almost) same set of "enemies" is not coincidental. It has been demonstrated that the writers of each piece of biblical Balaam material were priests, either Mushite or Aaronid/Zadokite.[34] The Balaam cycle recensions demonstrated that each recensionist added to, not subtracted from, the basic "stump" of the story or mosaic. And although two major trajectories can be followed throughout the remainder to the biblical period, enough remains of the "stump" so that one never has to lose sight of it as the anchoring tradition. Anywhere one reads in the Qumran library, one encounters the writings of a priest. Since these writers have voluntarily established a monastery in the Judean wilderness, due on no small part to their politico–sacerdotal worldview, they are priests who had no stake in the sacrificial cult side of the priestly office anyway. The most telling evidence, therefore, to suggest that with the first founders of the Qumran *yahad* [35] we are dealing with essentially scribe/priests of the type described above, is their copious library, and the way it has come to us modern researchers.[36]

The Nehemiah Chapter eight material tells the reader that many of the associates of Ezra the (priest) Scribe were Levites. The job of these Levites on the most important day of their lives, the day on which an assembly had been summoned officially before the Water Gate in Jerusalem to hear and witness the Torah of the God of Heaven read to the assembly, circulated among the assembly, and (at verses 7-9 themselves) "read from the book, from the Law of God, clearly; and they gave the sense,[37] so that the people understood the reading." Verse nine tells the reader that: "...the Levites taught the people..." One more piece of information must be supplied before we continue. It is found in Nehemiah 7:73. If one reads uncritically, the first thing that the will escape the reader is that four specializations within the post-exilic priestly ranks are enumerated here: priests, Levites, gatekeepers, and temple servants.[38]

The Qumran material reflects the work of two of these four groups: the priests and the Levites. It has been marked elsewhere in this study that this particular distinction within the priestly ranks was maintained by the producer of the P source *stratum* of the Pentateuch.[39] It may be that the priests referred to as Levites did not mind. At any rate, we have available no text containing a complaint by the group designated Levites which suggests that they had an insurmountable problem with this appellation.[40] Ezra, the redactor of the R source *stratum* of the Pentateuch, is cast as their Zadokite, not Levite leader and archscribe, and has no problem working with them.[41] Likewise, the intellectual, multilingual Levites appear to support Ezra's archscribal efforts. After all, all of them are ultimately official agents of the Persian government![42] Thus, a strong scribal class of priests is responsible for producing the Qumran library. One may add further, that there is evidence of both Zadokite priestly input and Levite priestly input.[43] Whatever the contents of the Qumran library, the contents are a joint Zadokite (=Aaronid)/Levite (=Mushite) venture and enterprise. Whatever distinctions existed during the days of P appear to no longer have been of concern during the days of the Qumran covenanters. **That war was not fought among them.**

Qumran, then, provides the reader with (among other significant things) a Balaam type who is the product of reconciliation between two formerly warring priestly factions. The Qumran Balaam influence does not reflect factionalism among traditionally warring priests. Rather, his typology is employed to ensure **unity**. The medium for accomplishing this is the *pesher*,[44] the commentary on literature, but employed to tell another story, or to present another etiology. At Qumran Balaam is not a shaped explosive charge aimed strategically at rival priesthoods, whether within or without Israel. At Qumran, there is the assumption and agreement of guilt and culpability on his part. But his influence still has a major part to play in terms of the outlook of apocalyptic warfare.

If we do not lose sight of the problem as it had developed to his point, however, we realize that we are ultimately still in the midst of a situation which pits priest against priest. However, we are no longer still embroiled in a situation where it is Israel priest against Israel priest, (Shilonites) or Israelite priest against Judaite priest, or even Shilonite priest against both Israel and Judaite priests, all of which have been demonstrated above. "Balaam" the type, therefore, is no longer necessary for the type of anti priestly arguments produced at Qumran. What is significantly different is that we are now witnessing literature which works through the problem of legitimate **Jewish** priest versus illegitimate **Jewish** priest! What has altered the earlier equations is a radical change in what is understood to be **Israel**! And the exigencies of the historical situation have brought that about.[45]

QUMRAN: THE FANTASTIC WAR   95

1)   Numbers 24:17 reads:

"I see him, but not now; I behold him, but not high: a star shall come forth out of Jacob, and a scepter shall rise out of Israel; it shall crush the corners of the head of Moab, and break down all the sons of Sheth.

2)   Numbers 24:18 reads:

Edom shall be dispossessed, Seir also, his enemies, shall be dispossessed, while Israel does valiantly.

3)   Numbers 24:8 reads:

God brings him out of Egypt; he has as it were the horns of the wild ox, he shall eat up the nations his adversaries, and shall break their bones in pieces, and pierce them through with his arrows.

All three "footnotes" come from material which comprises the Balaam cycle of Numbers 22–24. The Qumran worldview embraced that material and saw its usefulness in conducting their war. Looking at the contents of the three, one sees that the material quoted belongs to the **Book of the Wars of Yahweh** material.[46] Qumran is using the Numbers 24:8 "footnote" to describe combatants on the side of the Sons of Light. Its bellicose tone is apropos for the purposes of the War Scroll. Qumran employs the Numbers 24:18 material because it once again names one of (from the point of view of the priestly group writing this scroll) the archenemies of "Israel." Moab (and Sheth) complete(s) the list of primary archenemies, and links the Qumran tradition to that of the producers of the Numbers 22-24 material concerning Balaam, and to their *epigoni*, those who employed the cycle's contents following one of two trajectories about Balaam.

Other military oriented material certainly existed which could have been employed to make either of the three above points. My task, therefore, is to ascertain why **this** material and not some other material was employed in the War Scroll at this point. To accomplish this, let us first look at some particular phraseology of the Scroll column by column. Concerning the religious offices during wartime, [47] the producers of the Scroll wrote:

> After this high priest and his deputy they shall appoint an order of major **priests**, twelve in number, to serve constantly before God. Furthermore, twenty-six major officials duly assigned to service shall serve in their appointed offices; and after them shall be twelve **Levites**, one for each tribe, to serve constantly.

Concerning the battle signals[48] they wrote:

> When the lines of battle are drawn up to face the foe, line in front of line, then out of the center gap in the ranks there shall come into the lines seven **priests** of the descendants of Aaron...and: (a)

> And when these **priests** go out between the lines, seven **Levites** shall go out with them,...and: (b)

> And three officers selected from the **Levites** shall walk ahead of these **priests** and **Levites**. As well as: (c)

> And the **priests** shall sound a blast on [two of the trumpets] for calling to arms...and the **levitical** officers [shall go out with them]. (d)

Of the order of battle,[49] the covenanters wrote:

> After the priests have sounded a blast for them (i.e., the warriors) on the trumpets of [memorial],...Then the **priests** shall blow a second time,....And the **Levites** and all the people with ram's horns shall sound a loud blast.

Finally, on thanksgiving for victory,[50] one reads:

> And when the sun is hastening to set on that day, the high **priest** shall stand up, and the priests and the **Levites** that are with him,...

Compare the contents of these excerpts with the following one from the *TaNaK*:

> And Hezekiah established the divisions of the **priests** and the **Levites**, according to their divisions, every man according to his task, for the **priests** and for the **Levites**. (2 Chron. 31:2)

What all have in common is that an obvious distinction has been made between **priests** and **Levites**. The distinction came originally from warfare: warfare between the Aaronid priesthood and the Mushite priesthood. The distinction is introduced and maintained in literature belonging to the Aaronid tradition. It is never located in E or D source *stratum* material. Friedman wrote of the situation which brought this division about: "Solomon had removed the Shiloh (Levite/Mushite) priest Abiathar from Jerusalem and had given authority in the Temple entirely to the Aaronid priest Zadok."[51] This had occurred in the tenth century B.C.E. (ca. 966). P wrote at the court of Hezekiah during his attempt at religious reform. One major plank in his reform platform was centralizing the priesthood at Jerusalem. Thus, Friedman's statements "King Hezekiah was the best thing that ever happened to the Aaronid priests", and "Hezekiah followed Solomon's priestly preferences," [52] as well as the 2 Chronicles 31:2 account, provide sufficient information and reason for the bifurcation within the seventh century and later priestly ranks in Jerusalem in particular. Later material such as the D source *stratum* did not maintain this distinction; at least it did not reflect such a division literarily.

The priest/Levite division is maintained in 1QM. It reveals that a group of descendants of the Aaronid/Zadokite line wrote this material. Thus, the beginning of the **Manual of Discipline for the Future Congregation of**

Israel from Qumran should not surprise the reader:

> This is the rule for the whole body of Israel when, in the future, they lead their lives in the manner of the sons of Zadok, the **priests**, and of **those associated with them**...⁵³

Obviously, one of the "associated groups" was understood to have been Levites.

The Balaam material quoted within 1QM has a tradition connection with the P recension of the Numbers Balaam cycle. Any entry into the *arcana mundi* of why only these three Numbers passages from the Balaam cycle were employed must be approached from the standpoint of that P trajectory. The three "footnotes" demonstrate how severely the Balaam tradition within the P trajectory had been altered by the time of the writing of the War Scroll. Balaam the figure and Balaam the type no longer served as foils against other priestly outsiders. At Qumran no nebulous outsider was held up as a paradigm, neither to be emulated, nor to be spurned.⁵⁴ The Balaam of the recensions had all but disappeared: had become blended into the background of the Qumran P program. At Qumran the words ascribed to Balaam in poetically-written *mshlym* "footnotes" of Numbers had been severed from the one who supposedly had uttered them. Balaam had been demoted: his words had been promoted.⁵⁵ Words of a gazer *zofeh*/teleologist) had been lifted from one body of literature which depicted a wartime situation (Israel camped in the plains of Moab opposite Jericho, and following the Yahweh/holy war itinerary), and had been purposefully imbedded by gazer/apocalypticists in another body of literature which depicted another wartime situation. The reputed utterances of the *propriediv* Balaam at Qumran did not become dead letters once they were written down. A new living tradition about Balaam's words was generated among the P tradition, and new life was breathed into the word. The "footnotes" are written proof of that.[56]

Chapter 7. The Samaritan Literature and Balaam: Warring Priesthoods: The Hermeneutical Debates Continue

As soon as one considers the issue of the origins of the Samaritans, one is immediately cast into the continuing row between groups of priests. The Chronicler's (identified as an Aaronid priest) theological interpretation of the return from Babylonian exile is considered an idealized one, although much factual historical material is also embedded in his account. It would have the reader accept that only a handful of vinedressers and farmers remained in the territory of Judah to ensure a continued crop of wine and basic foodstuffs (Chron. 36:20ff.). Allied views contained in Ezra and Nehemiah paint a limited picture of what was going on in the territory of the former Kingdom of Israel, the administrative center of which continued under the Assyrians to be Samaria. There are those who take this idealized picture to serious task.[57] They argue that the Deuteronomic circle (to which Jeremiah belonged) was still active and influential during the seventy years of the Exile. It is certainly now known that accounts of the final days of the Kingdom of Judah and events several years later, bear the stamp of this circle.[58] This view tells us that only a small number of people (about 4,000) were taken into Babylonian exile.[59]

Bad blood between the North and the South has thus been seen as the major underlying reason for the separation between Jews and Samaritans. This bad blood has been traced traditionally to the period of Assyrian domination, and then as having been maintained during the following periods of Babylonian and Persian domination. 2 Chronicles 13 has been viewed as literature which gives voice to this situation. In the mouth of Abijah the king of Jerusalem, the Chronicler places the statement: "...we are keepers *(shomrim)* of the charge of Yahweh our God, but you have forsaken him." The charge was directed toward Jeroboam I king of Israel. M. Delcor in *"Hinweise auf das Samaritanische Schisma im Alten Testament,"*[60] suggested that: "particular emphasis of the speech was on the true priesthood being maintained at Jerusalem, whereas

Northern Israel had illegitimate priests serving false gods." Priesthood legitimacy and what constituted that legitimacy were at root of whatever issues animated 'Jews' against 'Samaritans' and *vice versa*.

The ancient cultic center of Shiloh, which had provided critique for both Samarian (Bethelite and Danite) and Jerusalem priesthoods (either from without or within) was still active during the exilic period. Thus, one reads in the exilic–period–edited Book of Jeremiah at 41:5 (writing of events ca. 583 B.C.E.): "eighty men arrived from Shechem and Shiloh and Samaria, with their bodies gashed, bringing cereal offerings and incense to present at the temple of the Lord." Shechem and Shiloh were old Levite priestly centers, while Samaria, the former Israelite capital, was then the administrative center of the Babylonian overlords. Laden with such goods, it would appear that priests were enroute to the (remainder of the) temple to engage in sacrificial offerings there. Some "official" priesthood officiated there. If the Chronicles–Ezra–Nehemiah texts can be trusted, some priests (and Levites!) remained in the territory of Judah. Apparently they carried on sacerdotal functions there although the political administrative machinery had been set up at Mizpah under Gedaliah. Ezra 9:1 refers to "the people of Israel, and the priests and the Levites" who had not "separated themselves from the people of the lands." These, too, appear to have been people who had not experienced an exile, although they could have been those priests and Levites who accompanied either Sheshbazaar or Zerubbabel. Mushite priests visited (ruined) Jerusalem to sacrifice. Priests and Levites remained in Judah as well as mixed with the other populations. We get the picture of busy priestly groups in an area where, according to the returning–from–Exile priests, there was a sacerdotal wasteland. Still, according to Coggins,[61] after performing an analysis on all of the TaNaK materials relevant to possibly identifying the Samaritans, the evidence was: "...never better than ambiguous and may well be nonexistent." Even the polemical enemies of the

Samaritans associate them with a northern tradition. The problem is that most (whether ancient Jewish or modern multipartisan scholarly) researchers still identify Samaritan with Samarian. And there is no evidence for this. Samarians were those who lived in Samaria (whether indigenous from the time of Omri, or those foreigners who occupied it later). Samaritan must be derived from the term *shomrim* (guardians, keepers, observers, watchers [of the correct observance of the dictates of *torah*]).[62]

Since literary research into the identity and origin of the Samaritans yielded nothing conclusive, investigators turned to archaeology to augment continuing studies. As to the occupation of Shechem, archaeological data puts "a community which we may properly describe as Samaritan...at Shechem during the third and second centuries,..."[63]

What may scholars conclude from the foregoing? In the period between the third century and the beginning of early Christianity and early rabbinic Judaism, Judaistic was multifaceted and polymorphous. The MT materials and the Qumran Scrolls discussed thus far provided evidence of two groups within pre-Christian era Judaism who disagreed on ideas of priesthood and number (and wording!) of certain books. What their respective canons imply is that both agreed that the Pentateuch was pivotal in importance. Add to this the picture of the Sadducees,[64] whose origins are not earlier than Hasmonean times (anymore than those of Qumran), and one becomes aware of three priestly groups who, by the literature they cherish most, agreed that the Pentateuchal traditions were primary in importance.

Recent studies of the Samaritans have seen fit to step out of the mainstream of traditional studies of the Samaritans and to take a fresh look at their origins and beliefs.[65] While much of what they believe comes from studies of Samaritan works produced by them much later than the period with which this work is concerned, it is now becoming generally acknowledged that the Samaritan community of the post-third century to the pre-Christian first century comprised one of several sub groups within the diversity of Judaism. They manifested a particular intra-Judaism conservatism, a part of which identified the sanctuary of the true (for them) Jewish priesthood on Mount Gerizim.

By the second century B.C.E. there was unquestionably a Mt. Gerizim-based Samaritan community over against a Jerusalem-based Jewish community, "The rivalry between them, affecting as it did both the interpretations of the holy traditions and the claims of different sanctuaries with their priesthoods... [66] Nowhere in their pre-Christian era literary traditions is that rivalry more evident than in the Samaritan Pentateuch.

a. Balaam in the Samaritan Pentateuch

The Samaritan Pentateuch (SP) preserves a text tradition somewhat different from the Masoretic Text (MT). [67] There are numerous points of agreement between SP and MT as well, but for studies in the interpretation of the Balaam figure, the differences are more noteworthy.

1) The Text Characteristics. The Samaritan Pentateuch is not a familiar document to many readers. Thus, some discussion of its characteristics are necessary before examining how the Balaam figure is presented in this material. The available texts of the SP are written in an archaizing Canaanite alphabetic script. A major characteristic is that two forms of writing the consonantal text are employed: what are often termed *plene* (full, marking long vowel sounds), and *defectiva* (defective, i.e., not marking long vowel sounds). In the Semitic languages a word containing the stem or root (*shoresh*) QRB, 'nearness', may be read several ways if the text is written without some means of recognizing the inflected form of the *shoresh*. And in many ancient, Semitic, alphabet-written texts that is typical.

> The adjective *qrb* means near.
>
> The noun *qrb* means relative (i.e., near kin).
>
> The verb *qrb* means he approached (i.e., drew near).
>
> The noun *qrbn* means sacrifice (i.e., that brought near the altar).
>
> The noun *qrb* means a fight/battle (i.e., approach, draw near in a hostile manner).

The problem with such a writing convention is that vocalization (a clue to meaning) is difficult and uncertain. The SP employs four consonants 'a (*aleph*), light h (*heh*), w (*waw/vav*), and y (*yod(h)* to mark certain long vowel sounds. It is a good attempt at better vocalization, but it is far from perfect. 'a marks the phoneme /a/ at the beginning of words. h marks the phoneme /a/ at the end of words. w marks the phoneme /u/. And y marks the phoneme /i/. That seems simple and reasonable enough. But 'a also marks /o/ (as in *l'a=lo* [no]/ The diphthong /ey/ in *bereyshit* (in/when beginning) is also marked by 'a. h also marks the phonemes /o/ in *'ayfh* [eyfo] (=where), and /eh/ in *mwrh* [moreh] (=male teacher). w marks the phoneme /o/ also (like h on occasion). And y marks two diphthongs as well: /e/ and /ay/ in *byt* [pronounced bait] (=house of), and *lfny* [lifenai] (=before me) respectively. These four letters are known as *immot hakkriyyah*: mothers of reading. SP employs these "mothers" just as MT employs them. There appears to be no specific pattern of use of the *plene* spelling, however. SP is less consistent in its application of them to militate against ambiguity of meaning. More will be demonstrated concerning this below.

SP differs from MT in the title of the scroll in which the Balaam cycle appears. SP's fourth book is entitled *bamidbar sinay* (In The Sinai Wilderness). MT's traditional Hebrew-written title is simply *bamidbar*.

Numerous points of difference characterize the two texts. Exponents of both "higher" and "lower" criticism would have a field day analyzing the fifty (50) places where SP diverges from MT in Chapter 22 of *bamidbar sinay*. Chapter 23 of SP is in dissonance with MT at fifty one (51) places. Following at a close third, in terms of numbers, are the forty-four (44) points of difference in Chapter 24. [68] These points of dissonance exhibit characteristics which I have grouped and studied under three headings:

1) Spelling Differences
2) Grammatical Differences
3) Deliberate Word-Choice Differences.

Since all three appear in each chapter of the SP Balaam cycle, I shall exploit their characteristics using Chapter 22 as a model demonstration text. [69]

a) Spelling Differences. Nowhere better does SP differ from MT than in the convention of spelling. Moreover, a focus on spelling points up the numerous inconsistencies in spelling (*plene* over *defectiva*, *defectiva* over *plene* [and in the same sentence to boot!] within SP itself. This is not to suggest that the MT is trouble free on this issue: my focus is merely on the SP. Eighteen (18) occurrences of differences appear in Chapter 22. When MT has a superior spelling over SP, an asterisk follows the line. Different possible meanings are separated by a diagonal line.

		MT	SP	Meaning
1.	22:5	*'amw*	*'amwn*	his people/Ammon
2.	22:5	*mmly*	*mmwly*	opposite me

3.	22:10	*tzpr*	*tzpwr*	bird
4.	22:11	*hnh*	*hn*	something important is about to follow/they (f.) are
5.	22:14	*wyqwmw*	*wtqmw*	and they rose*
6.	22:18	*ml'a*	*mlw'a*	filled
7.	22:18	*gdwlh*	*gdlh*	large/he grew large*
8.	22:20	blank	*ml'ak*	messenger
9.	22:23	*lhtth*	*lhtwth*	to turn her
10.	22:24	*bms'awl*	*bms'al*	in a narrow path*
11.	22:25	*lhkth*	*lhkwth*	to strike her
12.	22:26	*wywsf*	*wysf*	and again*
13.	22:26	*wsm'awl*	*wsm'al*	and to the left*
14.	22:28	*lbl'am*	*'al bl'am*	to Balaam
15.	22:31	*šlph*	*šlwph*	drawn (sword)
16.	22:31	*wysthw*	*wysthwy*	and he fell
17.	22:32	*šlwš*	*šlš*	three*
18.	22:37	*hl'a*	*hlw'a*	is it not...?

Although SP generally improves upon the spelling of MT through use of the *immot hakkriyyah*, here we note six instances where MT provides a clearer text. In one instance (22:31) the addition of a (*yod(h)*) to this word renders it nonsensical. It is probably a scribal error.

b) Grammatical Differences. Grammatical differences between SP and MT point up (1) the state of preservation of the text tradition employed by the Samaritans; (2) the level of knowledge and competence of the scribal groups handling and reproducing the scrolls of the SP; (3) the program and expected goals of the Samaritan intellectuals, and (4) how the Balaam figure facilitated their self-perceived purpose and program. The differences in Chapter 22 are:

1. 22:4   MT   b'at hh<u>w</u>'a   at **that** time
           SP   b'at hh<u>y</u>'a   at **that** time

[Change of demonstrative pronoun *that* from MT masculine to SP feminine. MT is grammatically correct here.]

2. 22:5   MT   hnh   what follows is important!
           SP   <u>w</u>hnh   **and** what follows is important!

[SP adds a conjunction to this particle usually translated *behold*, probably for emphasis.]

3. 22:6   MT   w'ašr t'ar yw'ar   and whoever you curse is cursed
           SP   w'<u>at</u> 'ašr t'ar wy'ar   and (object marker) whoever

[SP adds an object marker (*'at*) which produces a better grammatical sentence.]

4. 22:7   MT   wqsmym   and divinations
           SP   wqsmy<u>hm</u>   and **their** divinations

[SP adds the possessive pronominal suffix for clarity.]

5. 22:11 MT   hnh <u>h</u>'am <u>h</u>ytz'a and **the** people **who** came out

| | SP | hn *'am* ytz'a | **they, a** people, came out |

[SP prefers the indefinite mode of presentation here. MT prefers to employ a definite mode and the use of a relative pronoun.]

| 6. | 22:11 | MT | *'ath* | now |
| | | SP | *w'ath* | **and** not |

[SP adds the conjunction *and*, again probably for emphasis.]

| 7. | 22:12 | MT | *l'a* | not |
| | | SP | *wl'a* | **and** not |

[SP adds the conjunction *and*.]

| 8. | 22:10 | MT | *l'avr* | to cross/transgress |
| | | SP | *'a'avr* | **I shall** (not) cross/transgress |

[SP casts this in the first person singular imperfect, while the MT form is the infinitive.]

| 9. | 22:22 | MT | ky *hwlk* hw'a | because he **is going** |
| | | SP | ky *hlk* hw'a | because he **went** |

[SP prefers the past tense to MT's participle.]

| 10. | 22:28 | MT | *lhl'am* | to Balaam |

| | | SP | ’<u>a</u>l bl’am | to(ward) Balaam |

[SP prefers the full form to MT's shortened preposition.]

| 11. | 22:30 | MT | h<u>h</u>skn | was I ever accustomed |
| | | SP | hskn | I was accustomed |

| 12. | 22:32 | MT | lstn ky <u>yrt</u> hdrk | to be an adversary because the **way is perverse**... |

[MT's rather oblique presentation is replaced by the more forceful method of *direct discourse* here signalled by the two possessive pronominal suffixes in SP]

| | | SP | lst<u>nk</u> ky <u>br’a</u> drk<u>k</u> | to be **your** adversary because **your** way is evil... |

| 13. | 22:33 | MT | lfny | before me |
| | | SP | <u>m</u>lfny | **from** before me |

[SP prefers to add the preposition *from* here.]

| 14. | 22:38 | MT | hykl | am I indeed able...? |
| | | SP | bywkl | will I indeed be able...? |

[SP prefers the imperfect passive form of this question to MT's present interrogative.]

| 15. | 22:38 | MT | bpy | in (a) mouth |
| | | SP | bpy<u>y</u> | in **my** mouth |

[SP provides a second *yod(h)* in the form of a possessive pronominal suffix.]

16.   22:41   MT   *wyr'a mšm...qtzh h'am*
      SP   *wyr'a mšm ('at) qtzh h'am*
      and he saw from there (object marker) the nearness of the people.

[SP adds the untranslatable *object marker*.]

c) Deliberate Word–Choice Differences. There is evidence of conscious and deliberate change of wordings in SP over against MT. Oftentimes the changing `provided an attempted fine-tuning of a given text to reflect the Samaritan community's point of view. Any major clues as to the Samaritan community's use of "Balaam" must be expected and sought in the manner in which the thinkers deliberately deviated from the underlying Palestinian text tradition from which SP is derived. In Numbers 22 there are six (6) noteworthy examples.

1.   22:20   MT   *'alhym*   deity/deities
              SP   *ml'ak 'alhym*   messenger of deity/deities

2.   22:22   MT   *'alhym*   deity/deities
              SP   *yhwh*   Yahweh (the specific deity)

3.   22:33   MT   *'atkh hrgty w'awth*   I would have slain you and let her live.
              SP   *'atk hkyty w'ath*   I would have waited for you and her I would let live.

4.   22:35   MT   *tdbr*   you will speak

		SP	*tšmr ldbr*	will be careful to speak
5.	22:38	MT	*bpy, 'tw...'adbr*	in a mouth with which I shall speak...
		SP	*bpyy, 'atw...'ašmr*	in my mouth that I shall guard to say...
6.	22:39	MT	*wyb'aw*	and they came to/arrived
		SP	*wyby'ahw*	and he (Balak) brought him (Balaam)...

With the deliberate work choice phenomena one intuits a specific worldview concerning the Samaritan community's interpretation of Balaam, and how it used the tradition(s) concerning him. The text and its contents present another trajectory of interpretation of the Balaam tradition.

2) *Analysis*. The program of all Samaritan hermeneutics may be traced to three major and important deviations of SP from MT. 1) In SP Exodus 20:17 there is a command to build a sanctuary on Mount Gerizim. 2) In Exodus 11:30 one reads that at the end of this verse in the MT (which ends"...beside the oak(s) of Moreh?" SP adds *mwl škm*, opposite Shechem. 3) And Wuerthwein [70] states that there are nineteen passages in Deuteronomy:"...where the choice of the holy place is set in the past and the reference to Shechem (an ancient religious sanctuary and center for the Israelite amphictyony during the periods of the judges), meaning on holy ground, and the place which Yahweh chose (to be the meeting place between heaven and earth), betray priestly concerns.

Throughout Chapter 22 we must bear in mind my arguments about the recensions of the entire cycle (*Infra* Part 2, Section 1). SP Chapters 22–24 constitute yet another recension, but one must work hard to uncover its meaning and uses of the Balaam figure and type. In order to accomplish this, I shall present an analysis of the present data and their significance for these Balaam studies.

Chapter 22

verses 2-21 *In Fear of Israel, Balak Sends for Balaam to Curse Them*

(These examples are distilled from the above 3-part analysis of SP text characteristics. Here no MT material is highlighted.)

- (5) Ammon is specifically named (Spelling)
- (7) and *their* divinations in their hands (Grammatical)
- (11) *they, a* people, came out (Grammatical)
- (18) I shall not transgress/rebel (Grammatical)
- (20) messenger/angel of the deity (Deliberate Word-Choice)

22-35 *Balaam Is Rebuked By His Ass*

- (22) because he went (Grammatical)
- (22) Yahweh (the specific deity) (Deliberate Word-Choice)
- (30) I was accustomed (Grammatical)
- (32) because *your* way is evil (Grammatical)
- (33) I would have waited for you and let her live (Deliberate Word-Choice)
- (33) *from* before me (Grammatical)
- (35) you will be careful to speak (Deliberate Word-Choice)

36–41   *Balak Welcomes Balaam*

    (38)   will I indeed be able...? (Grammatical)

    (38)   in *my* mouth that I shall guard to say (Deliberate Word–Choice)

    (39)   and he (Balak) brought him (Balaam) (Deliberate Word–Choice)

Chapter 23

(Here I offer a somewhat fuller analysis with explanation, but in line with the presentation of the evidence from Chapter 22. Both (SP) and (MT) materials will be juxtaposed in order to highlight important differences.)

1–6   *Balak Makes Preparation for Curse*

    (1)   (SP) make (not build for me of MT) (Deliberate Word–Choice)

    (2)   (SP) stand by your wickedness/wrongs (this word 'awlh also means burnt offering, sacrifice, holocaust). (MT) has 'alh, sacrifice. (This may or may not be a Deliberate Word–Choice) MT 'altk: SP 'alwtk.

    (3)   (SP) perhaps Elohim (not Yahweh of MT) will come to meet me (Deliberate Word–Choice) Perhaps Yahweh did not meet propriedivs.

    (4)   (SP) And the angel/messenger of Elohim (not Yehweh) *found* (not appeared to) Balaam (Deliberate Word–Choice)

    (5)   (SP) And the messenger/angel of Yahweh (not Elohim) put a

word (not to be understood as oracle) in the mouth of Balaam. (Deliberate Word–Choice).

(6) (SP) and he (Balak) stood by his wickednesses/wrongs (MT) is singular and reads sacrifice. (Deliberate Word–Choice).

7–10 *Balaam's First Mashal*

(10) (SP) substitutes the form *mrb'at ysr'al* (a construct form) for

(MT) *'at rwb'a* (the stock). (Deliberate Word–Choice). Both meanings are uncertain. RSV offers 'fourth' for *rwb'a*, but states that it might also mean 'dust clouds.' (SP) would then mean either 'fourth part *of*', or 'dust clouds *of*.

(10) (SP) reads *yš'arym* for (MT) *yšrym*. That is, direct ones or upright, straight, honest ones, respectively. (Deliberate Word–Choice) But these are probably variants which might have been employed by contemporaries simultaneously.

11–17 *Balaam, Disappointed, Makes More Elaborate Preparations*

(12) (SP) reads *brkt brwk* (you have blessed the (already) blessed) over against (MT) *brkt brk* (you have indeed/surely) blessed them. Both renderings are powerful. (SP), however, consciously manipulates this verse to add more power and punch to those who are (once again) blessed! (Deliberate Word–Choice)

(13) (SP) what Yahweh puts in *my mouth* (*bpyy*), as opposed to the

less forceful (MT) *bpy* (in a mouth). (Deliberate Word-Choice and Grammatical Difference)

(13)   (SP) omits (MT) another place *from which* you will see them. Apparently the relative pronoun *'ašr* carried no weight in (SP) (Grammatical Difference)

(16)   (SP) and the *messenger* of Yahweh called to Balaam differs from (MT) and the Lord met Balaam. (Deliberate Word-Choice) This is preceded in v.16 by the differences "stand here while I *call*..."

18–24 *Balaam's Second Mashal*

(20)   (SP) I received a command to bless, I shall bless and not revoke it, is countered by (MT) I received a blessing and I blessed. The tense shift by (SP) shows (Deliberate Word-Choice as well as Grammatical Differences).

(21)   (SP) I shall not observe/see vanity/sinfulness in Jacob (MT) He did not observe/see......(Grammatical Differences and Deliberate Word-Choice)

25–24:2 *Balak, Angered, Makes New Preparations*

(25)   (SP) Neither are they cursed, nor blessed at all (MT) Neither curse them at all nor bless them at all (Deliberate Word-Choice and Grammatical Differences)

(26)   (SP) which *the deity (h'alhym)* will say, over against (MT) which Yahweh will say (Deliberate Word-Choice)

SAMARITAN LITERATURE AND BALAAM 117

(27) (SP) Balak did that which Balaam "*spoke*"...upon the altar (MT) Balak did that which Balaam "*said*"...*at* the altar (The Deliberate Word–Choice of spoke (*dbr*) over said (*'amr*)

Chapter 24

3–4 *Balaam's Third Mashal*

(4) (SP) consciously omits the (MT) The oracle of one who hears the words of deity (Deliberate Choice To Omit Words–Deliberate Word–Choice)

(8) (SP) El *leads/guides him out* of Egypt (*nhhw*) (MT) El *brings him out* of Egypt (*mwtry'aw*) (Deliberate Word–Choice)

10–14 *Balak Is Provoked and Balaam Explains*

(10) (SP) you have blessed the blessed (MT) you have blessed (Deliberate Word–Choice)

(11) (SP) three times (*rglym*) (MT) three times (*p'amym*) (Deliberate Word–Choice)

(13) (SP) Yahweh *my God* will say (MT) Yahweh will say (Deliberate Word–Choice)

(13) (SP) I shall say *it* (MT) shall say (Deliberate Word–Choice)

15–17 *The Doom of Moab*

(17) (SP) and people will bow and prostrate themselves (*qdqd*)(i.e,

all the sons of Sheth) (MT) and people will be mowed down, made level (*qrqr*)(i.e., all the sons of Sheth (Deliberate Word–Choice)

18–19   *Mashal Concerning Edom*

(18)   (SP) *'asw* (unknown word) (MT) *s'ayr* (Seir the country)(A Deliberate Word–Choice) probably attempting to restore a damaged text [both words contain the common letters *s* and *'a*, and *waw/vaw* and *yod(h)* which in many ancient texts (such as those from Qumran) may be confused.] But this is very tentative here.

20   *Mashal Concerning Amalek*

21–21   *Mashal Concerning the Kenites*

23–24   *Mashal Concerning Assyria*

Many historians have believed that the Samaritans *seceded* from contemporaneous Judaism during the fourth century B.C.E. [71] A group of priests determined that the situation concerning what is meant to be the people of Yahweh and who constituted these people was at hand, and acted forcefully and decisively to establish that people. Yet, oddly, no argument has been forwarded that they were apocalypticists, like the Qumran covenanters. We've already seen that (later) the people who established the Qumran community made similar decisions. At an even earlier time, Onias IV of the

Aaronid/Zadokite line also acted in such a manner by establishing a temple of Yahweh in Heliopolis in Egypt.[72] This group of priests who preserved the text of the Pentateuch and other literature, and who provided leadership for the Samaritan community obviously was at odds with the general priestly leadership within third century B.C.E. Judaism(s). "Balaam" in this material must be pursued within the framework of that with which we've become thoroughly familiar, priestly warfare. We've demonstrated with the Balaam cycle just how vicious such warfare could and did become. The very fact that the Samaritans preserved and reworked the Pentateuchal material suggests that intra-priestly interpretive differences existed. Let us see whether the old wars and positioning of the earlier priesthoods were still alive and well as we consider the Balaam cycle in SP Numbers 22-24.

One sees with the (SP) that numerous points of difference between (SP) and (MT) exist. Although numerous spelling differences were demonstrated to exist, they didn't affect the meaning of the text severely, with most of them being nothing more than full versus ancient spelling conventions and practices. What is much more noteworthy are the grammatical conventions and deliberate word-choices made by the preparers of the (SP). Anyone who works with ANE scrolls knows that such drastic and dramatic divergencies signal profound hermeneutical statements (whether within biblical texts or without). The above analysis has demonstrated that deliberate word-choices outnumber any type of deviation for pointing to hermeneutical differences.

One thing is immediately apparent: the *shomrim* saw in Balaam a dangerous figure. He is manipulated by them (through conscious word-changes) to look like a pawn; like someone who is never really in charge of anything. They controlled when it was appropriate for Balaam to *speak* with the deity directly. Thus, they employed the deliberate word-choice 'angel/messenger of the deity' to produce an *entrepreneur* whose function it was to maintain distance between deity and *propriediv*. The argument for the importance of keeping, guarding, watching, observing (*shamar*) the word of the deity, as opposed to (any)one having such power independently, is also stressed. It may be inferred from this convention that the *shomrim* considered themselves guardians of the COVENANT. They employed four names of deity in their Balaam cycle: 1) Yahweh, 2) Elohim, 3) El, and 4) (the) Deity. They do this, however, in no discernible pattern, and in the same sentence, two forms may be employed. Emphasis on what is spoken by Balaam is apparent in that he is constantly depicted as exercising caution about what it is that he will say, what is placed by deity in his mouth. The sacrifices of Balak are (by deliberate word-choice) downgraded to the status of the result of wickedness and wrongs, bespeaking an attitude toward sacrifices offered by any priests other than themselves to be at odds. The expression *brky brwk* makes light of any possible possession of power-of-the-spoken-word on the part of Balaam by implying that he was only *blessing the already blessed*, thus doing nothing! This position is stated once again in 23:25 where one reads: "Neither are they cursed, nor blessed at all." But one of the most damaging pieces of evidence is the complete omission by (SP) of the words: "The oracle of one who hears the words of deity" (24:4) *Prima facie* this would appear to be a barb hurled at the office of the prophet. Moreover, when one combines this occurrence with others in the (SP) Balaam cycle mentioned above, it becomes apparent that (SP) presents a front against those who are reputed to have spoken (especially directly) with a deity. It is through the middle agent (the messenger/angel) of the deity that communication takes place. One may not be certain, however, just who this messenger is. Later Samaritan thinkers would reflect on this and conclude that the messenger was Moses and none other. Thus, 24:8's: "El leads/guides him out of Egypt would appear to precurse this view. But that is not all. Anyone who subscribes to a belief in the efficacy of these peoples' actions (including speaking oracles) will suffer disappointment. Their sacrifices (or directions to others' sacrifices) produce wickedness. Even a situation such as 23:13 ("what Yahweh puts in **my** mouth), which at first sight appears to validate that Balaam is indeed a *bona fide* prophet, must be seen as anti-prophetic. It points more to the power of Yahweh than to the power of Balaam. Their argument would go something like this. "If Yahweh wanted to speak through your mouth as he did through the mouth of the ass, he has the power to do so, but nothing that you say on your own, and no oracle which Yahweh does not speak through your mouth is of any importance. Therefore, you, Balaam, are of no importance!" As a priestly-led group, it is understandable why *BaMidbar Sinai* 22-24 would contain anti (other) priestly polemics, and why the sacrifices attempted by them would not be useful in divination. Yet agreement with other priestly groups is much more evident in (SP) as a whole. But why does the (reputed) speaker of the word of deity come off so very badly at their hands?

The office of prophet in ancient Israel (and the *shomrim* must be included in this group) was a limited one. Although its beginnings are obscure, and signs of development within the office are evident at a later time (Amos 7:14 ff.), the death knell is delivered to it in Deutero-Zechariah 13:2ff:

> And on that day, says the Lord of hosts, I will...remove from the land the prophets and the unclean spirit. And if anyone again appears as a prophet...his father and mother who bore him shall pierce him through when he prophesies;...but will say, 'I am no prophet,...'

This demise of the prophetic office took place sometime during the fourth century. [73] Unlike (MT)'s Balaam cycle, which shows no hostility to the prophetic office as a whole, (SP) is openly hostile toward the office. This is one clue to the appearance of the Shomerim at a time later than the fourth century. The textual analysis has produced a text which denies that the deity spoke to the archprophet type represented by Balaam.

In the third century B.C.E. Aaronid/Zadokites were still in charge of the Jerusalem cultus. We do not know to what extent these Aaronids controlled the scribal priestly/political apparatus. Since it took later Aaronids (the Qumran group) much later to secede gradually from the main priestly group in Jerusalem during the days of the Maccabee/Hasmoneans, it is likely that the Samaritan priestly leadership consisted of a priestly elite who were are odds with the controlling Aaronids. Beyond this point the waters of interpretation became extremely murky. One is tempted to rush headlong and proclaim that once again Mushites and Aaronids reached some specific sacerdotal *impasse*, that some Mushite sympathizers found it impossible to live with this *impasse*, and decided to leave. We shall not give in to this temptation, but shall recall the *caveat* contained in the excellent study of Coggins instead.

Below, in the section which discusses the Asatir, arguments are forwarded that the Samaritan writers engaged in attempts at harmonization. I find it odd that exegesis which was engaged in to set up a new temple cultus (and thereby only correct place to establish it) was directed toward the end of achieving harmony. I find in my research no attempt on the part of the Samaritan leadership to harmonize anything! Even a perusal of their writings discounts such thinking. These people attacked, they were not interested in accommodating anyone, nor did they retreat. What their works will demonstrate is that they attacked, especially the image and type which had been known as the prophet. Because of the notoriety and previous uses of the Balaam type, the producers of the (SP) recension of Numbers 22–24 focused on the Balaam figure to make their anti prophetic case. The so–called prophetic material of the

Hebrew Scriptures was not employed by them as a *corpus* to attack. The Samaritan writers will employ some works belonging to the Deuteronomistic History to produce commentaries and chronicles which mirror their own worldviews. Some works will be ancient, and some will belong to the first Christian century and even later. Balaam was not forgotten by these other Samaritan writers either.

b. *Balaam in Samaritan Material Outside the SP*

Balaam and a figure based on the Balaam figure and type appear in other Samaritan literature. All, however, are based on the Balaam figure of the Samaritan Pentateuch as described above.

1) The Balaam of the Samaritan Book of Joshua. A work known as the Samaritan Chronicles [74] recasts the contents of several books contained within the *Nevi'im* section of the *TaNaK* to tell a Samaritan story. It has as one of its main functions to demonstrate that (and why) Moses was the only **prophet** in Israel. All other so-called prophets as depicted in the prophetic material of the Hebrew Scriptures (and other traditions with which the Samaritans disagreed) were gross phonies! The Chronicles also paint a picture of a group of schismatics led by, of all priests, Eli the chief priest of Shiloh. And they were at odds with the descendants of that group. A part of the Chronicles collection is known as the Book of Joshua. [75]

The Book of Joshua, Chapters 3-4 deal with Balaam and the Moabites, and not with Joshua at all. "Chapters 1-8", says Bowman, "may be from a different source,..., because only Chapter 9 begins "The beginning of the Book of Joshua the son of Nun." [76] This work mentions Balaam, and is dated to medieval times (though supposedly containing material which dates much earlier).

2) **The Discourse Concerning the Angels.** This discourse attempts to describe angels as having five (5) characteristics; mobility, articulation, the organs of speech, hearing, and sight. The writer then continues:

> In the Angel which appeared to oppose Balaam He proved standing up, and (the having) two hands, according to His saying in the story concerning Balaam, "And he saw the Angel of the Lord standing in the way, with his drawn sword in his hand." (Numbers 22:31) [77]

3) **The Asatir, the Samaritan Book of the Secrets of Moses.** The *Asatir* Chronicles I also mentions Balaam and causes a great deal of speculation about exegesis in general. Vermes writes, for example: "It has been claimed that the story of Balaam may lead us back to the "scriptural origins of the Aggadah," or, in other words, that the primitive exegesis may "coincide with that of the last redactors" of Scripture. [78] But to demonstrate just how much harmonization effort had gone into the Samaritan treatment of the Balaam type for their purposes, S. Lowy wrote concerning the Samaritan literature: "As compared with the exegesis of other groups utilizing Scripture like Micah vi, 5 and Nehemiah xiii, 2 that of the Samaritan, of course, relies on the Pentateuchal sources only. But in these sources alone there is quite enough material for creating a harmonized picture of Balaam." [79] For this reason, Lowy argues that:... "Balaam is depicted as the arch-villain. This, however, does not prevent either group from utilizing his "oracles" as prophecies of the future. The two contradictory portraits seem to have caused little conflict in the minds of the ancient exegetes."[80]

In the Asatir one finds a fine example of how biblical phrases were utilized by the Samaritans to provide (desired) exact dates for certain occurrences. One is based on the Numbers xxv 1-9 account of the rebellion of the Israelites at Shittim. Vermes comments: "Many details are added, including the exact date and hour of this happening, which resulted, according to the Asatir, from Balaam's advice to Balak. Balaam knew that God hates defilement; he accordingly advised Balak to make his people "commit whoredom." [81] Major literature on the Asatir includes Moses Gaster, *Asatir*, **The Samaritan Book of Secrets** (London: Royal Asiatic Society, 1927), and Ben-Hayyim. "*Sepher Asatir*," TARBIZ, xiv-xv (1943-44):pp 13, 29.

4) The Birth Story of Moses and Balaam. It is not without import that this story contains references to Numbers 24:17: "...a star shall come forth out of Jacob, and a scepter shall rise out of Israel;..." The birth text holds:

> For I have seen the star of Israel in the ascent, and his kingdom growing strong. Nigh is the apostle that is sent to them and the way of his star is on high, and at his hand shall be redemption for them.[82]

After the conception of Moses the writer continued:

> And after 19 days, evidence was established that the child from father had been begotten in the womb of his mother. A star showed his glory in the heavens, and the Egyptians were astonished at his appearance,....[83]

The reference to the star of Jacob is contained within one of four *meshalim* depicted as Balaam oracles within the Balaam cycle. Only the Balaam materials contained in the Pentateuch (SP or MT!) are used by the Samaritan writers. Other Balaam figures and types they do not appear to know even though later writings of the Samaritans belie they did possess those traditions contained in the *Nevi'im* section for example. [84] Within the Pentateuchal Balaam traditions, only the Balaam of the cycle is known to them. They assumed that all references to Balaam (Numbers 31; Deuteronomy 23:4–5) were in reference to that Balaam. The Balaam(s) of Micah and Nehemiah, for example, were either totally unknown to them, or were totally unimportant.

The literature about the birth of Moses is organized around the theme of light. As such, it tends to affirm the "light motif" of the Numbers 24:17 *mashal*, but focuses on:

Amram 1. "...and the **light** shines from his face,...

Moses 2. "...apostle shall proceed from him and **shine forth**."

Moses 3. "But to every stranger he gives **light**..."

Amram 4. "...because from him shall arise of **light**."

Moses 5. "For I have seen the **star** of Israel in the ascent."

Moses 6. "...and the way of his **star** is on high,...

Amram 7. "...and God aided him and the **light** from God passed from Amram."

Jochebed 8. "But she became pregnant with Moses and was great with child, and the **light** was present."

Moses 9. "A star showed his **light** in the heavens,..."

God 10. "And God said to the **Hosts of Heavens**:..."

Galaxies 11. "The **Galaxies** were shown to be in exceeding about Moses great joy, and all of them did

> obeisance to him for his **light** was the origin of theirs."
>
> Amram 12. "The house of Amram were dwelling in **light**, and the fullness (of the **light**) was directed on him."
>
> Moses 13. "The mother of **light** has come." (i.e., Moses as the **light** of the first day.) [85]

With the immediately-above in mind, one may approach another nebulous (but somehow familiar) figure introduced into this particular material. The story informs the reader: "Now there was with the wicked Pharaoh a sorcerer who had come into contact with the knowledge of the *Book of Signs*; and he knew the science of divination and omens." [86] In a note to this sentence, Bowman explains:

> It is this sorcerer (diviner) who makes reference to having "seen the **star** of Israel" and "A **star** showed its glory in the heavens." The sorcerer/diviner is identified in the text as a man named Pilti. This Pilti is mentioned nowhere else, and the rabbis, especially, never heard of him. [87]

Pilti shares many characteristics in common with the Balaam figure available in the cycle. In fact, Pilti does not make sense except in the light of what the reader knows about Balaam-of-the-cycle. Pilti is in essence a figment of the imagination of the Samaritan scholars who crafted a story about their hero, Moses, around the contents of one of the *meshalim* attributed to Balaam in the cycle. Their linking mechanism is the *"light motif"* mentioned above. Thus, a radical thesis would trace the leadership of the Samaritan community to a group extremely sympathetic to the views of Moses espoused by the earlier-mentioned Mushite priesthood of earlier interpretation, and which was centered on Shiloh. This is worth pursuing further. About Pilti and Balaam one reads that:

> 1) Both make oracular statements concerning the successful future of Israel (in Pilti's case through Moses, in Balaam's case though the people led by Moses).
>
> 2) Both are presented as diviner/sorcerer plus, and have reputations which precede them, and which cause monarchs who believe themselves and their countries to be threatened by the leadership of Moses.
>
>> (a) "yea, this man is strong, and the light shines from his face, and a faithful upright apostle shall proceed from him and shine forth. Then there shall be released from oppression for the people of Israel and the kingdom of the Egyptians shall be of no worth..."[88] and:
>>
>> (b) "Respect belongs to this man for he will have much honor, because from him shall rise the light from which the heavens and earth are illuminated. For from his loins will come forth the chosen apostle; and at his hand shall his people be relieved from all affliction." [89]
>
> 3) Both are summoned before (other) monarchs to do their bidding.
>
> 4) Both are depicted as having great and celebrated oracular skills which when encountering the will of God (i.e., Yahweh) contain no efficacy at all.
>
>> Replying to Pharaoh's distress at his divinations, Pilti states: Banish your fears. Hearken to the replies of your question. If what I say is right, the destruction of your kingdom is near, and you and your council shall perish. [90]

Like Balak at the hands of Balaam (Numbers 24:10), so is Pharaoh at the hands of Pilti:

1) "When Pharaoh heard this word he arose in haste, and was afraid,...[91]
2) "What you declare affrights me." [92]
3. "And violently he arose and was angry the whole of forty days."[93]
4. "So after this (i.e., the conception of Moses) Pharaoh convened an assembly and he called every wizard and sorcerer and magician and was violent concerning the reports of this affair." [94]

Pilti is presented in this material as a seer, an enchanter, and a diviner. As a seer he states:

Only I have seen something about the wondrous event of it; my knowledge is faint. For I have seen the Apostle...[95] and:

This is the vision which tells and shows that Israel shall be cast into the sea.[93]
As an enchanter:

He (i.e., Pharaoh) ordered Pilti is the enchanter; bring out from where you are a speaker;...11[96]
[But against the will of God he could not stand.][97]
And in his depicted role as diviner (and seer!):

Now this diviner was called Pilti.[98] and: Well have you answered and well have you seen that I might by your divination. [99] Pilti is cast in this material, then, as an individual extremely familiar with, and able to travel through, the *arcana mundi* with great facility and with efficacy; a Balaam type. Although Pilti is reputed to have many divining and allied skills, his reputed power to curse (like that of Balaam) is overturned by the will of God. Thus we read:

> Israel shall be cast into the sea; (the intended curse) while fire and water are scattered by him, and in the midst of the sea his people stand. (The overturning of the curse by God) This is the vision which tells and shows that Israel shall be cast into the sea. [100]

[This is based obviously on the same idea as the play on words [brk vs.brk].

This literary device seen in the Pilti account expands this idea. Once again a divination is performed, and its intended results have been turned into "clover" for Israel.] And likewise:

> ...let him (a speaker under Pilti's enchanting control] say that men of Israel are to be prevented from approaching a woman, lest he (Moses) he born.[101] (The overturning of which is seen in) By his [Pharaoh's] excellence and power, this is the thing which he did... But against the will of God he could not stand. And by the hand of the Lord the Helper a man went and joined together Amram and Jochehed;...and Amram knew his wife and God aided him and the light of glory passed from Amram; and all the wizards were in haste (to report to Pharaoh). [102]

The text is anti wizard, diviner, odd prophet, outsider mantic, seer, enchanter, gazer, magician, and perceiver, because it makes a big issue of presenting them and their reaction to what has been perceived by Pharaoh to be a challenge to his rule and leadership, on the one hand, and to their divining skills to relieve him of his anxiety as their employer and patron on the other. The text demonstrates its (and its producers') disdain for them by having them leave the story abruptly, and replacing them with Israelite midwives. No sorcery, etc. is able to solve Pharaoh's quandary; recourse to the *arcana mundi* does not work. A practical approach is set upon. Thus one reads further: "The midwives (a practical solution) were summoned by Pharaoh to do what diviners could not do." They, too, however, failed.[103] Note here how the attitude toward prophets seen in the analysis of (SP)'s Balaam cycle is still maintained in dealing with types. Thus, the Balaam type, Pilti, is hurled backwards into the framework of "history," a history which now precedes the very birth of Moses, to tell the "rumblings" of a story which anticipated Yahweh's actions not only at the birth of Moses (protection of the birth of a savior, or perhaps messenger), but on the trip from Egyptian bondage to the occupation of the land of Canaan. This new story told of a day when Moses (and those whom he led) would be saved once more from another propriediv, wizard, magician, seer, and enchanter, Balaam the son of Beor, at a much later time along the route which characterized the wars of Yahweh. One notes, then, that the theme of war is still alive in this material. The Samaritan thinkers appropriated the same **Book of the Wars of Yahweh** itinerary, but, having a different hermeneutical program, employed the Balaam figure as a way of achieving the aims of their program. At Shechem Balaam the figure met, and was married to Balaam the type. We observed with the Qumran materials that Balaam the figure was not considered as important as Balaam the type, whose words were infused with new meaning and purpose at a later time to tell a different story, and to spearhead a different *Weltanschauung*. That *Weltanschauung* was Aaronid/Zadokite. The Samaritan *Weltanschauung* appears to have been Yahwistic and Shilonite/Mushite-influenced. This is not to suggest, however, that a direct line from the earlier-mentioned Mushites to the Samaritans can be traced or demonstrated. But instead of employing Balaam the figure always, they employed the Balaam type in a way which anticipated the appearance of Balaam the propriediv as they continued to tell their story. If all this correct, the Samaritan materials (and especially those which focus on the Balaam figure and type) find once again the strand of Mushite/Shilonite/Levite priestly tradition, which was believed to have been lost during the JE and D source strand periods of priestly conciliation in Judah any time after 722 B.C.E. (but up to the time of Hezekiah, or the D worldview heyday under Josiah). This does not suggest that the Samaritan community in its distinct form appeared at such an early time. The Samaritan interpretation(s) hold(s) alive a hope by those who study the intellectual history of the Israelite priesthoods that the literature of each trajectory concerning priestly legitimacy (either Mushite or Aaronid) was still demonstrable long after the fourth century B.C.E., and long before the peculiar late Zadokite/Aaronid/Qumranite viewpoint of history written by a priestly group whose arguments for legitimacy began centuries before, but whose thought came to literary fruition centuries later. The Birth of Moses does not exist among the Samaritan thinkers by accident. Balaam not only lived in the recast Numbers 22–24 Balaam cycle of the Samaritan Pentateuch, but elsewhere in Samaritan thought as it groped with its essentially priestly–presented, religio–traditional written materials which continued to reflect priestly debates over sacerdotal legitimacy in ancient Israel. With this in mind, one can now discern the distinct outlines of the continuation of a priestly argument which, after the fourth century B.C.E., still clung tenaciously to the argument and belief that through them, and only them, priestly sanctification would come to Israel. Moses, their (priestly) ancestor (not Aaron), had been threatened by formidable enemies (in the form of Pharaoh and Pilti), had survived not only them, but also had survived the practical approach of employing midwives to destroy certain children (whether by miraculous birth or not!). Moses had survived Balaam and his awesome powers during his time in Balak's service, and had survived all that to found a priesthood in the land of the Canaanites to the unblemished worship of Yahweh, and by the legitimate priestly leadership of the Mushite faction of the Israelite priesthood]. It is possible that the Samaritans viewed themselves as the continuators of that Mushite priesthood. If so, they had earned this distinction because they were the heirs of the greatest survivor of all time, Moses their ancestor! But of course, at present this is mere speculation. More research is necessary before definitive statements could be made about definite links between the Samaritans and the Mushite/Levite/Shilonite trajectory.

5) *Memar Marqah* (**The Sayings of Marqah**). [104] Discussing the phenomenon of *hapax legomena*, S. Lowy wrote of how Marqah built a midrash on the interpretation of the word Chemosh, the name of the god of the Moabites (Numbers 21:29). [105] Actually, the full name of this deity is Chemoshmelek, information derived from the celebrated Moabite Stone. (*104*) Marqa, however, understood this word to consist of the preposition *k* (as, like), and the word for yesterday, *'ams* (pronounced *emes*). This produced for Marqa the expression "like Mosh: around which Marqa built one of his famous interpretations. Taking as his point of departure reasons why Moabites feared the Israelites (itself a part of deliberations on Exodus 15), Marqa held:

> The leaders of Moab trembling seized them (Ex. xv, 15). Where did Moses get this knowledge? If it had not been for his Prophethood, he could not have said it then. Thus the True One recorded what Balaam said about Israel: It shall crush the corners of Moab (Num. xiv, 29) There was knowledge of the destruction underlying his saying: "You are undone, O people, like

yesterday" (ibid). Yesterday was Moses' saying "Woe to you"; here (i.e., in the Song of Moses) it is complete destruction. [106]

Once again the reader notes how the words of Balaam were separated from any Balaam activity by Marqa, and were pointed in a different direction, putting Marqa on a hermeneutical par with the Qumran thinkers of 1QM.

6) *Summary*. The Samaritan materials are a gold mine of literature concerning both Balaam and the Balaam type. They demonstrate that the issues of prophecy and divination, priesthood and diviner continued to be of concern to this community. Balaam as a type was employed by them to lambaste and lampoon the "prophetic," not the "priestly," however, regardless of the fact that they were a priestly–led group themselves who were at odds with other priestly groups. Samaritan materials outside the SP present a program of interpretation which does not attack the exactly "priestly". Instead, it attacks every other functional type associated with mantics: prophets, gazers, diviners, wizards, seers, and magicians.

Text traditions vary widely in the Samaritan material. Although there have been numerous attempts to identify them on the basis of text tradition studies, such as those of Cross and Purvis, McDonald and Gaster, [107] the "theory of local texts" remains an hypothesis to be fleshed out by sustained treatment by Cross and Purvis. [108] It is for this reason that although the general term Hebrew Scriptures is used frequently in this work, I also refer to the *TaNaK* often and in those cases where it was impossible to argue for which type of text was in the hands of various groups interpreting the Balaam figure or type. And McDonald must still complete his study of the Chronicles. [109] On the basis of the present state of research, it is impossible to reduce the appearance of the

Samaritans to a sudden dispute ending in an equally sudden schism. Since no suddenness is evident, it is also impossible to specifically identify the Samaritans as descendants of any specific one of the known warring priestly groups previously discussed, whether pre-exilic or post-exilic, although this is tempting. Their anti prophetic stance is also an area of study which deserves more attention. One thing is certain; that stance corresponds with the age which followed the general decline of prophecy as reflected in Deutero-Zechariah 13:2ff., and the (SP) Balaam cycle certainly reflects that sentiment.

Chapter 8. The Book of Enoch (I Enoch): The War to Destroy All the Godless

The influence of one Balaam trajectory is immediately seen when one reads the first vision of Enoch. [110] The *Prooimium* and central theme is the great judgement. This is the same theme noticed in the Deir 'Allā text, though in fragmented (text) form. The Enochic type brings together a number of strands of interest observed in earlier studies of material and groups producing it in which Balaam the figure or type appears. The work's beginning "(1) The words of blessing, according to which Enoch blessed the righteous elect who, on the day of tribulation, are to destroy all the godless", [111] recalls the *Weltanschauung* of the Qumran covenanters. These, one remembers, incorporated three "footnotes" which had been borrowed from the Balaam cycle into a fleshed out vision of their own. They saw themselves as the righteous elect engaged in a war of wars which would bring on a day of tribulation for their godless enemies by effecting their utter defeat. [112]

Verse (2)'s contents, some of the most relevant for my study, will be displayed side by side with their Hebrew Scriptures counterparts for immediate comparative clarity.

Enoch 1:2	Numbers 23:15-16
And he took up his discourse and said: [Oracle of Enoch], a righteous man whose eyes were opened by God, and who saw a vision of the Holy One in heaven, which the angels showed me, and from the words of the [watchers and] holy ones I heard all; and I under-	And he took up his discourse, and said, "The oracle of Balaam the son of Beor, the oracle of the man whose eye is opened, the oracle of him who hears the words of God, and knows the knowledge of the Most High, who

stood what I saw; not for this generation, but for a generation remote do I speak.¹¹³	sees the vision of the Almighty, falling down, but having his eyes uncovered:

The reaction to the Numbers 23:15-16 by the Qumran community was to include the contents of verses 17ff. in its apocalyptic scheme of holy war. The author Enoch ennobles the Balaam type, as it were, by appropriating characteristics attributed to him, and by boldly casting him in the light of such a credentialed seer/gazer. The enemies of the Numbers text are Moab, Sheth, Edom and Seir. These, we saw with the Qumran War Scroll, were the same enemies who would be defeated first in that apocalyptic war. The Enoch text, which follows 1:2, combines the concerns of both Qumran and Deir 'Allā; Qumran in that the enemies of the elect will be destroyed, Deir 'Allā in that the destructive conflagration will be meted out to a kind of heretofore elect who had rebelled against the gods. One can weave in and out of all three texts with facility and intuit just how easily one text can affect the others as one moves toward the first century B.C.E.

The same formula borrowed from Numbers 24:15 occurs twice more in the Enochic materials; Chapters 93:1-2 and 93:3ff. Chapter 93:1-2 is short enough to present in its entirety:

(1) And after he had given over his Epistle (to Methuselah), Enoch took up his discourse, saying:

(2) Concerning the children of righteousness and
       the eternal elect
Sprung from the plant of righteousness

> and uprightness,
> These things will I recount and make
> known to you, my children:
> I, Enoch, was shown in a heavenly vision,
> And from the words of the watchers and
> holy ones I came to know everything,
> And from the tables of heaven I read
> and understood everything.

Once more the themes of righteousness, the elect, and uprightness connect the Enochic text with themes from Qumran self-concepts encountered in the War Scroll, while themes of having been shown a heavenly vision, and words from the (multi-meaning) holy ones, directly connects the Balaam *propriediv/hozpriediv* type. Only the reading from heavenly tablets with (visionary) comprehension, is foreign to both themes.

Chapters 93:10; 91:11-17 comprise **The Apocalypse of Weeks**. It (the apocalypse) begins:

(93:3) And then Enoch took up his discourse and said: I was born the seventh in the First Week; And till my time justice was delayed.

Thereafter, ten weeks (or ages, epochs) follow during which various advances and setbacks to human history are laid out briefly. Themes familiar from the War Scroll are read in 93:10 ("...in the Seventh Week, a perverse generation shall arise,... And at its close the elect shall be chosen..."; and in 91:11 ("And they [the elect] will uproot the foundations of oppression, And the structure of falsehood therein to destroy it utterly"). The war theme involving the righteous continues in 91:12 where, during the Eighth Week (a week of righteous) judgement is meted out to the wicked, for "a sword will be given to all of the righteousness." The Ninth and Tenth Weeks will be weeks of righteous judgement both on humans and on the **watchers**, at the end of which "the first heaven shall pass away, And a new heaven shall appear," (91:16). "And thereafter there shall be many Weeks; to all their number there shall be no end forever," (91:17). Such, then, is the fruit of the Balaam type's vision.

Enoch as a Balaam type keeps company with Pilti of the Samaritan material. Both types demonstrate the powerful appeal of the Balaam figure as groups following trajectories of interpretation of his character and significance continued through ancient Israelite history. The Samaritans, an essentially prophet-hating group, fabricated out of the Balaam figure of their *euberarbeitete* (=over worked, over laid, reworked, recended) Pentateuch a negative type whose function was to pre(curse), literally and figuratively, the appearance of a *propriediv* who, during the sojourn of Israel, was made to look stupid and ineffective by the power of Yahweh. It was a most negative view of all who engaged in what would have been understood to have been the prophetic consciousness.

The trajectory out of which the Enochic Balaam type emerges is (attitudinally) more allied with the Qumran covenanters than with the Samaritans as described above in the present study. For this apocalyptic trajectory, the Balaam figure served as the perfect type through which the goals of revealed knowledge could be mediated. Whereas the Samaritans manufactured the type and then hurled it into the past to set up the individual responding to the prophetic impulse (other than Moses their hero), the Enochic trajectory manufactured the type and depicted the figure as "not for this generation, but for a generation remote do I speak."*114* This figure was hurled into the future.

Whether directly or indirectly influenced, Enoch the book derives two other characteristics from the Balaam figure, type, and materials. Chapters 37–71 are termed the Parables of Enoch, while Chapters 83–90 become known as The Dream–Vision of Enoch. Concerning the parables, there are three located at 37–44, 45–57, and 58–69. In the Aramaic version, found at Qumran and known as 4Q En., at Chapter 1, verse 2, the word rendered *mtlh* (=*matlah*), by the standard phenomenon of consonantal shifts in the Semitic languages, is rendered by *mshl* (=*mashal*) in Hebrew. The reader might recall that I made the decision to employ this term consistently throughout my analysis of the literature which constituted the Balaam, cycle. [115] Rather than employ such terms as "parable," "gnome," "aphorism," "oracle," or "discourse," I thought it best to render the Hebrew term only. Due to the possibility of an inaccurate rendering of the term now in the Enochic material, I continue to adhere to this decision, now on the basis of the Aramaic *mtlh*. Enoch, like Balaam, delivers *mshlym* (=*meshalim*).

From Balaam is also borrowed the practice of entering the world of dream–visions. According to Black, they represent "the longest and the most self–consistent part of the Book." [116] In a zoomorphic history of the world, set within the framework of Enoch's instructions to Methuselah his son, he presents "a series of visions in which the principle protagonists are symbolized by animals,..." [117] These visions, which Enoch shares typologically with the Balaam of Deir 'Allā, cover a period from the Deluge to a last judgement sometime following the period of the Maccabean Revolt. Be it known, however, I focus only on the "agency" of the Balaam type's knowledge, not on the "contents." Balaam as figure, type, and actor, in the hands and hermeneutic of the Enochic School, had proved to indeed have been a man for all (their) seasons.

PART 4: BALAAM HERMENEUTICS FOR LATER AGES

Chapter 9. "Balaam During and Beyond the Middle Platonic Period: The Inability to Jettison the Theme of War

a.   *Balaam in The New Testament*

With the millennium change from B.C.E. to C.E., interest in Balaam does not cease,[1] and his figure and type do not receive rest from would be hermeneutist detractors. Three such detractors contributed the New Testament works of Revelation, Jude, and 2 Peter.

At Revelation 2:14 (one of three apocalyptic works [Qumran and Enoch being the other two] which incorporate the Balaam figure or type), as part of a critique sent to the "angel" of the church at Pergamum, the writer holds:

> But I have a few things against you: you have some there who hold the teaching of Balaam, who taught Balak to *put a stumbling block before the sons of Israel, that they might eat food sacrificed to idols and practice immorality."* (Emphases are mine)

These practices are serious enough for the writer to hold that "He who has the sharp two-edged sword" (Rev. 2:12) will "come...soon and war against them (the Balaam-like teachers) with the sword of (his) mouth" (Rev.2:16). This indictment contains the same complaints mirrored in Acts 15:20 and 15:29; that of food sacrificed to idols, and immorality. "Balaam" here serves as the type who opposed such restrictions and actually reflects the attitude of the writers of Romans 14:14; 20-21; and Acts 10:28. At any rate, this Balaam is woven on the loom of those who are embroiled in the issue of requirements for proselytes coming into various Greco-Roman forms of Hellenistic Judaism(s). To be sure, Balaam-of-the-cycle is associated with sacrifices. On more than one occasion, he gives instructions to Balak to sacrifice. But not to idols! Rather, he sacrifices to Yahweh. And even though the writer of Numbers 31:8ff. is thoroughly irate, the charge against Balaam is not immorality. He "tempts" the males of "Israel" to rebel (against the covenant), not immorality! This is Balaam dressed in later hermeneutical garb to be the fall guy for other problems encountered by a later "Israel".

The writer of the little epistle of Jude 1:11 packs a lot of complaints into one line of text. Reviling "heretics" and "false teachers" of all kinds, he argues that they: "...walk in the way of Cain, and abandon themselves for the sake of gain to Balaam's error, and perish with Korah's rebellion." The themes are jealousy/murder/guilt (Cain), greed (Balaam's accepting fees for mediating Yahweh's work, thus making it a commercial venture [this was certainly not the equivalent to tithing, the acceptable "insider" method of accepting fees for mediating Yahweh's will!]), and punishment (in the case of Korah, for rebelling against the proper leadership of the people "Israel" [i.e., Moses]). Evidently for him, Balaam's guilt was false teaching, and he was viewed by this writer as one of three past archetypes.

2 Peter is possibly the (chronologically) latest work in the New Testament. In addition to containing all of Jude (and being written by a different author than 1 Peter), it argues against all "heresies", especially those which deny the coming of Christ. At 2:15, Balaam is implicated in influencing people to forsake the right way. Specifically: "they have followed the way of Balaam, the son of Beor, who loved gain from wrongdoing, but was rebuked for his own transgression; a dumb ass spoke with human voice and restrained the prophet's madness." Like the writer of Jude, 2 Peter's author understood that Balaam accepted gratuities, and that this had been wrong. In addition, the writer stressed Balaam's humiliation at the mouth of the ass who shares billing with the Balaam-of-the-cycle.

b.   *Josephus' Antiquities and Balaam*

For Josephus, Balaam was the greatest of the prophets, raised to great reputation because of the truth of his predictions (Book IV: VI:2).[2] He added a few twists to the account contained in the Balaam cycle, such as:

1) a statement that Balaam was afraid of having incurred God's wrath after the speaking ass incident, and prepared to return to his homeland instead of continuing on to Balak.

2) a speech by inspiration in VI:4, characteristic of history writing of the Hellenistic Period, and certainly characteristic of Josephus' writings.

Other details are shown by way of comparison. In the Balaam cycle, Balaam goes to meet Balak because Yahweh wanted him to go: he goes as Yahweh's agent. Josephus, like the author of the text underlying Balaam-of-the-wall, understood Balaam to have been a partner in a covenant: Balaam-of-the-wall with the gods, Josephus' Balaam with Balak (cf. "But then Balak was displeased, and said he (Balaam) had broken the *contract* he had made..." (VI:5). Also, Josephus' Balaam makes only *two* attempts to fulfill his contract: the second only because he had a sense of professional duty. Then, like Balaam-of-the-wall, Balaam foretells calamities (the former, to befall his people, the latter, to "befall the several kings of the nations, and the most eminent cities" (VI:5). For Josephus, Balaam's predictions had been verified by history up to his (Josephus') time, and the remainder would come to pass in coming events (VI:5). And after failing to curse Israel for Balak and his associates (=blessing Israel at the direction of Yahweh), Balaam-of-the-cycle departs for home (Num. 24:25). Josephus' Balaam also departs for home after the second attempt to curse, but just before crossing the Euphrates he summons Balak and his associates, tells them how they may deliver small setbacks to Israel, but can never affect a curse on them. In another Hellenistic "speech" recalling the

Deuteronomist's rehearsal of the ups and downs of Israel's history, Josephus' Balaam reviews the history of Yahweh's people up to the first century C.E. (i.e., to Josephus time). The major agent of the setbacks (for Balak's time) will be the Midianite women. The short account of Balaam's connection with these women in Numbers 31:6, 2 Peter 2, Jude 11, and Revelation 2:14 is extended into a large account in Josephus (VI:6–13), a trait which he shares with the writer of the Samaritan Chronicle and with Philo.

c.   *The North African Platonists and Balaam*

During the Middle Platonic period and beyond, thinkers, both Jewish and Christian, in the buzzing and humming North African city of Alexandria, found that the Balaam figure and type were just as useful in framing and articulating certain of their religio–politico–intellectual worldviews as we've demonstrated above had been the case with the warring priesthoods of ancient Israel. Each turned the light of contemporaneous Platonic hermeneutics onto the figure and type of Balaam. All argued that the figure had been historical: typological hermeneutics upgraded him to the level of the concerns and argumentative methods of each writer's period. They exercised no surcease. The writings of Philo (?B.C.E.–c.50 C.E.), Origen (185?–254? C.E.), and Clement (150?–220? C.E.), three such Platonists, therefore pullulate with learned opinions concerning Balaam.

For Philo, Balaam was a figure to be held in contempt: he was nothing more than a wizard. To speak of him as a bona fide prophet was to insult that noble office. Divine wisdom came more through the mouth of an ass rather than through a wizard who could have had no contact with the Divine. *De Somniis* contains Philo's quintessential statement on prophecy and communiciation between the divine and human realms. But it is in his *De Vita Mosis* that he attacks Balaam vigorously. Balaam, for him, was a dreamer, but his dreams did not contain legitimate communication from the Divine. Bereft of a divine origin, his prophetic utterances were held up as exemplars of the oracles of the Gentiles. The main and characteristic weakness of such oracles is that they are irrational. In essence, Balaam symbolizes the base, negative traits of "religion" viewed from the comfortable perch of the "insider." The higher, positive traits are symbolized by the figure Moses. It was Moses who—without the agencies of dreams, incantations, sacrifices and the like—"spoke" with the God-of-the-Mountain "face-to-face." Thus, in typical Platonic fashion-reinterpreted with a prejudice for the primacy of the noetic inclination—Philo casts Moses as the "overman" (representing prophetic/rational tendencies supported by the world of ideas). Balaam he casts as the "underman" (representing the earthly/irrational tendencies which could only appear in the world of shadows and ignorance).[3]

Describing the "prophetic" in Moses, Philo could write:

> No pronouncement of a prophet is ever his own; he is an interpreter prompted by another in all his utterances, when knowing not what he does, he is filled with inspiration, as the reason withdraws and surrenders the citadel of the soul to a new visitor and tenant, the divine spirit, which plays upon the vocal organism and raises sounds from it which clearly express its prophetic message.[4]

On the "prophetic" in Balaam, he wrote, conversely, that he was a:

> False slanderer... Behold the armed angel, the reason of God standing in the way against you, the source through whom both good and ill come to fulfillment. See where he stands... the tests you use are false and your impatience is without reason. If you had learned from the first that it is not your life-pursuits which bring your share in good or ill, but divine reason, the ruler and statesman of all you would bear with more patience what befalls you...[5]

Origen sought to uphold the historicity of Balaam. Unlike Philo, he argued that Balaam had been a true (Gentile) prophet. Whatever his inclinations toward wizardry and divination might have been, Origen held, by the time the reader encounters the Balaam of the Septuagintal Numbers account, only what God wants him to say and do occurred.

The Balaam of Origen speaks God's **word** and does God's **will**, but he is also capable of engaging in magic, divination and wizardry. In a reasoning process similar to that employed by Paul in Galatians and Romans with relation to the significance and use of the figure Abraham for his theory of salvation, Origen needs and employs a Balaam and his oracles, especially the Numbers 24:17 **star which shall come forth from Jacob**, to demonstrate that a precursing of the incarnation to the Gentiles had occurred. After establishing that portion of his argument, he delved, like Philo, into an allegorical hermeneutics. "Balaam" and the "ass" took on philosophico-theological significance by representing —among many antithetical pairs—false belief having been converted to Christian belief and the Gentiles respectively. Origen introduced a

Balaam in the service of Christ (when it was convenient to his argument: he could also victimize him!). His major role as a Gentile prophet was to not only herald and precurse Christ to them, he also served as the founder of the Magi— especially those who adored the divine infant as depicted in Matthew. However, because he was a true prophet, Jews, too, could benefit from his **legitimate communications**. The functional "first shoe."

As Origen's argument proceeded, he allowed Balaam's other functional "shoe to drop." This aspect of Balaam, the magician/diviner/wizard enabled Origen to portray him as one also in the service of evil. By doing so, Balaam was made to serve both good and evil inclinations. As magician plus, he consciously directs Balak on several occasions to prepare sacrifices at specific "high places" for the evil purpose of manipulating or influencing a deity. As prophet, a legitimate, but obviously temporary title, he can only utter blessings on Israel with efficacy. Having framed his rhetoric this way, Origen articulated an allegory of the deadly battle between good and evil as a battle royale between the "Israel" inclination and the "Balaam" inclination within the human family.

d. *Rabbinical Literature and Balaam*

At some time later than the mid first-century C.E., "Balaam" was employed to refer to someone else! Here we have the reversal of someone else being employed to refer to Balaam: Pilti of the Samaritan material. Without getting lost in the labyrinthine volumes of the Talmud Bavli, I solicit instead the statement concerning early Christianity and its background in the first note on Chapter 2 of Samuel Sandmel's **We Jews and Jesus**. He writes:

> There are a few direct mentions of Jesus in

the Talmud, and a few passages about one Balaam which some have interpreted to be cryptic, and hence indirect, mention.[6]

In a rather lengthy critical note, Loewe[7] goes into some detail about the Balaam- Jesus contrived idetification. Casting doubt on its reliability, he writes:

> ...this is why Balaam may have been used as a designation of Jesus. On this see R. Travers Herford, **Christianity in Talmud and Midrash**, London, 1903; pp. 63ff.which deal with these Balaam-Jesus passages. But Bacher, in his review **J.Q.R., O.S.**, vol. XVII, 1905, pp. 171ff.), does not always agree with Herford's identification, and I believe that Herford has–at least in some instances–accepted Bacher's view that Balaam does not invariably refer to Jesus.

History requires one to understand that the Rabbis were responding to attacks upon Palestinian and Babylonian schools of Jewish thought which were antithetical and reactionary to thought coming out of Mediterranean Christian churches and academies headed by the early Church Fathers as well as by Jewish Hellenists. A work such as R. Travers Herford, **Christianity in Talmud and Midrash** (London, 1903), illustrates this point quite clearly. The opposite side of this issue is encountered in the writings of Philo, Origen, and Clement of Alexandria of Egypt.

Balaam appears also in Rabbinical material which takes up the issues of

(1) the nature of God— *Tanh. B.*, Balak, 69 *a fin*:

> When Balaam went with the princes of Moab against God's will, God was angry, 'and the angel of the Lord stood in his path as an adversary against him' (Num. XXII, 22). Thus the angel of mercy turned into an adversary. So God says to the sinner: 'Thou hast caused me to take up a trade that is not mine.'[8]

(2) the law–Zeb. 116a.

> When the Law was about to be given to the Israelites, a loud noise went forth from one end of the earth to the other; terror seized the peoples in their palaces, and they sang, as it is said, 'In their palaces [A.V. his palace] all say Glory' (Ps. XXIX, 9). They gathered together to Balaam and said, 'What is this tremendous noise which we have heard? Is a new flood coming upon the earth?' He replied, 'God has sworn that He will never bring another flood.' Then they said, 'But, perhaps He is going to bring a flood, not of water, but of fire?' He replied, 'He has sworn that He will never again destroy all flesh.' Then they said, 'What then was the noise?' He replied, 'God has a

precious treasure in His storehouse which has been stored up there for 974 generations before the creation of the world, and now He proposes to give it to His children.'...Then they said, "May God bless His people with peace' (Ps. XXIX, II).[9]

(3) proselytes

Balaam, as a prophet, is said to have been superior to Moses: he—and six others—were sent to the Gentiles.[10]

(4) life to come and judgment–San. X1,1,2 and 99b and 105a

All Israel will have a share in the world to come. The biblical proof is Isa. LX, 21 'They shall all be righteous.' The following have no share in the world to come. He who says the Resurrection of the dead is not indicated in the Law (see p. 600), he who says the Law is not from heaven [i.e. divine], and the Epikouros. R. Akiba said: Also he who reads the alien books, and he who whispers over a wound, and says the words of Exod. XVI, 26. Abba Saul said: He too who pronounces the Divine Name [Yahweh] out loud. Three kings and four private persons have no share in the world to come. The three kings are Jeroboam, Ahab, and Manasseh. R. Judah said: Manasseh has a portion in the world to come (II Chron. XXXIII, 13). The four private persons are Balaam, Doeg, Ahithophel and Gehazi...Three kings and four private persons have no share in the world to come. The three kings are Jeroboam and Ahab and Manasseh. R. Judah said: Manasseh has a share in the world to come, as it is said, 'And he prayed unto God, and God was entreated of him, and heard his supplication, and brought 327 again to Jerusalem into his kingdom' (II Chron. XXXIII, 13). They said to R. Judah: God brought him again to his kingdom, but He did not bring him to the life of the world to come. The four private persons are Balaam and Doeg and Ahithophel and Gehazi.[11]

(5) comparison to Moses–Sifre to Deuteronomy 357, f. 150a/ and Num. R.[12]

(6) and the angel– Tanh B., Balak, 70 a.

Balaam said to the angel: 'I have sinned' (Num. XXII, 34), for he knew that nothing can stand between a man and punishment save repentance. For the angel has no power to touch any sinner who says, 'I repent.'[13]

(7) as philosopher– Lam. R., Introduction,

R. Abba b. Kahana said: No philosophers have arisen among the nations to equal Balaam and Abnimos, the weaver. They said to them, 'Can we attack this people?' They replied, 'Go to their house of assembly. If the children are chirping there with their voices, you will not be able to destroy this people, but, if not, then you will, for their fathers made them rely upon this saying: "The voice of Jacob; the hands are those of Esau." When the voice of Jacob is heard in their houses of assembly and of study, then the hands of Esau are powerless; but when no voice chirps there, then the hands of Esau can act' (Gen. XXVII, 22).[14]

(8) prophet to the Gentiles[15]

(9) character (of Balaam)[16]

According to Loewe:

Here we see that Balaam is regarded as superior to Moses: it is no doubt a later addition to the Sifre passage which makes Moses, the prince in the palace, too grand to bother about culinary details, which concern the menial cook, i.e. Balaam. In Num. R. XIV, 20, where the account in the Sifre is elaborated, it is distinctly stated that Balaam was as (great as) Moses, so that the Gentiles should not have an excuse for saying, 'if only we had had a prophet like Moses, we would have served God' (cp [1603]).

e. *The Medieval Balaam*

Herein I have already mentioned one work on Balaam which is probably datable to the Middle Ages: The Samaritan Book of Joshua wherein Chapters 3–4 deal with Balaam and the Moabites.[17] This work is known as Chronicle IV, and is dated by Macdonald to the fourteenth–century C.E.[18] The use of Chronicle IV material may reveal another Balaam figure or type. [As of this writing, I have been unable to acquire this text.]

The work known as **The Tales of the Prophets of al–Kisa'i**[19] contains a story about Balaam. It contains several of the features known from the Balaam–of–the–cycle, but it differs from the cycle text(s) in several respects. In my previous work I summarized the differences in the final note.[20] It suffices to reproduce a portion of that summary here:

Among these (i.e., the differences) are Balaam's wife (who, after Balaam is refused permission to go the first time, persuades him to ask for permission again); viziers (as opposed to simple messengers, or even princes); a winged angel whose wings block the East and West; gifts for Balaam's wife; Iblis interpreting the significance of the angel's sudden departure, allowing Balaam to continue his journey; combined stories of how Balaam's counsel included using the Moabite women as bait for the Moses host (stories which, in the Numbers book, are spread over more material than chapters 22–24); a "certain book" which the "children of Israel" read, the precepts of which if not followed, will cause calamity to befall them; Balak will be established because "Israel" will rebel against the deity; a man of Simeon having sexual congress with an especially beautiful Moabitess, both of whom were impaled together on a spear wielded by a faithful man of Judah; routing of Balak's army, and his and Balaam's subsequent death.

It will be remembered that the story of the man of (the tribe of) Simeon is contained in Numbers 25:6–18, and Balaam's death is (gratuitously) included in a list of (Midianite!) kings killed in battle against the Moses host in Numbers 31:7–8. Although they stand outside the Balaam cycle, they are not totally new features to overall study of Balaam-of-the-Hebrew Scriptures. "Balaam" did not escape Muslim hermeneutics either.

f. *Balaam in Modern Literature*

Balaam has not escaped the attention of modern writers. The storyteller Joel Chandler Harris, famous for stories about Uncle Remus and Brer Rabbit, authored an anthology of stories under the title *Balaam and His Master.*[21] The Balaam of his story was a Black slave born on the Cozart plantation. The Balaam figure, the theme of war, and a number of "hints" borrowed from the cycle are evident in the story.

As to the figure, Harris' Balaam is charged with his (senior) master's orders: "Balaam," said Mr. Cozart, "this baby will be your master. I want you to look after him and take care of him" (pp. 11, 26). A special relationship develops between Balaam and his (younger) master which lasts a (short) lifetime. Berrien Cozart grows up to become a "wild ass" of a man. He is dismissed from college and returns home to Billville where the family estate is located. His father refuses to allow him to remain at home, and sends him back to college to redeem himself and the family honor. Balaam returns with him. "On the high hill beyond the "town branch" Balaam leaned out of the back [of the wagon] and *looked back* at Billville." (p.24) The image of the *tzofeh* is thus captured. Balaam "sees" something that Berrien Cozart does not. The next time either of them sees Billville, it is the last thing that either sees.

But instead of going back to college, the son takes his father's money (divinations in his hand?) and begins a gambling career in several southern states. Balaam watches over him and protects him at all cost. When the young Cozart loses all, he devises a scheme to "sell" Balaam for a sizable sum. It is all a "skin game" and scam, however, for Balaam, after being sold, is to gain freedom by escaping, and by the aid of a carefully-written letter to be kept in his possession, he is (theoretically) able to travel in the open unhindered and to rejoin his master in a prearranged city, only to repeat this scam as often as

Berrien Cozart needs the "divination services" (=more money to bankroll himself after having lost everything in a poker game) of Balaam. Never forgetting his charge, Balaam replied to his master's proposed scheme in *mashal*-like fashion: "you kin sell me, but de man dat buys Balaam will git a mighty bad bargain." (p.25), and "I been ˜long wid you all de time, an' ole marster done tole me w'en you was a baby dat I got ter stay wid you." (p.26) These statements may be compared with those made by Balaam-of-the-cycle in reply to Balak's statements and complaints.

After escaping, Balaam, alias someone else, is picked up on the road by a man known as the Judge. Although Balaam thinks that he had made an "ass" of this man by denying that he resembles Berrien Cozart's slave, a statement the Judge continues to make as they travel, the Judge, a gambler himself who knows Balaam's true identity, allows him to accompany him to a town close to where Balaam is to meet the master. The Judge then allows Balaam to continue on to meet Berrien Cozart. He does this because of a female cousin Cozart likes, and because he admires Cozart's rascality.

Berrien Cozart had paid Balaam fifty dollars (more divinations in the hand) "in specie" in order to get Balaam to go along with the skam (p. 28). The escape was announced in a local paper called the "Intelligencer" but no response was ever made (p. 29). And Balaam finally was rejoined with his master after crossing "the River." In this case it was the Tennessee River.

War characterized the entire life of Berrien Cozart. He was at war with everyone in the world except Balaam. As a professional gambler/college dropout, Cozart waged war by dealing from the bottom of the deck, and engaging in every activity designed to relieve his opponents of their cash. This led often to brawls and to several deaths at Cozart's hands. Once, onboard a river steamer, Cozart was engaged in his incessant war, was accused of cheating, killed a man, and had to run for his life. Hiding among a group of barrels on the lower deck of the steamer after having thrown a heavy object into the muddy river to give the impression that he had jumped overboard, believing this, the dutiful Balaam sprang into the river in search of his charge and master. The master did nothing to make Balaam think otherwise.

After a search through several states by legal authorities, Berrien Cozart is chased and finally captured very near Billville. Having shot a pursuing lawman through the head, he was finally captured and incarcerated in Billville. The last one reads of prisoner Berrien Cozart, he is lying dead on the floor of his cell. A large hole in the outer wall of the jail building, which at first had given he observer the idea that Cozart had attempted to escape, was seen to have been the entryway for someone to have joined Cozart. Balaam had broken into the jail to be with his master, and was also found dead on the floor beside his master. He had not relinquished his charge. He had done nothing that his master had not dictated. Here the Balaam figure was cast as the archetypical faithful man (i.e., servant of his master also).

The final modern example of continuing concern with Balaam themes and types is provided by Moshe Leshem.[22] For him:

> The Enlightenment and emancipation, the twin secular godheads that drew the Jews out of the ghetto, forced the Children of Israel to seek an answer to a difficult question: How could they maintain a Jewish identity while assimilating European culture and values that were not merely alien to Rabbinical Judaism but often irreconcilable with its teachings? Many Jews wrestle with the problem to this very day as individuals; so does Israel in its vocation as the Jewish state. (p. 10)

Leshem's main focus is on Israel the Jewish state, and its status as one nation "among the nations," but separate from them. He argues that since the establishment of Israel as a state, it has sought to be counted among the nations, especially the "United Nations", but that it has not received the same treatment as other charter members. Its major problem is being viewed by other members as unfair to its most immediate neighbors, the Palestinians. The Palestinians are politically in the same situation, as for example, the Kurds, the Lithuanians, the Letts, and the Estonians, all national groups without truly free and unquestioned borders. This list could be expanded to include Native Americans, Black South Africans, certain Shi'ite Muslims, and Ethiopians. The difference, Leshem maintains, is that nobody cares about the Kurds. And were he writing today, he would know that all three Baltic states the Kurds and Shiites of Iraq, and Black South Africans are indeed involved in the task of declaring their national independence once again. But at the time of his writing, his assessment that the international political community didn't care about them either was accurate. Of all these groups, however, the Palestinians are unique, because they and Israel came into existence at the same time, and now, as a result of a number of political moves and the fortunes or lack there of of war, Israel appears strong in the eyes of the world, while the Palestinians are viewed as those who have been pounced upon unfairly by the aggressive Israelis. Thus, holds Leshem, when Israel engages in politico–military activity engaged in by other member nations of the United Nations, such as the Soviet Union's actions toward the Baltic States, or Libya's occupation of large portions of Chad, no loud voice is raised in the Security Council in outraged protestation. Israel's acquisition of the West Bank, Gaza Strip, the Golon Heights and large portions of Egyptian territory as result of the 1967 war, or the ill–fated invasion of Lebanon in 1982 have been met by vitriolic barrages of declamation by Nations members. Whether fairly or unfairly, Israel is now in a situation where it realizes that it stands virtually alone, whether it does exactly the same thing as other nations or not, whether it reaches out to other nations or not: Israel is politically damned if it does, and damned if it does not.

For Leshem, this predicament recalls Numbers 23:9, the so called Blessing of Balaam: "Israel is a people [that] shall dwell alone, and shall not be reckoned among the nations." It should be remembered that the *shoresh brk* has the double meaning of "cursing" and "blessing." This *Zweideutigkeit* or doublemeaning is evident in the Balaam cycle and gives the story of Balaam some of its powerpunch. Leshem's analysis of modern Israel's political predicament utilizes once more the ambiguity of this potential *Zweideutigkeit* to raise the questions: Has the *brk* which Balak originally requested been effected?, and has Israel brought this *brk* upon itself?

One of Leshem's strongest statements concerning Israel's present situation is summed up thusly:

> Whatever the correct interpretation of Balaam's curse after 1967 it was cited by religious nationalists as proof that Israel's isolation was preordained, and therefore was not the result of any "sin" of commission or omission of which the Jewish state might be guilty in the eyes of the world. "Dwelling alone" was thus hailed as the normal condition for the Jewish state--though it surely was not the kind of normality Zionism's founding fathers had in mind, nor what the Yishuv had worked so hard to create. (p. 246)

Although religious Jews, Leshem argues, may find solace in this development, and may increase their ever strong embracing of the contents of Jewish Scriptures and their traditions' interpretations, the orthodox should be dissuaded from their attempt:

> to move Jewish history in a circular route back to the self-centered security of faith that is possible only in a ghetto. Such may be a valid route for an individual, but it is not a road on which the vehicle of the nation-state can travel. For if Israel were to dwell alone, the danger is that it won't ere long dwell at all. As the American poet Robert Frost reminds us: "Before I'd build a wall I'd ask to know what I was walling in or walling out." (p. 263)

We have not read or heard the last of the resilient Balaam image, but we have revealed more than just the tip of a hermeneutical iceberg.

According to Berchman, Clement considered Balaam as both a legitimate prophet and an illegitimate sorcerer. As prophet, Balaam could herald the incantation and function as the[23] progenitor of the Magi (who adored the infant Jesus as prophets, not magicians). He was also the agency through which the word of God came to the Gentiles. The figure of Balaam for Clement helped his establish his argument of the historicity of Christianity in the face of Jewish and Hellenistic opposition. Once again Balaam had been brought into the service of apologetics.

CONCLUSION

The preceding study has demonstrated that Balaam the son of Beor was an ancient Near Eastern monarch whose charisma so touched his own subjects, as well as members of the priestly class of at least one neighboring monarchy, Israel, that his name and type served as the organizing principle around which mantologists studied and debated the issues of prophecy, priesthood, divination and magic for a considerable lengthy period. Other names are equally well-known. Methuselah for his reputed longevity, Moses for his law-giving, David for his statescraft, Cyrus II, the Great for his Edict of Toleration, Judah the Maccabee for his zeal for religious freedom under *torah*, Flavius Josephus for his apologetics, and Jesus for his prominent place in issues on messianism. Of these (and many more) who have achieved solid notoriety, only Jesus ranks with Balaam. Both share many traits. Warring groups of priests between the 10th and 6th centuries depicted Balaam as "their man" to be emulated, or "the man" to be spurned/shunned. Either group viewed him as ideal for their purposes. Likewise, the Jesus of each "canonical" Gospel is the hellenized result of "their (the evangelists') man" to be emulated. He was either the "hidden messiah" (Mark), the "second Moses" (Matthew), the "pedagogue *par excellence*" (Luke), or the confident, lecturing, pre-existent *Logos* (The Fourth Gospel). And like Balaam, they depicted him as king also. But the opposing "gnostic" Jesus denied much that the "evangelistic" Jesus affirmed. The gnostic docetists' (= those who argued that [among other things] Jesus only **appeared to** be human) Jesus vied with the NT canonical Jesus as medium for enlightening humans about the latest communique from a deity concerning "salvation" (= escape from the numerous snares of the physical, hellenistic world, or occupying a foreigner-free [= without Roman overlordship], god-given land of Palestine with a Jewish priest/king as its ruler). And both have been depicted as magicians. (see Morton Smith) [1]

Before one gets lost in the analogies, however, certain significant differences must be pointed out. Jesus is depicted as a **figure**. There is no accompanying **type**. Jesus is depicted as riding on an ass (two asses if one trusts Matthew **21:5!**): Balaam's ass is depicted as having the ability to tell him that their nomenclatures should have been metathesized. Depending on the evangelist, Jesus' death was either undeserved but nevertheless significant (the Synoptics), or necessary **and** significant (the 4th Gospel). Balaam's death, along with that of his fellow, collaborating kings, was according to Numbers 32:8, deserved. Jesus dealt with rulers who had him killed. Balaam was killed along with kings/rulers with whom he dealt. Others took Jesus' message into the greater Hellenistic world, blended it with the rhetorical teaching of a Christ-centered, possible salvation, and effected another developmental, Jewish trajectory (Paul, Peter, *et al.*). Mantological conclusions **about** Balaam as either figure or type constituted portions of traditions for or against prophecy, divination, and magic by various priesthoods from at least the 10th century B.C.E. well into the European Middle Ages. Only during the 10th and 8th centuries in Judah was he a figure to be emulated. As type, Pilti and Enoch serve well. Of these, however, only Enoch reflects a positive Balaam typology. No new religious system ever grew up around Balaam. At best, he remained most useful as a "boundary marker" for those who wrote about him whether that was the writer of the J source *stratum* or Moshe Leshem.

The discovery at Deir 'Allā provided an opportunity to revisit the known Balaam traditions, to raise some old questions about them anew, and to raise some new questions about some old answers that earlier scholarship had provided. Deir' Allā's Balaam was cast as a monarch who headed a "covenanted community." The covenant **partners** comprised a council of deities who intended to redress a grievance against the "covenanted community" by way of cosmic conflagration. Though badly damaged, the text in reconstructed form depicted a Near Eastern monarch/seer who communicated with a community of gods by way of dreams. It was his sad task to inform "his people" of their coming doom, and he anguished over it.

The issues of location of the discovery of the on plaster-written text in Jordan, the fact that Balaam therein is the son of Beor also, that he is a *hzh*/seer who communicated with deities through dreams, and who functioned as a member of a covenanted community in the capacity of priest/king/seer/spokesperson/covenant mediator, guaranteed for him a place in the mantology of ancient Israel.

The Balaam-centered mantology was evident as the Documentary Hypothesis was revisited by way of the Friedman thesis. Factoring a necessary re-view of the Balaam traditions into Friedman's revision of the J, E, JE, P, D, and R *strata*, Balaam as figure and type took on meanings heretofore unnoticed by previous scholarship. An exegetical essay revealed that pursuing the hermeneutical history of the Balaam traditions was inextricably bound to the concerns of communication theory and praxis in ancient Israel from the 10th to the 5th centuries B.C.E. The several uses of "Balaam"-of-the-*strata* were shown to have been formulated in response to various wars during this five-century period. The possibility of Balaam-the-outsider having been depicted as a mantic who communicated with the god Yahweh is explained only by the contents of the non-Israelite, Deir' Allā text described above. A covenanted seer/priest/monarch (whether inside or outside) was an ideal type around which the Israelite priest/hermenenticists organized their own covenant-centered concerns. Deir 'Allā's Balaam helped make sense of why ancient Israelite priests employed him as the foil for their polemics. Frankly, it is difficult to think of another figure or type who would have captured the imagination and served the needs of so many of the sacerdotal *literati*. The Moses figure was useful showing the qualities of organization around covenant laws; that of Joshua for military leadership and covenant-making. David was renowned for his statescraft and crafting of state religion, while Hezekiah and Josiah provided the model of reformer. But all of these, and other distinguished Israelites, including kings and prophets, are all mediated to the reader through priestly authors/editors; Balaam was the silver thread running through their *Weltanschauungen* and organizing principles. Their hermeneutic of the Balaam cycle, the extra-Balaam cycle citings in Numbers, Deuteronomy, Nehemiah and Micah, and appearances of Balaam as figure or type at Qumran, in 1 Enoch, among the Samaritan writings, in Josephus, Al Kisa'i, and Philo, as well as in Harris' short story, or as the organizing principle around which Leshem raises serious socio-political questions about modern Israel's internal and external policies, would not have been possible employing the above-named, distinguished personalities. Balaam was truly the man for all priestly-needed seasons. It was he, as figure and type, who provided all those concerned with the platform for debating the most crucial issue which confronted the Israelite portion of the greater, ancient Middle Eastern society; Who is the **legitimate** spokesperson for deity (or deities)? The desired "answer" to this question would have ensured sacerdotal security for one competing group and hegemony over all others, and thereby over the people served(?) by that priesthood.

No sooner than one group of Israelite priests had secured that coveted position and had won the sacerdotal duels with the help of the Persian government, another challenge to their hegemony was presented by the Qumranites, and still later by the Samaritans. Both priestly-led groups refracted the "answer" to the main question of legitimate spokespersonship through their own hermeneutical prisms. The results were decentralized from Jerusalem-centered, post-exilic, theocratic government, or from the Levite-led, Maccabee-Hasmonean government between ca. 140-68 B.C.E. Either way separate communities were formed/founded, the former at Qumran, the latter at Shechem. Again, Balaam--in vestigial form--was pressed into the service of the

Qumranites. It was not the Balaam-of-the-cycle, however, but Balaam in "footnotes." The utterances attributed to Balaam in the *meshalim* section were separated from the context of the cycle and given new context by these schismatics. What remained was only the war theme: Balaam to avoid a war between Moab and the Moses-led host on the one hand, and exclamations attributed to Balaam (who was not mentioned!) in the service of the framing of a cataclysmic, eschatological war to end all of the other wars. 1QM, the so-called Qumran War Scroll, contained the details of the challenge to Jerusalem by the first group.

The Samaritans or *shomrim*, thought long and hard about the "question." Their "answer" to it was as Narcissus-like as that of their predecessors, the writer/editors of JE, P and D, as well as that of the Qumranites who followed them with 1QM. Whereas their competitive predecessors had not openly denied the "prophetic" dimension of the priestly office—although many had taken issue with colleague exponents of it (cf. Michaiah at 1 Kings 22 and Jeremiah 23 to cite but two instances)—the Samaritans did so openly and vehemently. Through the encounter between Pilti and Moses, the Samaritan writers expressed their great disdain for wizards, sorcerers, and diviners. They were no fans of the prophetic type either, as seen in their treatment of Balaam in the Samaritan Pentateuch. As to the issue of communication through prophets, they only acknowledged Moses as having been selected by Israel's deity as spokesman. And that deity's directive to build a sanctuary on Mount Gerizim opposite Shechem, they claimed, signalled their having been chosen as the legitimate spokespersons for deity. The contemporaneous "Balaams" (= Zadokite-led, Jerusalem-based priesthood) merely divined in Jerusalem. What they said and did were of no importance.

Like the covenanters of Qumran, among whose writings 1 Enoch also appears, it was more the utterances attributed to Balaam than the figure himself which were seized upon by its author. And in similar fashion, "Balaam" became a vehicle for more apocalyptic concerns. One is on safe ground to view both 1 Enoch and 1QM as works belonging to the same trajectory.

By the time the Middle Platonists, Philo and Origin, grappled with the Balaam figure, a long history of hermeneuticizing him could already be traced back to beyond the 10th century B.C.E. But once the hellenistic mind was brought to bear on what had been heretofore a Middle Eastern, semitic enterprise bound up chiefly by competing priesthoods, Balaam appeared in different garb.

The writings of Flavius Josephus, the New Testament, Philo, Origen, Clement and the rabbis continued to mirror a Greek-influenced world-view to varying degrees. The New Testament follows the anti-Balaam trajectory, but makes him culpable for having caused "Israel" to sin by eating food which had been sacrificed to idols. We saw this concern mirrored in the Acts of the Apostles also. And like the process pursued in that work, Josephus embellished his writings about Balaam with speeches, lengthy in nature also (cf. V1:4 of *Antiquities*).

With its concerns for applying Middle Platonic views of government, community and religion of the greater hellenistic world to Palestinian and Babylonian Jewish village life, Balaam, for the rabbis was a most minimal footnote who served merely as a circumlocution for, perhaps, only Jesus.

Al Kisa'i, like the author of Balaam-of-the-wall from Deir 'Allā, certainly presents a Balaam heretofore unencountered. There is certainly nothing that would have been odd about Balaam the monarch having had a queen. We are merely told nowhere else except in Al Kisa'i's writing that he did. In fact, it is credited to her influence that Balaam goes to meet Balak. That this account of Balaam is contained in a work which deals with prophets demonstrates that the work certainly did not grow out of the Samaritan trajectory with its anti prophet worldview.

CONCLUSION

The ancient Canaanite, Israelite, Jewish (semitic and hellenistic), Samaritan, Christian, and Muslim "Balaams" having served their respective uses prior to the advent of the modern world (understood in a Western sense), modern writers found him useful also. What appeared as a clever short story from the pen of Joel Harris, became, in light of the foregoing hermeneutical history, an extremely perceptive construction by the author. Harris did not miss Balaam's sense of duty, his faithfulness to executing an assigned task, his wisdom or his ability to "see". And Harris, making a socio-political statement as well, made his Balaam a black slave (= *ebed*/servant [of Yahweh] in Hebrew) to demonstrate both "Balaams'" faithfulness, while simultaneously showing and maintaining their outsider/insider status as well. And wisdom was depicted in the form of the black Balaam's deviant speech patterns, the equivalent of which were the seven *meshalim* of the Balaam cycle. It is to Balaam's credit that his figure was found to be the right stuff around which to spin a yarn even in this century.

It is not surprising that a Jewish writer, contemplating the state of Israel's stormy beginnings by decree of the United Nations, its membership among those nations, yet inability to be fully accepted as a member of those nations, would frame his study of this problem by asking whether Balaam's curse had only been deferred all these years and had not really been overturned. Although Leshem's work falls into the category of modern political scientific inquiry, the Balaam figure, even here, functioned to assist a modern scholar of political science to frame the question of Israel's place and future among the (modern) nations.

This study of Balaam has accomplished its aims of demonstrating that:

(1)   Balaam was a famous monarch/seer reputed to have been an

effective diviner.

(2) As a result of his divining efficacy, he became a legend among the members, especially the priests, of the petty kingdoms of the eastern Levant between the 10th and 5th centuries B.C.E.

(3) Ancient Israelite priesthoods warred with each other over the issue of sacerdotal hegemony: wars reflected in the source *strata* of the Pentateuch and "Balaam's" role within them.

(4) Later priestly trajectories continued to craft insider/outsider arguments around the Balaam figure and type.

(5) In some cases, Balaam's words were severed from his figure and type and were utilized by the Qumranities, the Samaritans, the writer of 1 Enoch, or

(6) The figure was embellished by later Samaritans (Pilti), Josephus (the Balaam speech), and Al Kisa'i.

(7) Balaam was remotely remembered by certain writers of works contained in the New Testament, the Babylonian Talmud, and medieval Samaritan works.

(8) Modern short story and political-scientific writers found Balaam the figure, or words attributed to him helpful in articulating social and political concerns.

Balaam proved to be an entity who was ideal for functioning as a fulcrum for numerous movements, ancient, medieval, and modern, in organizing various facets of the question of the social, religious, and political role(s) of one reputed to have mediated the word and will of the god of Israel.

PREFACE

1. Alexander Rofe, **The Book of Balaam (Numbers 22:2–24:25). A Study in Methods of Criticism and the History of Biblical Literature and Religion**, (Jerusalem: Simor Ltd., 1979 [in Hebrew]).

2. Michael S. Moore, **The Balaam Traditions: Their Character and Development**, SBL Dissertation Series (Atlanta: Scholars Press, 1990). Allied to these two is Judith Baskin's work **Pharaoh's Counsellors: Job, Jethro, and Balaam in Rabbinic and Patristic Tradition**, (Chicago Scholars Press, 1983).

3. William F. Albright, "The Oracles of Balaam," **JBL** LXIII/III (1944): 207–233, and Judith Baskin, "Origen on Balaam: The Dilemma of the Unworthy Prophet," **VC** 37 (1983), pp. 22–35.

4. An exception to this is Roland Devaux's work on **Ancient Israel**, 2 Vols. (New York: McGraw–Hill, 1965 c. 1961), and to some extent T. J. Meeks' **Hebrew Origins**, (New York: Harper & Row, 1936).

5. Recently, the papers from this conference were published under the title **Religion, Science, and Magic: In Concert and in Conflict,** Jacob Neusner *et al.*, eds., (New York and Oxford: Oxford University Press, 1989).

6. Robert M. Berchman, "*Arcana Mundi*: Between Balaam and Hecate: Prophecy, Divination and Magic in Later Platonism,"(1989), and John T. Greene, "Balaam: Prophet Diviner, and Priest in Selected Ancient Israelite and Hellenistic Jewish Sources" (1989), and "Balaam as Figure and Type in Ancient Semitic Literature to the First Century B.C.E., with a Survey of Post–Philo Applications of the Balaam Figure and Type" (1990), both in the **SBL Seminar Papers** Volumes. I explored uses of the Balaam traditions both within and without ancient Israel, while Berchman studied the Middle Platonic sources in Alexandria.

INTRODUCTION: A Man, A Monarch, A Marked Paradigm, A Monument
Balaam the Son of Beor

1. Cf. The New Testament citation of **Hebrews** 5:6;10;7:1; and especially 7:3; as well as 7:10;11;15; and 17b.

2. James M. Robinson, ed., **The Nag Hammadi Library**, Rev. ed. (San Francisco: Harper, 1990).

3. Cf. Jo Ann Hackett, **The Balaam Text From Deir 'Allā**, (Chicago Scholars Press, 1980), P. Kyle McCarter, Jr., "The Balaam Texts from Deir 'Allā: The First Combination," **BASOR** 239 (1980): 49–60, and André Lemaire, "Fragments From the Book of Balaam Found at Deir 'Allā," **Biblical Archaeology Review** (Sept.– Oct. 1985) Vol. XI No. 5: 26–39.

4. John T. Greene, **The Role of the Messenger and Message in the Ancient Near East,** Brown Judaic Studies 169 (Atlanta: Scholars Press, 1989).

5. This addition of the phoneme \m\ here, or of other phonemes to Semitic stems, is one method of overworking a text by later writers who used it for other purposes, especially those of a polemical nature.

6. This discussion is built ultimately on a practice commencing with David having brought the ark to Jerusalem dressed only in the priestly *ephod*. Later, he was followed by Solomon who served in a priestly capacity at the dedication of the new Temple of YHWH (1 Kings 8:1–26). These actions, as well as Josiah's reforming efforts, all mirrored the designation found in the Psalter (Ps. 110:4).

PART I: BACKGROUND

Chapter 1. A Discovery at Tell Deir 'Allā: Its Implications and Significance: The Coming War Between Heaven and Earth

1. André Lemaire, "Fragments from the Book of Balaam Found at Deir 'Allā," **BAR** (Sept.–Oct. 1985) Vol. XI No. 5, p. 39.

2. It has been suggested that the text was located in a scribal school, and that it possibly served as a text for copying exercises. This is pure speculation, however. The same was proposed for the Gezer Calendar also.

3. This portion of the translation of the reconstructed text is the work of Jo Ann Hackett, **The Balaam Text From Deir 'Allā**, Harvard Semitic Monographs 31 (Chicago: Scholars Press, 1980), p. 29.

4. The Council of Yahweh is studied in Frank Moore Cross, Jr., "The Council of Yahweh in Second Isaiah," **JNES** XII (1953), pp. 274–279; W. Hermann, ""*Die Goettersoehne*," **ZRRG** XII (1960), 242–251; Edwin Kingsbury, "The Prophets and the Council of Yahweh," **JBL** LXXXVIII No. 3 (1964), pp. 279–286; H. Wheeler Robinson, "The Council of Yahweh," **JTS** XLV (1945), pp. 151–157 in **Inspiration and Revelation in the Old Testament**, (Oxford: Oxford University Press, 1946); and also the discussion contained in Simon J. DeVries, **Prophet Against Prophet: The Role of the Michaiah Narrative (I Kings 22) in the Development of Early Prophetic Tradition**, (Grand Rapids: Eerdmans, 1978), pp. 7; 5; 40–42.

5. Hackett, **Deir 'Allā**, p. 29.

6. Cf. the same type of imagery in the complaint of the Egyptian wise man, Ipuwer, who lived during the Egyptian Early Intermediate Period. While contemplating the numerous disasters which had befallen Egypt in his day, he wrote: "The possessor of property is now one who has naught. Behold, servants have become masters of butler; He who was a messenger now sends another."

This example is derived from T.E. Peet, **A Comparative Study of the Literatures of Egypt, Palestine and Mesopotamia: Egypt's Contribution to the Literature of the Ancient World**, (London: Oxford University Press, 1931), p. 118.

7. Cf. Lemaire, "Fragments," p. 37.

8. Ibid., p. 38.

9. Cf. note 59 of PART 2.

Chapter 2. The Sacerdotal Class: Social and Religio-Political Protests in Ancient Israel: Hermeneutical Wars on "Paper"

10. Cf. note 123 of PART 2.

11. Richard Elliott Friedman, **Who Wrote the Bible?**, (Englewood Cliffs, NJ: Prentice Hall, 1987).

Chapter 3. The Development of Communication Theories and Praxes: Community Control: Wars for the Fidelity of the People

PART 2: Prophet, Priest, Diviner: Balaam as Test Case and Paradigm

Chapter 4. Philosophies of History and Communication in Ancient Israel: Priestly Wars and Nonaggression Pacts

1. Henri Frankfort, *et al.*, **The Intellectual Adventure of Ancient Man; An Essay on Speculative Thought in the Ancient Near East**, (Chicago: The Uiversity of Chicago Press, 1946).

2. This situation, we will see, happened with a vengeance in ancient Israel. The *Torah* and the *Nevi'im* sections of the *TaNaK* mirror this situation.

3. Or forced out, as in the case of the Levites under Saul and David, and of Abiathar under Solomon.

4. Geza Vermes, **Scripture and Tradition in Judaism,** *Studia Post-Biblica, Volumen Quartum* (Haggadic Studies), (Leiden: E.J. Brill, 1961), pp. 127–177.

5. The deuteronomistic circle is reputed to have been a prophetic group responsible for editing the block of material found in the Hebrew-written Bible embracing Deuteronomy through the end of 2 Kings plus the prophetic book of Jeremiah. This material is noted for its distinctive world-view crafted against the backdrop of the Mosaic covenant. In essence, "Israel's" ups and downs historically are explained as success (ups) when the Covenant is kept, and failure/punishment (downs) when it is not. A serpentine up–down, up–down scheme pervades and thus joins all of the above-mentioned material.

6. These terms and their significance for the Balaam text are derived from Michael Fishbane, **Biblical Interpretation in Ancient Israel,** (Oxford: Clarendon Press, 1985), p. 468.

7. Cf. "Literature" in G. Gray, **Numbers: A Critical and Exegetical Commentary,** (Edinburgh: T. & T. Clark, 1965 c. 1903), p. 307.

8. A. H. McNeile, **The Book of Numbers,** (Cambridge: At the University Press, 1931).

9. H. Cazelles, *La Sainte Bible: Lés Nombres,* Rev. 2d. Ed. (Paris: Lés Éditions du Cerf, 1958).

10. G. Vermes, **Scripture and Tradition in Judaism,** pp. 127–177.

11. John Sturdy, **The Cambridge Bible Commentary, Numbers,** (Cambridge: Cambridge University Press, 1976).

12. Nehama Leibowitz, **Studies in BaMidbar (Numbers),** (Jerusalem: World Zionist Organization, 1982 c. 1980).

13. M. Fishbane, **Biblical Interpretation in Ancient Israel,** (Oxford: Clarendon, 1985).

14. G. Von Rad, **The Problem of the Hexateuch and Other Essays**, (Edinburgh: Oliver & Body, Ltd., 1966 c. 1958).

15. Cf. the excellent work of Arthur Weiser, **The Old Testament: Its Formation and Development,** (New York: Association Press, 1961), p. 75; Cuthbert A. Simpson, **The Early Traditions of Israel**, (London: Oxford University Press, 1948), pp. 48–49; Robert Pfeiffer, **Introduction to the Old Testament: An Introduction,** (New York: Harper & Row, 1965), pp. 191–199; H. Gunkel, **The Legends of Genesis,** (New York: Schocken Books, 1964); E. Nielsen, **Oral Traditions**, (London: SCM Press, 1954).

16. R. E. Friedman, **Who Wrote the Bible?**, (New Jersey: Prentice Hall, 1987).

17. Some scholars argue a date of ca. 950, 850, 650, and 550 B.C.E. respectively for J, E, D, and P. But cf. Friedman, **Who Wrote the Bible?**, pp. 86–87 (J,E) and *passim* for a more recent argument.

18. R. F. Johnson, "Balaam," **IDB**, (Nashville: Abingdon Press, 1962), pp. 341–342.

19. G. B. Gray, **Numbers ICC**, p. 310.

20. A. H. McNeile, **The Book of Numbers,** *et passim.*

21. John Sturdy, **The Cambridge Bible Commentary**, pp. 4, 157.

22. R. E. Friedman, **Who Wrote the Bible?** See the chart he provides on p. 253.

23. G. Vermes, **Scripture and Tradition in Judaism**, pp. 127–177.

24. Leibowitz, **Studies in BaMidbar,** *et passim.*

25. Cf. John Marsh and Albert George Butzer, **The Book of Numbers**, **The Interpreter's Bible**, Volume II, (New York: Abingdon=Cokesbury Press, 1953), p. 247, wherein Butzer writes: "The plains of Moab is a term confined to P,..."

26. Cf. Sturdy, **Cambridge Bible**, p. 157.

27. These names of deity, Yahweh and Elohim, were the first clues noticed as early as 1753 by the French court physician Jean Astruc. An entire constellation of other characteristic data surrounds these two names of deity, however, to produce a plausible argument for more than one "document" in use as well as evident in this material.

28. See H. Keith Beebe, **The Old Testament: An Introduction to Its Literary, Historical, and Religious Traditions,** (Belmont, California: Dickenson Publishing Co., Inc., 1970), pp. 9-10.

29. Excellent works which discuss these versions and their production are Frank Moore Cross, Jr., **The Ancient Library of Qumran and Modern Biblical Studies,** (Garden City, New York: Doubleday & Co., 1961); and Ernst Wuerthwein, **The Text of the Old Testament,** (London: Basil Blackwell, 1957).

30. Ibid.

31. The Biblical books of Job, Proverbs and Ecclesiastes are characterized by the presence of such wise sayings. There were also famous communities in ancient Israel where scholars who produced wise sayings lived. The most famous is called by two names, *Kiriath-sepher* (literally village of the book, or book-town) and later, *Debir* (i.e., oracle or wise saying). Cf. Joshua 15:16 and Proverbs 25:1.

32. This addition of an \m\ here, or other letters to semitic stems, is one method of overworking a text (and deriving nouns) by later writers who used it for other purposes, especially those of a polemical nature. Cf. below in the section discussing the meaning of the Balaam cycle by the writer called P or Priestly Writer.

33. Again, I call attention to the rationale for the presence of many seeming anomalies in this cycle. Attention is directed to the Meaning(s) section of the present work where I discuss the reason why Balaam seems to have two

different homelands. See also A. S. Yahuda, "The Name of Balaam's Homeland," **JBL**, LXIV (1945): 547–551.

34. Cf. Yahuda, "The Name of Balaam's Homeland," and R.F. Johnson, "Balaam" in **Interpreters Dictionary of the Bible**, pp. 341–342.

35. John T. Greene, **The Role of the Messenger and Message in the Ancient Near East**, Brown Judaic Studies 169 (Atlanta: Scholars Press, 1989), pp. 81–83.

36. For quick reference to kings serving as priests also, see 1 Samuel 6:12–20; 1 Kings 8:5–63; as well as Psalm 110:4, where many scholars argue that this is in reference to David.

37. Cf. The **Revised Standard Version** of this cycle in the note at the bottom of page 167 of Thomas Nelson and Sons. Cf. also Gray, **Numbers**, p. 358.

38. I suspect that this is a cryptic reference to Nineveh or some other principal city in Assyria during the seventh century. My rationale for this is the discussion of the place of Assyria in the writing of P's version of the Balaam cycle. See, therefore, that discussion under Meaning(s) below.

39. Cf. note number 7 above for references.

40. Mt. Scopus in Jerusalem to this day bears the name with the same significance. At one time it must have served as a height from which certain "gazers" uttered their oracles. The more within the "scope" of the gazer, the greater was the extent of his/her power. Cf. the significance of going from higher to higher locales in the narrative framework of the discourses in the Balaam cycle.

41. Cf. Gray, **Numbers**, p. 341.

42. Cf. Sturdy, **Numbers**, p. 4 where he writes: "It is not however necessary to assign passages between J and E in this commentary." Later, on this same page, he writes: "This is the view taken by the writer of this commentary...it is simply more sensible to write in terms of `the older material' without attempting such

an uncertain division of the text."

43. The term "adversary" appears to signal some covenantal concern. Advocates and those who "stand in the breach" (cf. Ezek. 22:30; Ps. 106:23) comprise one body in a controversy, while the adversary speaks for the other. Oftentimes, the adversaries (within this covenant framework) are solicited by a deity, as in the case of the Book of Job, and vouchsafed considerable power.

44. Cf. 2 Samuel 19:23 and 1 Kings 5:18.

45. Cf. Greene, **Messenger**, pp. 191–204.

46. Cf. T. Witton Davies, **Magic, Divination, and Demonology Among the Hebrews and Their Neighbors**, (New York: KTAV Publishing House, 1960 c. 1898), p. 78. This is a dated work, but much of its contents are still of great value.

47. Cf. Numbers 21:14 where a portion of this poem may be read.

48. Ibid.

49. Cf. Numbers 24:16; Proverbs 2:5; 9:10; 30:3; Ecclesiastes 11:9; and Hosea 4:1; 6:6; where this prophet complains that those (i.e. priests) who are responsible for teaching the knowledge of Yahweh have abrogated their responsibilities.

50. There is an interstitial category in biblical Hebrew referred to as lyrical prose when that literature does not participate fully in all of the characteristics of pure poetry (i.e., *parallelismus memborum, chiasmus, bi* and *tri cola*, meter, stress, etc.), or prose. An excellent example in Hebrew is found in Genesis 2:23. To appreciate the problem, cf. James Kugel, **The Idea of Biblical Poetry: Parallelism and Its History**, (New Haven: Yale University Press, 1981), pp. 76–84. Cf. especially p. 76 where, bracketing the concerns of G. B. Gray's **Forms of Hebrew Poetry**, he asks: "Had then the ancient Hebrew three forms of composition–metrical poetry and plain prose, and an intermediate type differing from poetry by the absence of metre, and from prose by obedience to

certain laws governing the mutual relations between its clauses–a type for which we might as makeshifts employ the terms unmetrical poetry or parallelistic prose?"

51. See Theophile J. Meek, **Hebrew Origins**, (New York: Harper & Brothers, 1960), pp. 93–98 wherein he discusses the relationship of the Kenites to other Yahwistic groups.

52. Gray, **Numbers**, pp.377–378.

53. McNeile, **Numbers**, *et passim*; Gray, **Numbers**, pp.307–322, *et passim*; Cazelles, *Les Nombres* (*Les* ch. 22–24 *melent en un seul recit les elements, parfois discordants, provenant deux traditions, la<<yahviste>> et l'<<elohiste>>*, p. 105); and Sturdy, **Numbers**, pp. 1–9.

54. Cf. Butzer, **Numbers, The Interpreter's Bible**, p. 247, where Numbers 22:1 is attributed to P, with the rationale: "The plains of Moab is a term confined to P, and refers to the high steppes to the north of the Dead Sea and on the east of the Jordan. The position reported is opposite Jericho."

55. Cf. note 53.

56. Friedman, **Who Wrote?**, pp. 87–88.

57. A. S. Yahuda, "Balaam's Homeland," 547–51.

58. But cf. below (Meanings(s)) for another, and more specific rationale as to why.

59. *Propriediv* is coined in the spirit of words such as Rambam, Rashbam, Ramban, Rashi, etc., where, instead of names, titles of professions are used.

60. Friedman, **Who Wrote?**, p. 86 holds that J could possibly have been written by a woman.

61. Ibid., p. 87.

62. Ibid., p. 86.

63. Pages 85–87 of Friedman certainly deviate from the traditional view of the growth of the Pentateuch which is provided in graph form by C. F. North,

"Pentateuchal Criticism," in H. H. Rowley, ed. **The Old Testament and Modern Study**, (London: Oxford University Press, 1961).

64. Cf. Beebe, **Introduction**, pp. 92–95; Mitchell Dahood, S.J., **Psalms I, 1–50, The Anchor Bible**, (Garden City, New York: Doubleday & Co., 1964), pp. xxix–xxx; and James Kugel, **The Idea of Biblical Poetry: Parallelism and Its History**, (New Haven: Yale University Press, 1981).

65. The *mshl* displays most of the characteristics treated in the above works which discuss Semitic poetry, and Hebrew in particular, and how this poetry provides so few to no clues about the time in which it was written, or even where.

66. It is plausible that the first half of this *mshl* could have a northern provenance, but again, it is poetry, and the presence of the word "Israel," even when it is in parallelism with "Jacob," may mean the kingdom of Israel, or Israel the people of Yahweh. See R.F. Johnson, **Interpreter's Dictionary of the Bible**, p. 341, who writes: "The two poems in Num. 23, usually attributed to E, are obviously acquainted with the story of Balaam in the employ of the King of Moab, while the J poems in ch. 24 could have originated apart from this particular tradition about Balaam."

67. But cf. Friedman, **Who Wrote?**, pp. 174–187, and his discussion of the Tabernacle and its relation to the P source *stratum* of the Pentateuch. For the most comprehensive work on Confederated Israel, see Norman K. Gottwald, **The Tribes of Yahweh: A Sociology of the Religion of Liberated Israel, 1250–1050 B.C.E.**, (Orbis Books, 1979).

68. A. S. Yahuda, "Balaam's Homeland," **JBL** LXIV (1945): 547–551.

69. There is also speculation that the poem reflects the situation in Judah during the period of David's conquests of his eastern and southeastern neighbors, i.e., 10th century B.C.E. See e.g. Gray, **Numbers**, p. 370.

70. Strong evidence suggests that this was accomplished in the 10th century by

David. See 2 Samuel 1:1.

71. Assyria, under Sennacherib, conquered Judah in the campaign of 701 B.C.E. Moab, Edom, Ammon, Ashdod were among others affected. It is possible that the Kenites, who also lived in this region south of Judah, were willing to fight for independence. See Meek, **Hebrew Origins**, pp. 92-98.

72. Harry Orlinsky, **Ancient Israel**, (Ithaca, New York: Cornell University Press, 1960); Martin Noth, **The History of Israel**, (New York: Harper & Row, 1960); Herbert G. May, ed., **Oxford Bible Atlas**, (London: Oxford University Press, 1962); John Bright, **A History of Israel**, (Philadelphia: Westminster Press, 1959); and Yohannan Aharoni and Michael Avi-Yonah, **The Macmillan Bible Atlas**, (New York: The Macmillan Co., 1968) all continue to be first rate and reliable historical sources.

73. The responsibilities of the two co-High Priests, Zadok and Abiathar, under David would have been great, for it would have fallen to them as to how best to reorganize the priests of the lands conquered by David, and to absorb their traditions into the emerging national Yahwistic cult centered on Jerusalem. We get no picture of a national (or imperial!) policy of destroying other religious centers during the United Monarchy period. For example, Absalom fulfills a vow at Hebron, while Solomon has religious shrines built for all of his foreign wives, as a result of state marriages.

74. But the urgency was the result of a rapidly growing empire which was built mainly on military defeat. The Balaam figure by its very inclusion in J material--the earliest of the source *strata*--shows a "defeat" in reverse, a legend-tradition victory over the conquerors.

75. This would have been accomplished partially by what are called the J poems in Chapter 24 of Numbers.

76. Cf. the discussion on law and empire in Beebe, **Introduction**, pp. 105-106. Law, then, is only one side of the priestly function within an expanding empire.

How priests of the conquering group related to priests of the conquered groups is still an area worthy of further study.

77. Omri (876–869) made Moab a vassal state from which sheep and cereal grains came into Israel in large supply. His son, Ahab, (869–850) continued that control over Moab. After his death, however, Moab rebelled, and at least two of his successors, sons Ahaziah and Jehoram, were unable to dominate the country again.

78. Even a reconstruction of the constituent parts of the four source Documentary Hypothesis by Friedman includes almost all of the Balaam cycle within the E *stratum* (p. 253). Numbers 22:1 he assigns to the **Redactor** of the Pentateuch. Friedman, **Who Wrote the Bible**?

79. The Shiloh–oriented priests who produced E were anti–Israelite religious practices, but they did not (as their work demonstrates) oppose the Israelite monarchy. As priests, they could have opposed all priests who threatened their position as the premier priests of Israel and Judah. Since the J *stratum* is critiqued by the later E *stratum*, E's (now very nebulous at best) treatment of Balaam might have specific E–programmatic polemic which can no longer be recovered.

80. The fate of E after 722 B.C.E. is discussed by Flanders, Crapps, and Smith, **People of the Covenant** (New York: Oxford University Press, 1988), pp. 76–77. There JE is simply referred to as the "E narrative which is partially preserved in the Torah." Cf. also, Friedman, **Who Wrote the Bible?**, pp. 87–88; and 207–208.

81. Apparently, after 722 B.C.E., Judah had no choice but to absorb numerous refugees from the north which had been defeated by the Assyrians. Since the Aaronid/Zadokites heading the state priestly office in Jerusalem would have also been overrun with out of work priests from the Israelite state shrines, as well as from Shiloh, the purpose of the reworked Balaam tradition in J might have been

reworked once more for a similar purpose.

82. Anytime from Asshurnasirpal II (883–859) to Sargon II (722–705) B.C.E. for Israel; and continuing until Sin–shariskun 629–612 B.C.E. for Judah.

83. Or at least against the state appointed priesthood of the north, as well as against the kings of the north in their roles as "Highest" Priests.

84. Cf. note 80 above. It is less certain when a northern king would have controlled Edom. Sheth is another name for Moab.

85. Friedman, p. 88.

86. Cf. the discussion above in the Linguistic Analysis.

87. Cf. the Preface above, and the discussion to follow Meaning(s) below.

88. See above the material accompanying notes 77, and 84.

89. Friedman, **Who Wrote the Bible?**, pp. 162–163.

90. Cf. discussion in Flanders, Crapps, and Smith, **The People of the Covenant**, p. 75.

91. It was believed that P did not reflect anything pre–exilic. True, it reflected a great concern for centralization of the cult, but that was at a time, according to the history of the post–exilic era, when priests would most certainly have been preoccupied with consolidating the national cult, and that during a theocratic form of government. Such did not occur, it was believed on the basis of that understanding of history, until the coming of Zerubbabel and Joshua (Ezra 3:1 ff.). This traditional Documentary Hypothesis is reappraised.

92. Ibid., p. 190.

93. Ibid., pp. 207–216.

94. Ibid., pp. 89–192.

95. Ibid., p. 210.

96. This is essentially the main argument of Friedman's thesis. When all of the source *strata* were written before the exile, many heretofore prevailing arguments must be rethought in light of the arguments presented in **Who Wrote**

the Bible? and elsewhere in Friedman's writings, and those of his colleagues mentioned throughout his book as well.

97. Friedman, **Who Wrote the Bible?**, *et passim*.

98. Ibid., pp. 188-191.

99. Those priests who traced their ancestry to Moses had been excluded from important urban (i.e., capital city) priestly functions, and a share in any kind of power in directing the course of state Yahwism in either its Jerusalem version (lost after Abiathar was ousted ca. 966 B.C.E. in a failed attempt to have Prince Adonijah succeed David), or its Tirzah/Samaria/Bethel/Dan version (Here, too, the Shilonites had assisted Jeroboam in his bid for kingship, but were then rejected in favor of another state-appointed priesthood). These Mushite priests waged polemical warfare against rival (as they understood them) state priesthoods on two fronts. Essentially, P opposed their opposition to P's group.

100. See above, note 74.

101. Cf. Marsh and Butzer, **The Book of Numbers, The Interpreter's Bible**, Vol. II, p. 247.

102. This, of course, being due to the conclusions long held to be true and accurate as a result of Documentary Hypothesis studies until very recently.

103. Understanding the history of the Aaronid/Zadokite priesthood within the history of Judah leads one to understand the situation of that priesthood during the reign of Hezekiah, and that in the light of the Assyrian bid for power and conquest. Priesthoods battled for power in a manner similar to corporations taking over other corporations today. One should not underestimate the urgency with which P worked and wrote.

104. A reading of what is considered traditional P material reflects this concern. P is interested in nothing less than a sacerdotal monopoly for the Aaronids.

105. By doing so, P sent a strong signal that all priestly activities other than those now being conducted and supervised by Aaronids, and those at Jerusalem!,

were illegal.

106. Friedman, pp. 193-195.

107. Cf. also Friedman, pp. 199-200; 202-203, for more examples of P's reworking of JE.

108. "Princes" appears to have been included as some sort of literary prosthesis. Where it appears, it is really not necessary to tell the "main tree trunk" story. Eight such occurrences send to the critical reader a signal that "princes" are important to one of the contributors to the narrative framework of this cycle. Why, must be sought against the historical backdrop of the overall cycle.

109. Cf. Friedman's research and results on the overworkings of P, and the same "thumbprints" in this cycle.

110. In addition to the "thumbprints," when Assyrian political ambitions are factored into the equation, a picture emerges which would have presented numerous reasons why a, perhaps, dormant Balaam tradition, formerly employed by earlier Aaronids for a, then, relevant reason, would, during Hezekiah's(=neo-Assyria's time), have been pulled out, dusted off, and recast by this later Aaronid for yet one more example of what the position of the foreign priest, prophet, diviner should now be.

111. The Deuteronomist appreciated Hezekiah's efforts at both political and religious independence as well. He wrote at a later time, and was extolling the virtues of Hezekiah for another reason, however. He had a different hero, but one who was certainly related to Hezekiah. See below, note 134, for the identification of this writer and his connection with Hezekiah.

112. Cf. Friedman, 211.

113. Astruc, and some time earlier a German pastor in Hildesheim named Witter (1711), identified not only one source using the name Yahweh, and one using the name Elohim, but ten other sources which he claimed had been collected and included by Moses as he had composed Genesis.

114. Cf. the discussion by Gray, **Numbers**, pp. 377–378, and that in A. Dupont–Sommer, **The Essene Writings From Qumran**, (New York: The World Publishing Co., 1967), pp. 339–351.

115. Cf. Gerhard von Rad, **The Problem of the Hexateuch and Other Essays**, (New York: McGraw–Hill, 1966), pp. 3–4, where he argues that Deuteronomy 26:5b–9 contains in a terse form the same story contained in Genesis through Deuteronomy. The passage is therefore the Hexateuch in miniature.

116. Cf. Gwilym Jones, "Holy–war" or "Yahweh–war?", *Vetus Testamentum*. Vol. XXV (1975): 642–650.

117. James B. Pritchard, ed., **Ancient Near Eastern Texts Relating to the Old Testament**, (rev. ed., Princeton, New Jersey: Princeton University Press, 1955), p. 286.

118. Cf. Beebe, **Introduction**, p. 252.

119. In c. 966 B.C.E., as David had withdrawn from public life, but was still the king/emperor, two of his sons, Princes Adonijah and Jedidiah(=Solomon), struggled with each other to succeed him on the throne. David had failed to publicly name his official successor. Religious, and military personnel supported each candidate. One of the Co–High Priests, Abiathar (a Mushite), supported Prince Adonijah, while the other, Zadok (an Aaronid), supported Prince Jedidiah. Prince Jedidiah eventually succeeded David some six years later. He banished Abiathar to internal exile in the Aaronid priestly town of Anathoth, leaving the reins of priestly power solely in the hands of Zadok, the sole High Priest and his party. From then on, Mushites played minor roles in state religious politics. The view of P grew out of this long debate between the two factions. See the discussions in Roger N. Whybray, **The Succession Narrative: A Study of II Samuel 9–20; I Kings 1 and 2,** (Alec R. Allenson, 1968); and Von Rad, **Hexateuch**, pp. 176–189.

120. Friedman, pp. 188–206.

121. Ibid., pp. 197–198.

122. Cf. the discussion of events which led to this possible attitude toward jettisoning the Old Testament in Harold J. Grimm, **The Reformation Era-1500–1650**, (New York: Macmillan Publishing Co., Inc., 1973), pp. 52–72.

123. Cf. H. Graf Reventlow, *Das Amt des Propheten bei Amos, Forschung zur Religion und Literature des Alten und Neuen Testaments*, 80 (Goettingen, West Germany: Vandenhoeck und Ruprecht, 1962); Walter Brueggemann, "Amos IV: 4–13 and Israel's Covenant Worship," **VT**, XV (1965), pp. 1–15; and J.D.W. Watts, **Vision and Prophecy in Amos**, (Grand Rapids, MI: W.B. Eerdmans, 1958).

Evidence seems to point to Micah having been a priest in the small rural town of Moresheth. His concern was with corruption in big cities, especially Jerusalem and Samaria, and he critiqued the priests in those cities for not having provided proper leadership. Moreover, his language reflects priestly concerns also. See Micah 1:2–5 and 4:1–3.

Isaiah of Jerusalem (i.e., Isa. 1–23; 28–39) wrote that he had visions within the very walls of the Jerusalem Temple (building). Only a priest was allowed therein. See Isa. 6:1–9.

124. Cf. the (apparently) odd reading at Numbers 22:7: "with divinations in their hand."

125. Divining, *per se*, does not appear to have been considered a negative activity engaged in by prophets. It is, rather, the result(s) of the divining which is/are questioned. Cf. Micah 3:5–8.

126. The "diviners from the east" most probably points to the presence of Assyrian priests, as well as those from Assyria who had come to Jerusalem through Philistia (which was an on–again, off–again vassal of the Assyrians, or were, along with Judah and Moab, co–conspirators against the Assyrians).

127. The first major concentrated interest in divination in ancient Israel occurred

in the eighth century. Afterwards, it remained an abiding interest and issue until the end of the prophetic period.

128. Cf. Beebe, **Introduction**, p. 252, under The Third Crisis: "These reforms were undertaken guardedly at first in order to see what reaction Assyrian political agents in Jerusalem might have."

129. Friedman, p. 210.

130. Ibid., p. 210.

131. Ibid., pp. 193–203.

132. Ibid., pp. 202–203.

133. Ibid., pp. 193–195.

134. Thus, when Friedman writes (Ibid., p. 204): "We can explain this (i.e., P's additions to and subtractions from JE) partly in recognizing that the person who fashioned P rejected the angels, dreams, talking animals, and anthropomorphisms of JE," I find cause for the first time to disagree with his conclusion. The same "thumbprints" he ascribes to P with great accuracy are also evident in the Balaam cycle which does include a *ml'k*(=messenger/angel), and most certainly a talking animal.

135. Cf. Neil Q. Hamilton, "Temple Cleansing and Temple Bank," **JBL LXXIII** (Dec. 1964), Pt. IV: 365–372, for a study of temples, what they contained, and their place in the economic systems of the countries in which they were located in the ancient Near East and in the Mediterranean world.

136. Cf. note 128 above.

137. The Chronicles work as it presently stands, whether a part of a larger work termed Chronicles–Ezra–Nehemiah or not, is certainly concerned with its version of the Jerusalem priesthood's history to the time of its having been written.

138. Thus, my rationale for why there need be no attempt to further emend the text to harmonize J and E material as it presently stands. The intended

emendation of this text has already been accomplished by P. That emendation served an eighth century B.C.E. function during Hezekiah's reign. See also note 127 above.

139. That the Balaam of the cycle goes home, while in the other two Numbers passages he is brought in gratuitously, and shown (in reverse) to have given inefficacious counsel, and later to have deserved and received punishment by death, goes a long way toward revealing the purpose of the "Balaam" figure for P. "Balaam" recalled for P what Judas, Brutus, Benedict Arnold, Quisling, and Vichy recall for westerners over forty five today. But this was not all. "Balaam" was far more complex because his threat was viewed by P as far more complex.

140. Greene, "Balaam, '89," pp. 70–71.

141. Ibid., pp. 70–71.

142. Ibid., pp. 75–76.

143. Ibid., pp. 76–81.

144. Ibid., pp. 57–58; 93–95.

145. This will not change even when the Balaam figure departs, but the **type** remains as in the Samaritan figure Pilti. John Bowman, **Samaritan Documents,** Pittsburgh Original Texts And Translation Series (Pittsburgh: The Pickwick Press, 1977).

Chapter 5. Balaam Elsewhere in the Hebrew Scriptures:
The War Theme Continues

146. Greene, "Balaam," pp. 63.

147. John T. Greene, **The Role of the Messenger and Message in the Ancient Near East** (Atlanta: Scholars Press, 1989), pp. 81–83.

148. Greene, "Balaam," p. 63.

149. Numbers 31:8.

150. Numbers 31:18.

151. Apparently this work was expanded, and thus served as the vehicle for telling the story of the journey of Moses and his host from the mountain of Yahweh to a position in Transjordan opposite Jericho, before continuing across the Jordan.

152. Patrick D. Miller, Jr., **The Divine Warrior in Early Israel,** (Cambridge, Massachuetts: Harvard University Press, 1973).

153. Eleazar is said to have been the son of Aaron. Below, more will be stated concerning to which source stratum of the Pentateuch this segment belongs. Eleazar will be a key to identifying the author/editor of that stratum.

154. Friedman, **Who Wrote the Bible?**, pp. 120–121.

155. Ibid., p. 210.

156. Ibid., p. 210.

157. Ibid., pp. 210–211.

158. Greene, "Balaam," pp. 76–81; 81ff.

159. The extent to which priests would go to execute completely the complete cycle of activity connected with Yahweh/holy war is available in 1 Samuel 15:1–34. In typical (holy war) fashion, Saul, the newly-appointed *nagid* is charged: "Now go and smite Amalek, and **utterly destroy** all that they have; **do not spare them**, but kill both man and woman, infant and suckling, ox and sheep, camel and ass" (15:3). Saul failed to carry out the **herem** (ban, i.e., consecrating and devoting the spoils of war to Yahweh alone) and thereby violated the charge of the covenant, and earned the ire of Samuel. Saul spared Agag the king of the Amalekites, and also: "the best of the sheep and oxen..."

(v. 11). In order to set matters right, Samuel withdrew his support from Saul and said: "Bring here to me Agag the king...And Samuel hewed Agag in pieces before the Lord at Gilgal" (vv. 32–33). "Balaam," therefore, in Numbers 31 may do double duty, standing for both king and (outsider) *propriediv.*

160. Cf. J. Harvey, *"Le 'Rib–Pattern' requistoire prophetique sur la rupture de l'alliance," Biblica* 43 *(1962): 172–196, and* E. Wuerthwein, *"Der Ursprung der prophetischen Gerichtsrede," Zeitschrift fuer Theologie und Kirche* 49 (1952): 1–16.

161. Cf. Deut. 3:24, 4:36; 1 Kg. 8:42; 2 Chr. 6:32; Dan. 9:15; Ezek. 20:33, 34; Ps. 20:6, 71:12, 145:4 and 145:12 for testimonies to these "mighty acts." Descriptions of the **same** mighty act, reported in three different ways by the Yahwist (=P) writers are found in Exodus, [13:21, 14:13, 19b–25, 27b, 30, 31]; [13:17, 17–19, 14:10c, 16, 19A]; and [13:21, 14:1–4, 8–9, 15, 17–18, 21–23, 26–27a, 28–29] respectively. Cf. pp. 122–124 of H. Keith Beebe, **The Old Testament,** (Belmont, CA: Dickenson, 1970).

162. The homes of the J (Jerusalem) and E (Shiloh) *strata.*

163. Cf. Micah 1:5, 9, 13, 3:10, 12 (against Judah), and 1:5, 6, 14; 3:1, 8, 9 (against Samaria).

164. See especially the anti priesthood stance in Micah 3:11 "Its priests teach for hire," and 6:7 "Will the Lord be pleased with thousands of rams (**having been sacrificed**)..." The anti propriediv stance is read at 3:6–7: "Therefore it shall be night to you without **divination,** the sun shall go down upon the **prophets,**...the **seers,** shall be disgraced, and the **diviners** put to shame;...

165. Cf. Micah 3:5–6.

166. Greene, "Balaam," pp. 70–81.

167. Friedman, **Who Wrote?**, p. 123.

168. Ibid., pp. 125–127.

169. Ibid., pp. 123–124.

170. Greene, "Balaam," pp. 93-95.
171. Cf. Deuteronomy 23:4.
172. Greene, "Balaam," pp. 61-64.
173. Friedman, **Who?**, pp. 210-216.

PART 3: "Balaam" in Other Semitic Language-Written Materials

Chapter 6.   Qumran and the Balaam Traditions:
The Fantastic War

1. This division is certainly for purposes of description and nothing more. I am the first to realize that it could and should be subjected to numerous legitimate attacks; the first of which is that it is too simplistic and artificial. The point here is that certain biblical material exhibits certain characteristics which other biblical materials exhibit as both attempt to 'tell a story' and how they do it. See below, note 55.

2. Be reminded that this deuteronomistic body of material was presented in two "editions," Deuteronomistic History version one (designated D1), and version two (designated D2). Cf. the discussions in Friedman, **Bible?**, pp. 129, 137-149, and Brian Peckham, **The Composition of the Deuteronomistic History**, (Atlanta: Scholar Press, 1985), pp. 7-9 (D1); 21-68 (D2).

3. These dates coincide with the twentieth years of the reigns of Kings Artaxerxes I and II. Since neither Nehemiah 1:1 nor 2:1 supply more information, we must proceed with caution in dating the Nehemian material.

4. Cf. Greene, "Balaam," pp. 96-99 for a condensed treatment of these extra-Hebrew Scriptures texts, and the discussion which follows below.

5. Cf. the bibliography in Millar Burrows, **The Dead Sea Scrolls**, (New York: Viking Press, 1955), pp. 420-435. The classic introductory work is by Frank

M. Cross, Jr., **The Ancient Library of Qumran and Modern Biblical Studies,** (Garden City, New York: Doubleday, 1958); B. Jongeling, **A Classified Bibliography of Finds in the Desert of Judah: 1955-1969,** (Leiden: E.J. Brill, 1971); and J.A. Fitzmyer, **The Dead Sea Scrolls. Major Publications and Tools for Study,** (Missoula: Scholars, 1975).

6. The distinction between **priests** and **Levites** is maintained here also.

7. Cf. note 1 above, and Hannelis Schulte, *Die Entstehung der Gerichtsschreibung im Alten Israel,* **BZAW**, (Berlin: Walter de Gruyter, 1972); John Van Seters, "Histories and Historians of the Ancient Near East," **Orientalia** 50 (1981), pp. 137-185; and André Lemaire, *"Vers l'histoire de la redaction des livres des Rois,"* **ZAW** 98 (1986), pp. 221-236.

8. Cf. M. Avi-Yonah, "The `War of the Sons of Light and the Sons of Darkness' and Maccabean Warfare," IEJ (1952): 1-5, Flavius Josephus, **Antiquities** Book XIII and **Wars** Book I, I Maccabees (which covers the years 167-134), and II Maccabees (which covers the period 175-160 B.C.E.), and Bar Kokhbah, **The Battles of the Hasmoneans: The Times of Judas Maccabeus,** (Jerusalem: Ben Zvi Institute, 1980) (in Hebrew), which presents a detailed description of these battles.

9. Josephus, **Antiquities** Book XIII; and **Wars** Book I.

10. Josephus, **Antiquities** Book XIV, **Wars** Book I, and Martin Noth, **The History of Israel** (2d. Ed.) (New York: Harper Row, 1960), pp. 346-401, which covers the period from Alexander the Great to the Jerusalem victory of Pompey.

11. Zoroastrian influence provided Jewish apocalyptic with a cosmic dualism: a view which allowed the conception of a world as battleground between a good creative principle (Ormazd, or Ahura-Mazda), and an evil disturbing principle (named Angra-Mainyu, or Ahriman). These two principles competed for domination of the world. Cf. among others, the treatment of Zoroastrian

literature in A. C. Bouquet, **Sacred Books of the World**, (Baltimore: Penguin Books, 1954), pp. 104–118, and also Albert T. Olmestead, **History of the Persian Empire**, (Chicago: University of Chicago Press, 1948), John M. Cook, **The Persian Empire** (London: J. M. Dent, 1983), and Richard N. Frye, **The Heritage of Persia**, (London: Weidenfeld & Nicholson, 1966).

12. Cf. Mary Smallwood, **The Jews Under Roman Rule**, (Leiden: E. J. Brill, (1976); John J. Collins, "Jewish Apocalyptic Against Its Hellenistic Near Eastern Environment," **BASOR 220**(1975), pp. 27–36, and Erich S. Gruen, **The Hellenistic World and the Coming of Rome**, 2 Vols. (Berkeley: University of California, 1984).

13. Cf. note 3 above.

14. Which means that it was retrieved from Cave 1 of the Qumran Caves, and has the title *(M)ilhamat Bne Or Bi–Bne Hoshech*, i.e., **The War Between the Sons of Light and the Sons of Darkness.**

15. Cf. Paul D. Hanson, "Jewish Apocalyptic Against Its Near Eastern Environment," **RB** 78 1971), pp. 31–58; John J. Collins, Jewish Apocalyptic Against Its Hellenistic Near Eastern Environment," **BASOR** 220 (1975), PP. 27–36.

16. Cf. Delbert R. Hillers, **Covenant: The History of a Biblical Idea,** (Baltimore: Johns Hopkins Press, 1960); K. Baltzer, **The Covenant Formulary**, transl. David E. Green (Philadelphia: Fortress Press, 1971); and Moshe Weinfeld, "*B'rith*," in **TDOT**, Vol. 2, pp. 253–259.

17. J and E respectively.

18. Cf. Theophile J. Meek, **Hebrews Origins,** (New York: Harper & Row, 1960 c. 1936), pp. 148–183.

19. Cf. Friedman, **Who Wrote The Bible?**, p. 135.

20. The "Chronicles" would have been kept in priestly/scribal repositories near the temple complex in Jerusalem, available to those who possessed "library

cards," as it were.

21. Cf. 1 Samuel 10:1, 2, 5, 6, and 10.

22. Cf. Georg Fohrer, **History of Israelite Religion**, (New York: Abingdon Press, 1972), p. 359: "Ezra's reform finally set the mainstream of Yahwism on the course that turned its back on the insights and principles that had previously prevailed, above all on the message of the prophets." And John Bright, **A History of Israel**, 2d. ed. (Philadelphia: The Westminster Press, 1976), p. 322: "The official promulgation of a written law,...elevated the law until it became in post–exilic times...the first step in the concomitant process whereby the prophetic movement,...came to an end."

23. Thus, the Temple of Jerusalem was rebuilt between 520 and 515/14 B.C.E. and the sacrificial cult resumed.

24. Ezra the priest's duties do not involve him in sacrificial activities performed by priests.

25. Even the side of the bifurcated priestly function split, apparently, into two concerns. This first, the **scribal,** is summed up, although much later, in Ecclesiaticus: "On the other hand he who devotes himself to the study of the law of the Most High will seek out the wisdom of all the ancients, and will be concerned with prophecies;...He will reveal instruction in his teaching, and will glory in the law of the Lord's covenant" (Ecclus. 39:1–4a; 7–8). The second, the **apocalyptic**, is also **learned**, and is understood to be the continuation and "heir" of the "prophetic" inclination.

26. Cf. Paul D. Hanson, **The Dawn of Apocalyptic**, (Philadelphia: Fortress Press, 1975); D. S. Russell, **The Method and Message of Jewish Apocalyptic**, (Philadelphia: The Westminster Press, 1964); Harold H. Rowley, **The Relevance of Apocalyptic**, rev. ed. (New York: Harper & Row, Publishers, 1955); and "Apocalypticism," **IDBS**, pp. 27–34.

27. Cf. note 11 above.

28. That is, **apocalypse**, revelatory knowledge.

29. This, however, is only one battle consisting of seven (7) encounters in its present redacted form. See the discussion in Philip R. Davies, **Qumran**, (Guilford, Surrey: Lutterworth Press, 1982), pp. 118–125.

30. The *pesher* or sectarian commentary, the best example of Qumran editorial activity, is studied by Y. Yadin, "Some Notes on the Newly Published Pesharim of Isaiah," **IEJ** 9 (1959), pp. 39–42; J. Carmignac, *"Notes sur les Pesharim,"* **RQ** 3 (1962), pp. 505–538; and D. Flusser, "The Pesher of Isaiah and the Twelve Apostles," **Eretz Israel** 8 (E. L. Sukenik Memorial Volume, 1967), pp. 52–62 (in Hebrew); J. D. Asmusin, *"Ephriam et Manasee dans Le Pesher de Nahum,"* **RQ** 4 (1964), pp. 389–396; and G. Lambert, *"Traduction de quelques 'psaumes' de qumran et du 'pesher' d'Habacuc,"* **NRT**, (1952), pp. 284–297.

31. 1 QM 1:1.

32. Cf. Isaiah 14:29–31 (an oracle against Philistia) and Isaiah 15–16 (an oracle against Moab), and the discussion in Greene, "Balaam," (1989) pp. 90–92.

33. The Kittim, the final enemy of the Qumran sect, are discussed in R. Goossens, *"Les Kittim du Commentaire d'Habacuc,"* **NC** (1952), 137–170, and O. Eissfeldt, **The Old Testament, an Introduction,** (New York: Harper & Row, 1965), 419–420.

34. Greene, "Balaam," (1990) pp.70–92.

35. Cf. Y. Bear, *"Serekh ha-Yahad-*The Manual of Discipline. A Jewish-Christian Document from the Beginning of the Second Century C.E.," **Zion** 29 (1960), pp. 1–60 (in Hebrew), and Ralph Marcus, "Philo, Josephus and the Dead Sea Yahad," **JBL** LXXI/IV (1952), pp. 207–209.

36. Frank M. Cross, Jr., **The Ancient Library of Qumran and Modern Biblical Studies,** (Garden City, New York: Doubleday & Co., 1961).

37. "...*mbynym 'at–h'am ltwrhb...wswm skl wybynw bmqr'a*" (Nehemiah 8:7–8) is a bit more active than many translations into English would suggest. *mbynym*,

for example, is an active participle of a *hif'il* (causative *binyan* or inflection form). "They caused them to understand" (=*mbynym*) produces an image of much verbal give and take on the part of both Levite Scribe/Assistant to Ezra (the arch Scribe), and person for whom the teaching is intended. "And placing comprehension (on *torah*) they caused (the audience) to understand.

38. These four ranks (Scribes according to Nehemiah 8:7 and 8:9 come from both the **priest** and **Levite** ranks) producing the `priestly estates' suggest a highly stratified self-view of the priestly office in Jerusalem in the Ezra-Nehemiah and Post-Ezra-Nehemiah periods. Gatekeepers, and temple servants are priestly groups whose courses would have required their presence physically within the temple precints. Not so for the groups priest and Levite. These groups appear to have consisted of various specialized substrata groups. See Ezra 7:7 where singers are also mentioned.

39. Friedman, **Who Wrote?**, p. 210, and see discussion engendering note 18, above.

40. There exists no literary complaint, that is, until one reads critically the **Testament of Levi**, a part of the Testament of the Twelve Patriarchs contained in the Pseudepigrapha. The literary view contained therein was probably engendered by the success of the Maccabean revold and hasmonean success. The **Testament of Levi** laments the demise of, and looks forward to the restoration of Levite messiahs (=priest/kings). The Maccabee/Hasmoneans were Levites.

41. Friedman, pp. 217-245; 246-254; especially 218-255 for a discussion of Ezra the Aaronid priest.

42. Cf. Ezra 7:11-14 (and Nehemiah 2:5-9).

43. My previous study of the Balaam cycle has shown that "Balaam" was a "bat" in the grip of numerous "sluggers"; all attempting to bash out each other's brains, or at least to "bash" one another group into submission. The most

vicious "slugger" was P, and to him is traced the distinction between **priest** (a priest) and **Levite** (a priest!). This distinction, or at least dual appellation at Qumran appears to have been most acceptable in light of non-sacrificing priestly self-views expressed in their **writings.** "Balaam" is no longer the enemy–*typos.* Danger is now presented by the Sons of Darkness and the Kittim! Both terms were loaded.

44. See note 30 above.

45. With the Maccabbee/Hasmoneans, specific Levities found themselves enjoying titles such as High Priest and Priest–King, leadership positions in Jerusalem after the death of Onias III. The **Testament of Levi,** mentioned in note 40 above, is sympathetic with this historical situation.

46. Apparently this work was expanded, and thus served as the vehicle for telling the story of the journey of Moses and his host from the mountain of Yahweh to a position in Transjordan opposite Jericho, before continuing across the Jordan.

47. 1QM II (II:1–2).

48. 1QM VII (a)VII:8; (b)VII:10; (c)VII:11; (d)VII:12.

49. 1QM XVI: 2–9.

50. 1QM XVIII: 2.

51. Friedman, **Who?**, p. 211.

52. Ibid., pp. 211–212.

53. 1QS 1:1.

54. But see the Scrolls for a view of the Teacher of Righteousness at Qumran.

55. Below in the Samaritan materials we will view a continuation of this practice.

56. It is largely the material influenced by the P trajectory concerning Balaam which appears in the New Testament.

Chapter 7.   The Samaritan Literature and Balaam:
               The Warring Priesthoods:
               The Hermeneutical Debates Continue

57. Cf. R. J. Coggins, **Samaritans and Jews: The Origins of Samaritanism Reconsidered,** (Atlanta: John Knox Press, 1975), pp. 56, 66; P. R. Ackroyd, **Exile and Restoration,** (London, 1968), p. 150, note 50; and the discussions in M. Noth, **The History of Israel,** (2ed.) (New York: Harper & Row, 1960); and John Bright, **A History of Israel,** (Philadelphia: Westminster Press, 1959).

58. Friedman, **Who?**, pp. 136–149; Brian Peckham, **The Composition of the Deuteronomistic History,** Harvard Semitic Monographs (Atlanta: Scholars Press, 1985), pp. 21–68; Jeremiah; and Lamentations.

59. Cf. Ezra 2; 2 Kings 25:26; 11–12; 24:11–16.

60. Cf. M. Delcor, "*Hinweise auf das Samaritanische Schimsa im Alten Testament,*" **ZAW** 74 (1962), pp. 238ff.

61. Coggins, **Samaritans,** p. 100.

62. Cf. the discussion on page 234, and note 689 on that page, in S. Lowy, **The Principles of Samaritan Bible Exegesis,** *Studia Post–Biblica* (Leiden: E.J. Brill, 1977).

63. Coggins, **Samaritans,** p. 115.

64. Cf. Lee Lavine, "The Political Struggle Between Pharisees and Sadducees in the Hasmonean Period," **Jerusalem in the Second Temple Period: Schalit Memorial Volume,** ed. Aaron Oppenheimer *et al.* (Jerusalem: Ben Zvi Institute, 1981), pp. 61–83; Elias Bickerman, **From Ezra to the Last of the Maccabees,** (New York: Schocken, 1962); Abraham Geiger, **The Bible and Its Translations,** (Jerusalem: 1949), pp. 69–102 (in Hebrew); Louis Finkelstein, **The Pharisees,** 3 Vols. (Philadelphia: Jewish Publication Society, 3rd ed.,

1962), Vol. 2, pp. 637–753; Rudolf Leszynsky, *Die Sadduzaeer*, (Berlin: Meyer & Mueller, 1912); and Jean Le Moyne, **Les Sadduceens**, (Paris: 1972).

65. Cf. Moses Gaster, **The Samaritans: Their History, Doctrine and Literature,** (Sweich Lectures, 1923, London: The British Academy, 1925); John Macdonald, **The Theology of the Samaritans,** (New Testament Library, London: SCM Press, 1964); James A. Montogomery, **The Samaritans, the Earliest Jewish Sect: Their History, Theology and Literature,** (Philadelphia: J.C. Winston, 1907); Yishaq Ben–Zvi, *spr hšmrwnym: twldwthm, mwsbwtyhm, dtm wsprwtm*, (Tel–Aviv: '.y. *stybl*, 1935); James D. Purvis, **The Samaritan Pentateuch and the Origin of the Samaritan Sect,** Harvard Semitic Monographs 2 (Cambridge, MA: Harvard University Press, 1968). For a more recent treatment which critiques the conclusions of the foregoing works, see R.J. Coggins, **Samaritans and Jews: The Origins of Samaritanism Reconsidered,** (Atlanta: John Knox Press, 1975).

66. Coggins, **Samaritans Reconsidered**, p. 100.

67. James D. Purvis, **Origin of the Samaritan Sect,** pp. 16–87; S. Talmon, "The Samaritan Pentateuch," **JJS** ii (1951), pp. 144–150; Ernst Wuerthwein, **The Text of the Old Testament,** (New York: Macmillan, 1957) which mentions an edition by A. von Gall, *Der hebräische Pentateuch der Samaritaner*, produced between 1914 and 1918, and informs the reader that: "The oldest known manuscript in **book–form** is in the Cambridge University Library." (p. 32).

68. According to Wuerthwein: "The problem of the Samaritan Pentateuch is that it deviates from MT in about 6000 instances," and that "Some deviations from MT must be regarded as alterations which the Samaritans introduced in the interests of their own cultus." (p. 31).

69. The text differences between SP and MT are highlighted in *hmšh hwmšy twrh: sfr hšwmrwny* by Avraham and Ratson Sadaqa, (Jerusalem: Reuben Mass, 1965), pp. 38–43. The MT and SP texts are presented side–by–

side and the variations are presented in bold print.

70. Cf. Wuerthwein, **Text**, p. 31.

71. Cf. Purvis, **Origins**, pp. 98–118; Wuerthwein, **Text,** p. 32; and Coggins, **Samaritan Origins,** pp. 105–115.

72. Josephus, **Antiquities**, Book XIII: 3:1–3; **Wars**, Book I: 1:1; Book VII: 10:2–3 provide information concerning Onias IV's flight to Ptolemy at Heliopolis, and his receipt of permission to build a "New Jerusalem" there. This included a new temple.

73. The demise of this office is discussed in Greene, **The Role of the Messenger and Message,** pp. 172–174.

74. J. Macdonald, ed., **The Samaritan Chronicle II** (or *Sepher Ha–Yamim*), (*Beihefte* **ZATW** 107), (Berlin: 1969) A. Neubauer, "*Chronique samaritaine, suivie d'un appendice contenant de courts notices sur quelques autres ouvrages samaritains,*": **JA**, 6e ser., t. 14 (1869), pp. 385–470; Coggins, **Samaritanism Reconsidered,** 116–131.

75. Coggins, **Samaritanism**, pp. 117–120; John Macdonald, **The Theology of the Samaritans**, pp. 44–49; John Bowman, **Samaritan Documents,** Pittsburgh Original Texts and Translation Series (Pittsburgh: The Pickwick Press, 1977), pp. 63–85.

76. Bowman, **Samaritan Documents**, pp. 63–85.

77. Bowman, **Documents**, pp. 248–251.

78. G. Vermes, **Scripture and Tradition**, pp. 127ff.

79. S. Lowy, **Samaritan Bible Exegesis**, p. 43.

80. Ibid., p. 43.

81. Lowy, **Principles**, p. 188, and also note 512 of this page.

82. Bowman, **Documents**, p. 286.

83. Ibid., p. 287.

84. Cf. **Asatir, The Chronicles,** for example, in Moses Gaster, **The Astair, the**

Samaritan Book of the `Secrets of Moses' Together With the Pitron or Samaritan Commentary and the Samaritan Story of the Death of Moses, (London: 1972).

85. Bowman, **Documents,** p. 289.
86. Ibid., p. 285.
87. Ibid., p. 291, note 14.
88. Ibid., pp. 285–286.
89. Ibid., p. 286.
90. Ibid., p. 286.
91. Ibid., p. 286.
92. Ibid., p. 286.
93. Ibid., p. 287.
94. Ibid., p. 288.
95. Ibid., pp. 286–287.
96. Ibid., p. 287.
97. Ibid., p. 287.
98. Ibid., p. 287.
99. Ibid., p. 286.
100. Ibid., p. 286.
101. Ibid., p. 287.
102. Ibid., p. 287.
103. Ibid., p. 287.
104. Ibid., p. 288.
105. Some of the most often consulted sources are E. Baneth, *Des Samaritaners Marqah an die 22 Buchstaben den Grundstück der hebräischen Sprache anknüpfende Abhandlung.* **Heft** i. (Berlin: 1888); M. Hildesheimer, *Marqah's Buch der Wunder nach einer Berliner Handshrift*, (Berlin, 1898); J. Macdonald, ed., *Memar Marqah* (6 Books in 2 Vols.), *Beihefte zu ZATW* 84 (Berlin: 1963;

D. Rettig, *Memar Marqa*, (*Bonner Orientalische Studien. Heft* 8), (Stuttgart 1934); and I. Szuster, *Marqa–Hymnen aus der samaritianischen Liturgie uebersetzt und bearbeitet,* (Bonn: 1936).

106. Lowy, **Exegesis**, p. 366.

107. Cf. James B. Pritchard, ed. **The Ancient Near East: Anthology of Texts and Pictures** (Princenton: Princeton University Press, 1958), pp. 209–210, and see illustration number 74, p. 274.

108. Lowy, **Exegsis,** p. 366. .

109. Cf. notes 110 and 112, plus the discussion of the SP in Macdonald, **Samaritanism Reconsidered,** pp. 151–152, especially note 72 at the bottom of page 152 where he states: "It has not been worked out in a major study, but Cross has devoted a series of articles in journals to his views. See especially "The Contribution of the Qumran Discoveries to the Study of the Hebrew Text," **IEJ,** 16 (1966): pp. 81–95.

Chapter 8. The Book of Enoch (1 Enoch):
The War to Destroy All the Godless

110. Cf. Purvis, **Origin of the Samaritan Sect,** pp. 16–87, and notes 5, 8, 49, 55, 58, 83, 84, 88, 94, 107, 110, 111, 112, 116, 135, 139, 142, 143, 144, 146, 149, 150, therein which demonstrate his dependency on the work of Cross, his mentor, on this subject.

111. Cf. Coggins, **Samaritanism Reconsidered,** pp. 117–118, where discussing Chronicle II, he states: "Two sections have so far been published: the book known as Samaritan Chronicle II, Edited by Professor Macdonald...," and note 81 above.

112. The literature on Enoch is prodigious. Cf. Nathaniel Schmidt, "The

Original Language of the Parables of Enoch," **Old Testament and Semitic Studies in Memory of William Rainey Harper**, ed. R. F. Harper *et al.* (Chicago, 1908), Vol. ii, pp. 329-349; Edward Ullendorf, "An Aramaic *"Vorlage"* of the Ethiopian Text of Enoch," *Atti del Convegno Internazionale di Studi Etiopici (Academia dei Lineci, Problemi attuali di scienza e di cultura* **48**), (Roma, 1960), pp. 259-267; and for a most recent exhaustive study which was designed to upgrade the celebrated work of R. H. Charles, Matthew Black, **The Book of Enoch or I Enoch,** *Studia In Veteris Testamenti Pseudepigrapha* (Leiden: Brill, 1985). All quotes from I Enoch herein are from Black's work.

113. Cf. Matthew Black, **I Enoch,** p. 25.

114. Cf. Yigael Yadin, *Megillath Milhamath Bne Or bi-Bne Hoshech.* (Jerusalem: Bialik Institute, 1956); M. Avi-Yonah, "The `War of the Sons of Light and the Sons of Darkness' and Maccabean Warfare," **IEJ** (1952): 1-5, Flavius Josephus, **Antiquities** Book XIII Maccabees (which covers the period 175-160 B.C.E., and Bar Kokhbah, **The Battles of the Hasmoneans: The Times of Judas Maccabaeus,** (Jersualem: Ben Zvi Institute, 1980) (in Hebrew), which presents a detailed description of these battles.

115. Black, **Enoch,** p. 25.

116. Ibid., p. 25.

117. Cf. Greene, "Balaam '89," pp. 62; 65-67; 68-70; 72-76, and on Enochic material "*Mashal* in the Similitudes of Enoch," **JBL** 100/2 (1981), pp. 1193-1212.

PART 4: Balaam Hermeneutics for Later Ages

Chapter 9. "Balaam During and Beyond the Middle Platonic eriod: The Inability to Jettison the Theme of War

a. Balaam in The New Testament

1. Cf. Robert M. Berchman, "*Arcana Mundi*: Between Balaam and Hecate: Prophecy, Divination, and Magic in Later Platonism," **SBL Seminar Papers** 28, (Atlanta: Scholars Press, 1989), pp. 114–117; 122–124; 128–130. Berchman also includes in his study Clement and Origin of Alexandria's views of Balaam, pp. 124–127; 130–133.

b. Josephus' Antiquities and Balaam

2. Loeb Classical Library, and William P. Whiston, **JOSEPHUS: Complete Works**, (Grand Rapids: Kregel Publications, 1981 c. 1960).

c. The North African Platonists and Balaam

3. Cf. the statement in the Mishna quoted in Montefiore and Loewe, **A Rabbinic Anthology** (New York: Meridian Books, 1963), p. 167, which holds:

> When God created the world, He decreed that 'the heavens are the heavens of the Lord and the earth is for men' (Ps. CXV, 16), but when He intended to give the Law, He repealed the former decree, and He said, 'The Lower shall asscend to the Upper, and the Upper shall descend to the Lower, and I will make a beginning,' as it is said, 'And the Lord came down upon Mount Sinai, and he said unto Moses, Come up unto the Lord'

(Exod. XIX, 20). *Exod. R.*, *Wa'iqra*, XII, 3.)

4. Quoted from *De Specialibus Legibus* in Robert Berchman, "Balaam and Hecate," **SBLSP**, 1989, p. 128.

5. Quoted from *De Cherubim* in Ibid., p. 124.

d. Rabbinical Literature and Balaam

6. Samuel Sandmel, **We Jews and Jesus**, (New York: Oxford University Press, 1965), p.28.

7. Cf. C. G. Montefiore and H. Loewe, **A Rabbinic Anthology**, (New York: Meridian Books), pp. 575–576.

8. Cf. **A Rabbinic Anthology**, p. 57.

9. Ibid, p. 169.

10. Loewe writes in a note on page 653 that:

> In the Sifre (357, f. 150a) we read, on the verse at the end of Deuteronomy (XXXIV, 10), "There arose not in Israel a prophet like Moses, the following comment: `but among the Gentiles, one did arise. Who was this? Balaam. What was the difference between the prophetical powers of Moses and Balaam? Balaam knew who was speaking with him, Moses did not, for Balaam described himself as "he that heareth the words of God and knoweth the knowledge of the Highest"(Num. XXIV, 4). Moses did not know when God would speak with him until God actually spoke: "But Balaam knew in

> advance. When God spoke to Moses, Moses stood (Deut. v, 31): but Balaam lay down when God spoke to him (Num. XXIV. 4). Here we see that Balaam is regarded as superior to Moses....

11. Ibid, pp. 604–605.
12. Ibid, p. 653.
13. Ibid, p. 327.
14. Ibid, p. 517.
15. Ibid, p. 652.
16. Ibid, p. 652.

e. The Medieval Balaam

17. Cf. John Bowman, **Samaritan Documents**, Pittsburgh Original Texts and Translation (Pittsburgh: The Pickwick Press, 1977), pp. 63–85.
18. Cf. Macdonald, **Theology**, pp. 13, 46ff.; and 118.
19. Ibid., pp. 46–47.
20. W. M. Thackston, Jr., **The Tales of the Prophets of** *al–Kisa'i*, Library of Classical Arabic Literature (Boston: Twayne Publishers for G. K. Hall & Co., 1978), pp. 244–245.
21. Joel Chandler Harris, **Balaam and His Master. And Other Sketches and Stories,** (Boston: Houghton Mifflin and Company, 1891).
22. Moshe Leshem, **Balaam's Curse: How Israel Lost Its Way, and How It Can Find It Again,** (New York: Simon and Schuster, 1989).
23. Cf. Berchman, "Balaam and Hecate," on Origen and Clement.

CONCLUSION

1. Morton Smith, **Jesus the Magician**, (New York: Harper & Row, 1978), and John Hull, **Hellenistic Magic and the Synoptic Tradition**, (London: SCM Press, 1974).

BIBLIOGRAPHY

Aharoni, Yohannan and Avi-Yona, Michael, eds. **The Macmillian Bible Atlas.** New York: The Macmillan Co., 1968.

Ackroyd, Peter R. **Exile and Restoration.** London, Philadelphia: Westminster Press, 1968.

Albright, W.F. "The Oracles of Balaam." **JBL** LXIII/III (1944): 207–233.

Asmusin, J.D. "*Ephraim et Manasse dans le Pesher de Nahum.*" **RQ** 4 (1964): 389–396.

Avi-Yonah, M. "The War of the Sons of Light and the Sons of Darkness and Maccabean Warfare." **IEL** (1952): 1–5.

Baer, Y. "*Serekh ha-Yahad*–The Manual of Discipline. A Jewish–Christian Document from the Beginning of the Second Century C.E." **Zion** 29 (1960): 1–60.

Baltzer, K. **The Covenant Formulary.** Philadelphia: Fortress Press, 1971.

Baneth, E. *Des Samaritaners Marqaa an die 22 Buchstaben den Grundstück der hebräischen Sprache anknüpfende Abhandlung.* Heft i. Berlin: 1888.

Bar Kokhbah. **The Battles of the Hasmoneans: The Times of Judas Maccabaeus.** Jerusalem: Ben Zvi Institute, 1980.

Beebe, H. Keith. **The Old Testament.** Belmont, CA: Dickenson, 1970.

Ben-Zvi, Yishaq. *spr hšmrwnym: tyldwthm, mwsbwtyhm, dtm wsprwtm.* Tel-Aviv:'.y. stybl, 1935.

Berchman, Robert M. **From Philo to Origen: Middle Platonism in Transition.** Brown Judaic Studies, Chicago, CA: Scholars Press, 1984.

_____."*Arcana Mundi*: Between Balaam and Hecate: Prophecy, Divination, and Magic in Later Platonism." **SBL Seminar Papers** 28. Atlanta: Scholars Press, 1989.

_____. "*Arcana Mundi*: Prophecy, Divination in the *Vita Mosis* of Philo of Alexandria." **SBL Seminar Papers** 28. Atlanta: Scholars Press, 1988.

_____. "*Arcana Mundi*: Magic Divination in the *De Somniis* of Philo of Alexandria." **SBL Seminar Papers** 27. Atlanta: Scholars Press, 1987.

Bickerman, Elias. **From Ezra to the Last of the Maccabees**. New York: Schocken, 1962.

Black, Matthew. **The Book of Enoch or I Enoch**. *Studia In Veteris Testamenti Pseudepigrapha*. Leiden: Brill, 1985.

Bouquet, A.C. **Sacred Books of The World**. Baltimore: Penguin Books, 1954.

Bowman, John. **Samaritan Documents**. Pittsburgh Original Texts and Translation Series. Pittsburgh: The Pickwick Press, 1977.

_____. "The Exegesis of the Pentateuch Among the Samaritans and Among the Rabbis," *Oudtestamentische Studiën* 8, Leiden, 1950.

Bright, John. **A History of Israel**. 2d. Ed. Philadelphia: The Westminster Press, 1976.

Brooke, George J. **Exegesis at Qumran: 4QFlorilegium in Its Jewish Context**. Sheffield: **JSOT** Press, 1985.

Brueggemann, Walter. "Amos IV. 4-13 and Israel's Covenant Workship." **VT** (1965): 1-15.

Burrows, Miller. **The Dead Sea Scrolls**. New York: Viking Press, 1955.

Buttrick, George A. Ed. **The Interpreters' Dictionary of the Bible**. A-D. New York: Abingdon Press, 1962.

Carmignac, J. "*Notes sur lés Persharim*." **RQ** 3 (1962): 505-538.

Cazelles, H. *Lés Nombres*. Paris: Lés Editions du Cerf, 1958.

Coggins, R. J. **Samaritans and Jews. The Origins of Samaritanism Reconsidered**. Atlanta: John Knox Press, 1975.

Collins, John J. "Jewish Apocalyptic Against Its Hellenistic Near Eastern Environment." **BASOR** 220 (1975): 27-36.

Cook, John M. **The Persian Empire**. London: J.M. Dent, 1983.

Cross, Frank Moore Jr. **The Ancient Library of Qumran and Modern Biblical Studies**. Garden City, New York: Doubleday, 1958.

_____. "The Council of Yahweh in Second Isaiah." **JNES** XII (1953): 274–279.

Davies, Philip R. **Qumran**. Guilford, Surrey: Lutterworth Press, 1982.

Davies, Benjamin Ed. **Hebrew and Chaldee Lexicon**. Boston: Bradley & Woodruff, 1875.

Davis, T. Witton. **Magic Divination, and Demonology Among the Hebrews and Their Neighbors**. New York: **KTAV** Publishing House, 1960 c. 1898.

Delcor, M. "*Hinweise auf das Samaritanische Schisma im Alten Testament.*" **ZAW** 74 (1962): 238ff.

DeVries, Simon J. **Prophet Against Prophet: The Role of the Michaiah Narrative (I Kings 22) in the Development of Early Prophetic Tradition**. Grand Rapids: Eerdmans, 1978.

Dupont–Sommer, A. **The Essene Writings From Qumran**. New York: The World Publishing Company, 1967.

Eissfeldt, Otto. **The Old Testament: An Introduction**. Harper & Row, 1965.

Feldman, Louis. "Prophecy in Josephus," **SBL Seminar Papers** 27, 1988, pp. 424–441.

Finkelstein, Louis. **The Pharisees**. 3 Vols. Philadelphia: Jewish Publication Society, 1962.

Fishbane, Michael. **Biblical Interpretation in Ancient Israel**. Oxford: Claredon Press, 1985.

Fitzmyer, J.A. **The Dead Sea Scrolls. Mayor Publications and Tools for Study**. Missoula: Scholars Press, 1975.

_____. **The Aramaic Inscriptions of Sefire**. Rome: Pontifical Biblical Institute, 1967.

Flusser, David. "The *Pesher* of Isaiah and the Twelve Apostles." *Eretz Israel* 8 E.L. Sukenik Memorial Volume, 1967.

Fohrer, Georg. **History of Israelite Religion**. New York: Abingdon Press, 1972.

Frye, Richard N. **The Heritage of Persia**. London: Weidenfeld & Nicholson, 1966.

Friedman, Richard E. **Who Wrote the Bible**? Englewood Cliffs, New Jersey: Prentice Hall, 1987.

Garbini, Giovanni. "*L'iscrizione di Balaam Bar–Beor.*" *Henoch* 1 (1979): 166–188.

Gaster, Moses. **The Samaritans: Their History, Doctrine and Literature**. Sweich Lectures, 1923. London: The British Academy. 1925.

Gaster, T. H. **The Dead Sea Scriptures**. Garden City, New Jersey: Doubleday and Co., 1956.

Geiger, Abraham. **The Bible and Its Translations**. Jerusalem: 1949.

Ginzberg, Louis. **The Legends of the Jews**. 7 Vols. Philadelphia, Jewish Publications Society, 1946.

Glatzer, Nahum. N. **The Essential Philo**. New York: Schocken Books, 1971.

Goossens, R. "*Lés Kittim du Commentaire d'Habacuc.*" **NC** (1952): 137–170.

Gottwald, Norman K. **The Tribes of Yahweh: A Sociology of the Religion of Liberated Israel**, 1250–1050 B.C.E. Maryknoll, New York: Orbis Books, 1979.

Gray, J. **Numbers: A Critical and Exegetical Commentary**. Edinburgh: T. & T. Clark, 1965 c. 1903.

Greene, John T. **The Role of the Messenger and Message in the Ancient Near East**. Brown Judaic Studies 169. Atlanta: Scholars Press, 1989.

_____. "Balaam: Prophet, Diviner, and Priest In Selected Ancient Israelite And Hellenistic Jewish Sources." **SBL Seminar Papers**. Atlanta: Scholars

Press, 1989.

_____. "Balaam as Figure and Type in Ancient Semitic Literature to the First Century B.C.E., With a Survey of Post–Philo Applications of the Balaam Figure and Type." **SBL Seminar Papers**. Atlanta: Scholars Press, 1990.

Grueun, Erich S. **The Hellenistic World and the Coming of Rome**. 2 Vols. Berkeley: University of California, 1984.

Hackett, Jo Ann. **The Balaam Text From Deir 'Allā**. Chicago: Scholars Press. 1980.

Hamilton, Neil Q. "Temple Cleansing and Temple Bank." **JBL** LXXXIII (Dec. 1964) Part IV: 365–372.

Hanson, Paul D. **The Dawn of Apocalyptic**. Philadelphia: Fortress Press, 1975.

_____. "Jewish Apocalyptic Against Its Near Eastern Environment." **RB** 78 (1971): 31–58.

Harvey, J. "*Le Rîb–Pattern' requistoire prophetique sur la rupture de l'alliance.*" *Biblica* 43 (1962): 172–196.

Hermann, W. "*Die Goettersoehne.*" **ZRRG** XII (1960): 242–251.

Hesse, Franz, "*Wurzelt die prophetische Gerichsrede im Israelitischen Kult?*" **ZAW** 65 (1953): 45–53.

Hildesheimer, M. *Marqa's Buch der Wunder nach einer Berliner Handschrift*. Berlin: 1898.

Hillers, Delbert R. **Covenant: The History of a Biblical Idea**. Baltimore: Johns Hopkins Press. 1960.

Hoftijzer, Jacob. "The Prophet Balaam in a 6th Century Aramaic Inscription." **BA** 39 (1976) 11–17.

Jones, Gwilym. "Holy–war" or "Yahweh–war?" *Vetus Testamentum*. Vol. XXV (1975): 642–650.

Jongeling, B. **A Classified Bibliography of Finds in the Desert of Judah**.

1958-1969. Leiden: Brill, 1971.

Kingsbury, Edwin C. "The Prophets and the Council of Yahweh." **JBL** LXXXVIII No. 3 (1964): 279-286.

Kirshbaum, E. *"Der Prophet Balaam und die Anbetung der Weisen."* **RQ** 49 (1954), pp. 129-171.

Kugel, James. **The Idea of Biblical Poetry: Parallelism and Its History**. New Haven: Yale University Press, 1981.

Lambert, G. *"Traduction de quelques `psaumes' de Qumran et du `pesher' d'Habacuc."* **NRT** (1952): 284-297.

Lavene, Lee. "The Political Struggle Between Pharisees and Sadducees in the Hasmonean Period." **Jerusalem in the Second Temple Period: Schalit Memorian Volume**. Ed. Aaron Oppenheimer *et al*. Jerusalem: Ben Zvi Institute, 1981.

Lemaire, André. *"Vers l'histoire de la redaction des livres des Rois."* **ZAW** 98 (1986): 221-236.

_____. "Fragments from the Book of Balaam Found at Deir 'Allā." **BAR** (Sept.- Oct. 1985) Vol. XI No. 5: 26-39.

Leibowitz, Nehama. **Studies in BaMidbar (Numbers)**. Jerusalem: The World Zionist Organization, 1980.

Le Moyne, Jean. *Lés Sadduceens*. Paris: 1972.

Leshem, Moshe. **Balaam's Curse: How Israel Lost Its Way, and How It Can Find It Again**, (New York: Simon and Schuster, 1989).

Leszynsky, Rudolf. *Die Sadduzäer*. Berlin: Meyer & Mueller, 1912.

Levine, Baruch. "The Deir 'Allā Plaster Inscriptions." **JAOS** 101 (1981): 195-205.

Lowy, S. **The Principles of Samaritan Bible Exegesis**. *Studia Post-Biblica*. Leiden: Brill, 1977.

Macdonald, John. **The Theology of the Samaritans**. New Testament Library.

London: SCM Press, 1964.

_____. **The Samaritan Chronicle II (or Sepher Ha-Yamim)**. *Beihefte zu* **ZATW** 107. Berlin: 1969.

_____. ed. *Memar Marqah* (6 Books in 2 Vols.) *Beihefte zu* **ZATW** 84 Berlin: 1963.

Marcus, Ralph. "Philo, Josephus and the Dead Sea Yahad." **JBL** LXXI/IV (1952): 207-209.

_____."A Textual and Exegetical Note on Philo's Bible." **JBL** LXIX/IV (1950): 363-365.

Marsh, John and Butzer, Albert, eds. **The Book of Numbers. The Interpreter's Bible**. Volume II. New York: Abingdon-Cokesbury Press, 1953.

May, Herbert G. ed. **Oxford Bible Atlas**. London: Oxford University Press, 1962.

McCarter, P. Kyle, Jr. "The Balaam Texts From Deir 'Allā: The First Combination." **BASOR** 239 (1980): 49-60.

McNeile, A.H. **The Book of Numbers**. Cambridge: At the University Press, 1931.

Meek, Theophile J. **Hebrew Origins**. New York: Harper & Row, 1936.

Mendenhall, George. **Law and Covenat in Israel and the Ancient Near East**. Pittsburgh: The Biblical Colloquium, 1955.

Miller, Patrick D., Jr. **The Divine Warrior in Early Israel**. Cambridge, Massachusetts: Harvard University Press, 1973.

Montefiore, C.G. & Loewe, H. **A Rabbinic Anthology**. New York, Cleveland, & Philidelphia: Meridian Books, 1963.

Montgomery, James A. **The Samaritans. The Earliest Jewish Sect: Their History, Theology and Literature**. Philadelphia: J.C. Winston, 1970.

Mueller, Hans-Peter. *"Die aramäische Inschrift von Deir 'Allā und die älteren*

Bileamsprüche." **ZAW** 94 (1982): 214–244.

Naveh, Joseph. "The Date of the Deir 'Allā Inscription in Aramaic Script." **IEJ** 17 (1967): 256–258.

Neubauer, A. "*Chronique samaritaine, suivie d'un appendice contenant de courts notices sur quelques autres ouvrages samaritians.*" **JA** 6e ser., 7. 14 (1869): 3855–470.

Neusner, Jacob, *et al.* **Religion, Science, and Magic: In Concert and in Conflict**. Oxford: Oxford University Press, Inc., 1989.

Noth, Martin. **The History of Israel**. 2d Ed. New York: Harper & Row, 1960.

Olmstead, Albert T. **History of the Persian Empire**. Chicago: University of Chicago Press, 1948.

Orlinsky, Harry. **Ancient Israel**. Ithaca, New York: Cornell University Press, 1960.

Peckman, Brian. **The Comparative Study of the Deuteronomistic History**. Atlanta: Scholars Press, 1985.

Peet, T.E. **A Comparative Study of the Literatures of Egypt. Palestine and Mesopotamia: Egypt's Contribution to the Literature of the Ancient World**. London: Oxford University: Press, 1931.

Pfeiffer, Charles. **The Dead Sea Scrolls**. Grand Rapids, MI: Baker Books, 1962.

Pritchard, James B., Ed. **The Ancient Near East: An Anthology of Texts and Pictures**. Princeton: Princeton University Press, 1958.

Purvis, James D. **The Samaritan Pentateuch and the Origin of the Samaritan Sect**. Harvard Semitic Monographs 2 Cambridge: Harvard University Press, 1968.

Rabin, Chiam. **The Zodokite Documents**. Oxford: Oxford University Press, 1953.

Reventlow, H. Graf. *Das Amt des Propheten bei Amos. Forschung zur Religion und Literatur des Alten und Neuen Testaments* 80. Göttingen, West Germany: *Vandenhoeck und Ruprecht*, 1962.

Rettig, D. *Memar Marqa. Bonner Orientalische Studien Heft* 8. Stuttgart: 1934.

Ringgren, Helmer. "*Bileam och inskrifen fran Deir 'Allā.*" *Religion Och Bibel* 36 (1977) 85-89.

Robinson, H. Wheeler. "The Council of Yahweh." **JTS** XLV (1945): 151-157 in **Inspiration and Revelation in the Old Testament**. Oxford: Oxford University Press, 1946.

Rofe, Alexander. **The Book of Balaam** (Numbers 22:2-24:25). Jerusalem: Simor Ltd., 1979 [In Hebrew].

Rowley, Harold H. **The Relevance of Apocalyptic**. Rev. Ed. New York: Harper & Row, 1955.

_____. "Apocalypticism." **IDBSV**: 27-34.

Russell, D.S. **The Method and Message of Jewish Apocalyptic**. Philadelphia: The Westminster Press, 1964.

Sadaqa, Avraham and Ratson. *hmšh hwmšy twrh: sfr bmdbr: hmwsh hmswrtyh whnwsh hšwmrwny*. Jerusalem: Reuben Mass, 1965.

Sandmel, Samuel. **We Jews and Jesus**. New York: Oxford University Press, 1965.

Schmidt, Nathaniel. "The Original Language of the Parables of Enoch." **In Old Testament and Semitic Language Studies in Memory of William Rainey Harper**. Ed. R.F. Harper *et al*. Chicago: 1908.

Schulte, Hannelis. **Die Entstehung der Gerichtsschreibung im Alten Israel**. **BZAW**. Berlin: Walter de Gruyter, 1972.

Smallwood, Mary. **The Jews Under Roman Rule**. Leiden: Brill, 1976.

Sturdy, John. **Numbers**. Cambridge: Cambridge University Press, 1976.

Szuster, I. *Marqa–Hymnen aus der samaritainischen Liturgie uebersetzt und bearbeitet.* Bonn: 1936.

Talmon, S. "The Samaritan Pentateuch." **JJS** ii (1951): 144–150.

Thackston, W.M. Jr. **The Tales of the Prophets of Al-Kisa'i. Library of Classical Arabic Literature.** Boston: Twayne Publishers for G.K. Hall Co., 1978.

Ullendorf, Edward. "An Aramaic *"Vorlage"* of the Ethiopian Text of Enoch." *Atti del Convegno Internazionale di Studi Etiopici (Academia del Lincei.* **Problemi** *attuali di scienza e di cultur 48*). Roma: 1960.

Van Seters, John. "Histories and Historians of the Ancient Near East." *Orientalia.* 50 (1981): 137–185.

Vermes, Geza. **Scripture and Tradition in Judaism.** *Studia Post Biblica. Volumen Quartum* (Haggadic Studies) Leiden: E.J. Brill, 1961.

Von Rad, Gerhard. **The Problem of the Hexateuch and Other Essays.** London: Oliver & Boyd, 1956.

Watts, J.D.W. **Vision and Prophecy in Amos.** Grand Rapids: W.B. Eerdmans, 1958.

Weinfeld, Moshe. "*B'rith.*" **TDOT** Vol. 2: 252–259.

Weippert, Helga and Manfred. "*Die Bileam–Inschrift von Tell Deir 'Allā.*" **ZDPV** 98 (1982): 77–103.

Wuerthwein, Ernst. "*Der Ursprung der prophetischen Gerichtsrede.*" **ZThK** 49 (1955) 1–16.

_____. **The Text of the Old Testament.** New York: Macmillan, 1957.

Yadin, Yigael. *Megillath Milhamath Bne Or bi–Bne Hosehech.* Jerusalem: The Bialik Institute, 1956.

_____. "Some Notes on the Newly Published *Pesharim* of Isaiah." **IEJ** 9 (1959): 39–42.

Yahuda, A.S. "The Name of Balaam's Homeland." **JBL LXIV** (1945): 547–551.

GENERAL INDEX

(King) Ahab 10
(King) Bela 11, 23
(King) Hezekiah 43, 51, 55,67,74,98
Aaron 43, 44, 56, 96, 132, 190, 99, 214
Aaronid 7, 16, 36, 37, 42–44, 47, 55–57, 60–62, 73, 74, 92, 94, 98, 101, 119, 122,131, 132, 182, 84–186, 197
Abel 13
Abiathar 55, 56, 98, 174, 181, 184, 186
Adversary 4, 26, 27, 57, 110, 150, 178
Agag 38, 39, 190, 191
Ahab 10, 11, 16, 152, 182
Ahaz 11, 51, 52, 59, 61–64
Ahijah 11
Al Kisa'i 12, 165, 167, 169
Alexander Balas 85
Alexander Jannaeus 85, 86
Amalek 24, 25, 34, 91, 118, 190
Amalekites 38, 39, 190
Amaw 24, 59, 63, 77, 79
Ammon 19, 36, 66, 76, 80, 92, 106, 113, 181
Amos 6, 57, 58, 89, 121, 187, 210, 216, 218
Amram 126, 127, 130
Anathoth 6, 56, 186
Angel 13, 113, 114, 119, 120, 124, 142, 147, 150, 152,
Anthiochus IV Epiphanes 85
Apocalypse of Weeks 138
Aram 19, 24, 28, 33, 36, 62, 64, 215
Aramaic 2, 22, 140, 204, 211, 213, 216, 218
Aramean 23

Aristobulus I 85, 86
Aristobulus II 86
Arnon River 25, 31
Ashdod 52–54, 181
Ass 27, 30, 32, 48, 113, 121, 143–145, 147, 156, 157,163, 190
Asshur 35, 39, 41, 64, 78
Assyria 34, 38, 39, 41, 46, 47, 52–54, 59, 62–64, 67, 74, 78, 79, 91, 118, 177, 181, 185, 187
Ba'al 73, 74, 80
Babylonian Talmud 12, 169
Balaam 1, 3–5, 7–12, 8, 9, 12, 14, 15, 17–31, 33–48, 51, 53, 57, 58, 59–84, 87, 91,92, 94–96, 99, 101, 104–117, 119, 120, 121–129, 131–158, 160–177, 212–215, 217, 218
Balaam ben Beor 2, 5, 8, 10, 37 68
Balak 11, 18, 19, 24–26, 28, 31, 47, 59–63, 67, 70, 71, 75, 79–81, 112, 113–117, 120, 125, 128, 132, 142, 144, 145, 148, 150, 152, 155, 157, 160, 167
Bamoth 25, 31
Beor 3, 8, 10, 11, 2, 3, 5, 8, 23, 37, 42, 68–70, 73, 131, 136, 143, 162, 164, 171
Berrien Cozart 156–158
Billville 156, 158
Book of Secrets 125
bronze serpent 28, 49
burning 13
Cain 143
Calvin 57

Canaanites 31, 33, 69, 133
Christ 10, 143, 148, 163
Congregation 46, 60, 70, 98
covenant 4, 9, 10, 27–29, 34, 49, 50, 52, 73, 75, 76, 88–90, 120, 143, 144, 163, 164, 174, 178, 182, 183, 187, 190, 194, 195, 209, 210, 213
curse 10, 63, 77, 79–81, 108, 113, 114, 116, 129, 130, 139, 144, 160, 168, 207, 214
cycle 4, 17–20, 22–27, 29–32, 35, 36, 38, 39, 42–49, 51, 53, 57–62, 64, 65, 68–71, 73, 78, 80, 83, 87, 91, 92, 95, 96, 99, 105, 106, 112, 119–121, 126, 127, 131, 132, 135, 136, 140, 142–144, 154–157, 160, 165, 166, 168, 176, 177, 182, 185, 188–190, 197
Cyprus 29, 92
David 11, 16, 25, 39, 66, 68, 70, 88, 162, 164, 171, 174, 177, 180, 181, 184, 186, 194, 212
Dead Sea 36, 84, 179, 192, 193, 196, 210–212 215, 216
Deir 'Allā 4, 5, 24, 84, 136, 137, 140, 163, 164, 167, 171, 172, 213, 214, 215–218
deity 3, 4, 9, 11–14, 18, 22, 25, 29, 33, 39, 45, 61, 71, 81, 91, 111, 113, 116, 117, 119–122, 133, 148, 155, 162, 165, 166, 176, 178
Deutero-Isaiah 11, 89
Deutero-Zechariah 13, 89, 90, 121, 135
Deuteronomistic History 6, 77, 78, 84, 123, 192, 199, 216

Dibon 25
divine warrior 32, 71, 190, 215
Documentary Hypothesis 6, 21, 42, 48, 65, 164, 182–184
dream 4, 13, 140
Eber 35, 39, 78
Edom 11, 23–25, 31, 36, 38, 39, 41, 42, 62–64, 85, 91, 95, 118, 137, 181, 183
Egypt 31, 39, 51, 52, 54, 75, 76, 95, 117, 119, 120, 149, 172, 173, 216
El 2, 22, 117, 120
Eldad 10
Elohist 20
Emperor David 39
Eshnunna 11
Euphrates 24, 39, 80, 144
Exegetical Method 49
exilic 10, 11, 42, 43, 84, 89, 90, 93, 102, 135, 165, 183, 195
Ezekiel 11, 89
Ezra 7, 68, 83, 90, 93, 101, 102, 183, 188, 195, 197, 199, 210
fable 22, 26, 27, 30, 32, 35, 39, 45, 46, 48, 50, 51, 66
gazer 19, 27, 28, 66, 99, 130, 137, 177
Haggai 11, 89
Hammurabi 11, 25, 70
Hasmonean 103, 165, 197, 199, 214
Heliopolis 119, 201
High Priest 56, 85, 86, 90, 96, 97, 186, 198
Hiram of Tyre 11, 25
Holy War 50, 74–76, 81, 99, 137, 190
Hulda 10
Iamani 52, 53

GENERAL INDEX

Janus 12
Jeremiah 3, 6, 11, 29, 78, 89, 101,
  102, 166, 174, 199
Jeroboam I 101, 152, 184
Jerusalem 6, 7, 10, 11, 18, 19,
  42–47, 51–63, 67, 70,
  74–77, 85–87, 89–91, 93,
  98, 101, 102, 104, 122,
  152, 165, 166, 170, 171,
  174, 177, 181, 182, 184,
  187, 188, 191, 193–195,
  197–201, 204, 209, 212,
  214, 217, 218
Jesus 10, 148, 149, 161–163, 167,
  206, 208, 217
Jezebel 16
Jochebed 126
John Hyrcanus I 85, 86
John Hyrcanus II 86
Josephus 5, 12, 144, 145, 162,
  165, 167, 169, 193, 196,
  201, 204, 205, 211, 215
Josiah 16, 28, 77, 88, 132, 165,
  171
Judah 18, 24, 33, 34, 36, 41, 46,
  51, 53, 54, 58, 59, 61–64,
  67, 68, 72, 76, 79, 85, 88,
  89, 92, 101, 102, 132, 152,
  155, 162, 163, 180–184,
  187, 191, 193, 213
Kenites 34, 39, 64, 78, 118, 179,
  181
King 10, 11, 5, 8, 10, 11, 16, 18,
  21, 23, 24, 28, 38, 39,
  41–43, 46, 51, 52, 54, 55,
  60–64, 66, 67, 69, 70, 74,
  75, 86, 88, 89, 92, 98,
  101, 162, 164, 180, 183,
  186, 190, 191, 198
Kittim 29, 35, 39, 49, 64, 67, 78,
  91, 92, 196, 198, 212
Korah 143
legend 11, 25, 40, 169, 181

Levant 11, 41, 46, 92, 169
Levites 56, 58, 71–73, 93, 96–99,
  102, 174, 193, 197
"light motif" 126, 127
Light 8, 10, 3, 7, 17, 24, 30, 33,
  51, 64–66, 75, 91, 95, 105,
  120, 126, 127, 128, 130,
  137, 145, 168, 183, 184,
  193, 194, 198, 204, 209
Lipit-Ishtar 11
Luther 57
Lyeabarim 31
Manasseh 16, 47, 59, 64, 152
mantic 8, 10, 13, 18, 19, 27, 39,
  41, 50, 61, 63, 65, 66, 79,
  130, 164
Mantology 18, 44, 164
Mashal 23, 25, 28, 29, 32, 33, 35,
  49, 51, 71, 115–118, 126,
  140, 157, 204
Masoretic Text (MT) 104
Mattaniah 11, 86, 89
meaning 6, 12, 17–19, 23, 26, 29,
  48, 49, 51, 53, 57, 61, 63,
  65, 72, 80, 81, 92, 105,
  106, 112, 113, 119, 131,
  138, 160, 176, 177, 183
Medad 10
mediator 10, 13, 164
Melchizedek 10
Memar Marqah 133, 202, 215
Mesopotamia 77–79, 173, 216
Methuselah 137, 140, 162
Micah 4, 6, 29, 57–59, 75, 76, 80,
  87, 89, 124, 126, 165, 187,
  191
Michaiah 3, 11, 166, 172, 211
Mishna 205
Moab 18, 19, 21, 24, 25, 28, 31,
  38, 39, 41, 46, 50, 53, 54,
  63, 64, 70, 73, 75, 76, 80,
  81, 95, 96, 99, 117, 133,
  137, 150, 166, 175,

179–183, 187, 196
Moabite 53, 76, 79, 133, 155
monarch 3, 10, 11, 25, 38, 41, 49, 63, 70, 77, 162–164, 167, 168, 171
Moresheth 57, 75, 76, 187
Moses 5, 10, 28, 30, 31, 43, 45, 49, 53, 56, 65, 69, 70, 72, 73, 75, 120, 123–134, 139, 146, 151, 152, 154, 155, 162, 164, 166, 184, 185, 190, 198, 200–202, 205–207, 212
Mount Gerizim 104, 112, 166
Mount Hor 31
Mushite 16, 20, 36, 37, 56, 72, 73, 77, 92, 94, 98, 102, 122, 127, 131, 132, 133, 184, 186
Muslim 155, 168
Nag Hammadi Library 10, 171
Narrative Framework 22, 25, 30, 31, 34, 35, 65, 177, 185
Nathan 10, 11
New Testament 5, 6, 10, 12, 57, 142, 143, 167, 169, 171, 198, 200, 205, 214
Noah 13
Numbers 4, 10, 11, 17, 18, 20, 21, 23, 24, 26, 28, 31, 33, 35, 44–46, 48, 60, 54–67, 69–75, 77–80, 83, 84, 87, 91, 92, 95, 96, 99, 106, 111, 119, 122, 124–126, 128, 132, 133, 136, 137, 143, 145, 147, 155, 160, 163, 165, 170, 174, 175, 177–182, 184, 186, 187, 189, 190, 191, 212, 214, 215, 217
Oboth 31
Old Testament 6, 57, 172, 175, 176, 180, 186, 187, 196, 200, 204, 209, 211, 217, 218
Onias 118, 198, 201

Origen 145, 147–149, 167, 170, 207, 209

paradigm 3, 4, 10, 12, 15, 17, 99, 171, 173
parallelismus membrorum 23, 28, 75
Peor 25, 34, 60, 70–74, 80, 84
Persia 8, 87, 194,
Peshitto 22
Pethor 24, 59, 63, 77, 79
Philistia 52, 53, 64, 187, 196
Philo 8, 145–147, 149, 165, 167, 170, 196, 209, 210, 212, 213, 215
Philo Seminar 8
Pilti 12, 127–132, 139, 148, 163, 166, 169, 189
Pisgah 25, 31, 33
Poem(s) 34
Pompey 86, 193
post–exilic 42, 89, 90, 93, 135, 165, 183, 195
pre–exilic 43, 90, 135, 183
priest–kings 11, 89, 90
Propriediv 5, 37, 39, 47, 50, 57, 59, 66, 84, 99, 120, 131, 132, 138, 139, 179, 191
Qumran 4, 7, 22, 83–85, 87, 91–96, 99, 103, 118, 122, 131, 134, 136, 137, 138–140, 165, 166, 176, 186, 192–194, 196, 198, 203, 210, 211, 214
Qumranities 12, 169
River 24, 25, 31, 36, 39, 59, 63, 65, 77, 79, 80, 157, 158
River of Egypt 39
sacerdotal 3, 11, 6, 16, 47, 55, 56, 62, 72, 74, 88, 92, 102, 122, 132, 164, 165, 169,

173, 184
Sacred Tree 12
Sadducees 103, 199, 214
Salome 86
Samaria 52, 56, 78, 85, 101–103, 184, 187, 191
Samaritan Pentateuch 4, 7, 104, 123, 132, 166, 200, 216, 218
Sargon 52–54, 183
Saul 11, 16, 89, 151, 174, 190, 191
scribe(s) 2
seer 11, 2, 4, 19, 27, 50, 66, 129–131, 137, 163, 164, 168
Seir 38, 95, 118, 137
Seleucid 85
Sennacherib 46, 54, 181
Septuagint(s) 22
serpent 28, 32, 49, 53
setting 24, 35–39, 41, 43, 46, 47, 49, 51, 53, 56, 59, 68, 71
Shalmaneser 52
Shamash 4
Sheshbazaar 102
Sheth 38, 39, 41, 95, 96, 118, 137, 183
Shiloh 3, 7, 16, 20, 36, 37, 40, 41, 43, 55, 58, 66, 72, 75–77, 98, 102, 123, 127, 182, 191
shoresh 17, 104, 160
Simon 85, 86, 172, 207, 211, 214
Sinai–Horeb 9
Sodom and Gomorrah 13
Solomon 11, 16, 23, 25, 39, 47, 56, 58, 66, 70, 98, 171, 174, 181, 186
Spokesperson 3, 12, 14, 164, 165
suzerain 62, 63
Syria 24, 39, 49, 51, 62, 63

Syriac 22, 28
Tabernacle 60, 71, 72, 180
Talmud 12, 148, 149, 169
TaNaK 7, 6, 7, 13, 42, 49, 56, 83, 87, 98, 102, 123, 134, 173
telos 27
"thumb print" 45, 57
Tiglathpileser 52
torah 7, 87, 88, 90, 93, 162, 173, 182, 197
Tryphon 85, 57
typos 74–76, 80, 198
United Monarchy 39, 41, 42, 72, 181
United Nations 159, 168
Ur–nammu 11
vassal 40, 52, 59, 62, 182, 187
Vulgate 22
Wadi Maghara 39
Wagner 8
War 3–5, 7, 12, 2, 4, 9, 34, 50, 63, 65, 67–69, 71, 73–77, 81, 83–87, 91, 92, 94–96, 99, 131, 136–138, 142, 156, 157, 159, 166, 172, 186, 189, 190, 192–194, 203, 204, 209, 213
War Scroll 7, 84, 87, 91, 92, 95, 96, 99, 137, 138, 166
watchers 103, 138, 139
Weltanschauung 6, 7, 49, 131
wizard 13, 66, 129–131, 145, 148
Yahweh 14, 17–20, 22, 25–27, 29, 31–33, 35, 39, 46, 49, 50, 55, 60, 61, 63–68, 71, 73–77, 79, 81, 88, 95, 99, 101, 111, 112, 113–121, 128, 131, 133, 139, 143–145, 164, 172, 176, 178, 180, 185, 186, 190, 198, 211–214, 217
Yahweh War 65, 67, 71

Yahwist 20, 21, 52, 191
Zadok 55, 56, 98, 99, 181, 186
Zadokite 42, 55–57, 62, 72, 74,
　　　　85, 92–94, 98, 119, 131,
　　　　132, 166, 184
Zechariah 11, 13, 89, 90, 121, 135
Zedekiah (Mattaniah) 11, 86
Zerubbabel 102, 183
Zion 55, 196, 209
Zophim 25, 33

ANCIENT NEAR EASTERN TERMINOLOGY INDEX

'alh 114
'altk 114
'ams 133
'at rwb'a 115
'bd 23
'dm 24
'elohim 22
'l 22
'lywn 22
'rm 24
aleph 105
bamidbar sinay 105, 106, 121, 174, 175, 214
bene 36
bereyshit 105
bl' 11
bl'm 11
bny 'mw 19
bpy 110, 112, 116
brk 80, 81, 115, 160
brkt brk 115
bt' 26
bw' 17
dbr wl' yqymynh 18, 67
dbr yhwh 14
dbr–yhwh 26
ebed 168
El 2, 22, 117, 120
fin 150
glh 26, 27, 29, 49, 50
hartum 10
heh 105
hozeh 10, 28
ht' 26, 27
hyh 17
hzh 2, 164
immot hakkriyyah 105, 107
Kittim 29, 35, 39, 49, 64, 67, 78, 91, 92, 196, 198, 212
ktym 29
ktyym 29, 49
lfny 105, 110
matlah 140
melachim 88

mem 11, 23
meshalim 25, 29–32, 35, 37, 39, 41, 42, 48–50, 58, 59, 66, 126, 127, 140, 166, 168
mishle shlomo 23
ml' 17
mshl 23, 32–35, 38, 39, 41, 58, 62, 64, 140, 180
mtlh 140
mwl 112
mwrh 105
mwtry'aw 117
nabi' 66
nahash 32
Nebo 25
nhsh 28, 49
nhsh nhshym 28, 49
p'amym 117
Peor 25, 34, 60, 70–74, 80, 84
pesher 94, 196, 209, 212, 214
Pisgah 25, 31, 33
pth 26
qrb 104, 105
qrbn 105
qrqr 118
qsm 12, 28, 29, 49, 58–60
qwm 18
ro'eh 10
ruah 'lhym 61
s'ayr 118
shamar 120
shdy 22
shomrim 101, 103, 119–121, 166
shoresh 17, 104, 160
shtm 29, 49, 50
smihut 23
stn 26
torah 7, 87, 88, 90, 93, 162, 173, 182, 197
tzofeh 156
waw/vav 105
wl' 'sybynh 18, 67
wrt 26
y'sh 67

yahad 92, 196, 209, 215
Yahweh 14, 17–20, 22, 25–27, 29, 31–33, 35, 39, 46, 49, 50, 55, 60, 61, 63–68, 71, 73–77, 79, 81, 88, 95, 99, 101, 111, 112, 113–121 128, 131, 133, 139, 143–145, 164, 172, 176, 178, 180, 185, 186, 190, 198, 211–214, 217
yhwh 14, 22, 26, 32, 34, 48, 61, 111, 171
yod(h) 105, 107, 111, 118
yrt 26, 48, 110

yshr 28, 49
Zophim 25, 33

BIBLICAL AND POST-BIBLICAL INDEX

Genesis
3:1   28, 32, 183, 191, 201
36:32   11, 23, 25
41:16
Exodus
11:30   29, 112
17:2–7   60
17:8–16   34
20:17   112
Numbers
15:17
16:1–35   60
20:1   31
20:2   60
20:14   31
20:22   31
21:5–9   52
21:6   28
21:13B   31
21:14a.   31
21:19   28
21:20   31
21:29   133
22:5–7   11
22:41   31, 45, 111
22–24   4, 10, 17, 18, 35, 48, 65, 66, 70, 72, 75, 77–80, 83, 84, 92, 95, 96, 112, 119, 121, 122, 132, 155, 179,
23:6   45, 46
23:9   160
23:14   31, 45
23:15–16   136, 137
23:18b–24   33
23:19–20   18, 67
24:3b–10   80
24:8   91, 95 120
24:10   18
24:17   63, 91, 125, 126, 147
24:18   64, 91, 95

24:22–24   92
31   4, 23, 26, 54, 69–74, 80, 83, 91, 98, 107, 124, 126, 143, 145, 155, 172, 176, 190, 191, 196, 200, 201, 207, 213
31:8   70, 83, 190
31:16   71, 83
Deuteronomy
18:10   58
18:21ff   17
18:22a   17
23:2–4   76
23:3–4   79
23:4–5   4, 76, 84, 126
24:15   137
26:5–10   23
Joshua
13:22
24:9   69
24:10   128
I Samuel
9:6   17
9:9   10
2 Samuel
7:25   18
9–10   176
I Kings
1–2   3, 52, 83, 137, 198
8:56   17
22:19–22   3
2 Kings
10:10   17
18:1–8   53
2 Chronicles
31:2   69, 98
36:20
Nehemiah
13:1   81
13:2   4, 79, 80, 88
Job
1:6–12   3

15:8   3
Psalm
82:1   3
89:7   3
Isaiah
6:1–4
12   3, 20, 29, 43, 77,
        91, 107, 109, 110,
        115, 117, 127, 139,
        142, 152, 174, 177,
        191, 194, 198, 199,
        207
18:1–2 52
18:3–7 52
20:2–4
23:1   45, 46
30:1–7
31:1–3
37:1–2
44:26   18
45:23   18
55:11   18
Jermiah
2:10   29
15:15   17
18:18   6
23:18   3
23:22   3
36:24   3
41:5   102
Ezekiel
27:6   29
Hosea
4:1b   29
Micah
6:5   4, 75, 80
Zechariah
13:2ff 13, 90, 121, 135
Matthew
15:15   17
18:18   6
21:5   53, 163
41:5   102

Acts
2:10
10:28   142
15:20   142
15:29   142
Romans
14:14   142
14:20–21
27:6   6
II Peter
2:15   143
4:1b   29
Jude
1:11   143
Revelation
2:12   14
22:14   142, 145
2:16   142
Deir 'Allā
(Reconstructed Text)
Lines 1–7
I Enoch
1:2   61, 136, 137, 187
37–44   140
37–71   140
45–57   140
58–69   140
83:90
91:11–17 138
93:1–2 137
93:3   138
93:10   138
Josephus' Antiquities
        5, 144, 205
Book IV
VI:2   144
VI: 4
VI:5   144
VI:6–13 **145**
Madrashim

Lamentations Rabbah

Numbers Rabbah

Sifré
  152, 154, 206
Sifré to Deuteronomy
  152
Tanhuma B, Balak

Mishna Sanhedrin

X1, 1, 2 and 99 b and 105 a.
Tanhuma B, Balak
69 a–fin
70 a 152
Wadi Qumran
1 QM   196
1 QM II:1–2
VII:8   198
VII:10   198
VII:11   198
VII:12   198
XVI:2–9
XVIII:2
1 QS 1:1
4 Q En.

www.ingramcontent.com/pod-product-compliance
Lightning Source LLC
Chambersburg PA
CBHW030240170426
43202CB00007B/64